DREAMS BIGGER
THAN TEXAS

DREAMS BIGGER
THAN TEXAS

A STORY OF FAITH, PURPOSE, PERSEVERANCE AND
GROWTH INTO WOMANHOOD

RAHKAL C. D. SHELTON

Copyright © 2021 by Be The Inspired You Publishing

All rights reserved. This book or any portion thereof may not be reproduced or used in any manner whatsoever without the express written permission of the publisher except for the use of brief quotations in a book review or scholarly journal.

First Printing: © 2016

Printed in the United States of America

ISBN: 978-1-7376892-0-1

Library of Congress Control Number: 2016908319

Rahkal Shelton Roberson
Lawrenceville, Georgia 30043
www.rahkalroberson.com

Instagram: rcarladanielle
Twitter: rcarladanielle
Facebook.com/rahkal.shelton
www.youtube.com/c/rahkalshelton

Cover Concept: TMIX Studios
Editing: Bettye Underwood

All Scripture references are taken from the King James Version of the Bible (Public Domain) unless indicated.

New International Version (NIV): Holy Bible, New International Version®, NIV® Copyright ©1973, 1978, 1984, 2011 by Biblica, Inc.® Used by permission. All rights reserved worldwide.

New Living Translation (NLT): *Holy Bible*, New Living Translation, copyright © 1996, 2004, 2015 by Tyndale House Foundation. Used by permission of Tyndale House Publishers Inc., Carol Stream, Illinois 60188. All rights reserved.

All names and some identifying details have been changed to protect the privacy of individuals.

Dedication

To my nieces and granddaughters...

Every part of your life has a purpose; it's your legacy, your story to tell. So, create one worthy of sharing. Learn from your mistakes. When you fall, get up and be kind to yourself along your path. You are enough, valuable, divinely guided, beautiful, loved, fearless, wonderfully made, and created for a purpose.

Author's Note

Every aspect of this journey has been nothing short of astounding! Get this—the story isn't even over yet. I am still growing, learning, and discerning. My sole intention, goal, and purpose of this project is to inspire. Dreams Bigger Than Texas offers an intimate glimpse into my life, my hardships, struggles, accomplishments, and my commitment to persevering.

It is my hope that you'll finish this book encouraged to push through your own adversities, believing in yourself and empowered to keep going…no matter what!

Listen, we can either use our pain, hurt, and shame as a platform to stand on, or allow it to defeat and define us. I chose the former. You should, too. I want you to know that you are stronger than you think and that you have the power to change the things in your life that you don't like.

There is no such thing as a perfect life or a perfect person. We don't choose our families, race, talents, or physical abilities. However, we **can** choose what we do with them. Play the cards you were dealt. Make the most of the life you have. Be relentless in pursuing your dreams. Live, laugh, love, give, and most importantly, don't be afraid to start over when needed. Be kind to yourself. You got this. I believe in you, and your Creator does, too.

Table of Contents

Author's Note vii
Acknowledgments xi
Introduction xiii

Chapter One	Take Root	17
Chapter Two	Possum Town to Music City	43
Chapter Three	Devil on the Left	63
Chapter Four	Love, Is That You?	89
Chapter Five	Chi-City	103
Chapter Six	I'm Neva Coming Back!	141
Chapter Seven	Texas Southern University	155
Chapter Eight	US	187
Chapter Nine	Starting Fresh	209
Chapter Ten	Dreams Bigger Than Texas	231
Chapter Eleven	God, Are You There?	245
Chapter Twelve	Who Said Experience Is the Best Teacher?	257
Chapter Thirteen	Purpose	275
Chapter Fourteen	Believe 'Em the First Time	287
Chapter Fifteen	Faith Is	299
Epilogue	A Decade and a Year Later	315

About the Author 327

Acknowledgments

A number of wonderful people contributed in countless ways to my experiences in life and writing this book. First and foremost, I'm grateful to be in relationship with Jesus Christ, my Lord and Savior. Apart from him, I am and can do nothing!

To every soul whose presence I have encountered (temporarily, permanently, subtly, directly, or indirectly) whether receiving or lending, good, bad, or indifferent, thank you. I am appreciative of every opportunity to grow. To my extraordinary husband, Dr. Joe L. Roberson, Jr., thank you for your continuous support, selfless sacrifice, for changing my name, upgrading my identify, and unlocking the brightest version of me. I love you, bunny.

Introduction

It's been a ride, you hear me? A ride, and a wild one at that. First and foremost, thanks for hopping in and joining me. My desire is for you to finish this book and be inspired, encouraged, and motivated to write or rewrite your own story. I pray my transparency transforms you.

So, I began writing *Dreams Bigger Than Texas* in March 2007 and continued little by little through 2008. My writing came to a halt and collected dust for a few more years. I procrastinated. I allowed fear to incapacitate and further delay my writing. After all, I didn't want all my business in the streets. Honestly, I was uncomfortable with the thought of exposing myself. *Who are you to publish a biography at age twenty-four, and what's so doggone special about your story?* I thought, allowing the negative self-talk to reign. I didn't feel secure about everyone watching me grow.

Most importantly, I didn't know how to frame a story that was just beginning. But I knew I needed to release it. I don't remember exactly what it was, but something prompted me to start writing again in 2011 and once more in 2014. *It's time for real now. You keep meeting people who need to hear your story,* I told myself after years of stalling before finally pulling the trigger and successfully publishing on my third writing attempt.

While a lot has changed over the last fourteen years since I first started writing, I learned firsthand just how debilitating and deceptive fear really is. I also learned that timing is everything and that God is a restorer of time. He sure has a way of reestablishing what we let fear hold hostage.

I published *Dreams Bigger Than Texas* in 2016, nine years after its conception. The publishing process was grueling, but also an incredible ride. I had a sophisticated and independent marketing campaign that morphed into a movement of inspiring countless people to #dreambigger. Successfully, I crowdfunded over 9k in under eight weeks (solo), which helped with publishing and marketing costs. My social media content and consistency was booming. I went live weekly, updating fans, followers, and friends on my publishing journey. People near and far tuned in to be inspired and to cheer and support me in the publishing process. I produced and filmed three unique video trailers, booked press with major media outlets, and hosted a sold-out book release party in Chicago during a holiday and World Series weekend. Sounds awesome, right?

Well, nearly two months after the book's release, a tragic series of events occurred, causing an abrupt book tour cancellation and other life-altering implications that rocked my family and me over the next couple of years. But I'm still grateful for the entire experience, and I am reminded of the most important part of this journey...the testimonies and feedback of how my story touched people's lives. I watched friends start businesses, podcasts, and even write their own books because my faith inspired them. I say "faith" because I had no clue of what I was doing, at least not initially. I had never published a book. I had no way of knowing if things would really work, but I suspected they would.

I believe so passionately in the power of sharing stories and believe that since God gave it to me to share, it will be successful. Belief is so much more powerful and motivating than any interview or royalty check. Here I am believing again, five years later, and still refining my story. This time around, I'm more seasoned as a writer, more introspective and mature, more honest and unforgiving about

INTRODUCTION

delivering my absolute best to you. There is a freeing power through storytelling. I'm also a married woman now with a wonderful husband who is supportive, loving, covering, and backing my transparency. And the beauty in all this is that I'm not even who I am yet, and neither are you. Our stories will constantly be refined, and we can revise them whenever we choose. My hope is that you'll finish this book inspired to courageously write, live, create, and rewrite your own.

God Bless.

CHAPTER ONE

Take Root

I sat there with my full lips protruding from my round, brown face and my deep-set eyes periodically closing. Half cognitive, I was dozing off and very tired from a long night of celebratory partying. *Just please don't cry and try not to look over at them,* I told myself as loud chants and screaming filled the hot and humid mid-size gymnasium. "Go, Dee, go!" I keyed in on my name being shouted in the midst of thousands of cheers, all belonging to those attending a very proud moment of a daughter, son, niece, nephew, grandchild, or friend.

I recognized that distinctive voice from anywhere — the same voice that took me back to a time when I was backhandedly slapped, falsely accused, and yelled at for locking Carlos out of the house. Carlos, my father, a 5-foot-9, brown-skinned, slender man whom I hardly knew intimately, finally got in after kicking, threatening, and pounding on the door. My mother, Tina, reluctantly let him in, quickly insisting, "Dee did it. She pulled up a chair, stood on it, and locked the door." Carlos definitely wasn't buying that excuse. Furious, he rushed over like a charging bull, slamming Tina's head into the heavy metal door, which tore through her skin just above the brow. Blood flowed like a low-pressure faucet from her forehead to her bottom lip. The room went silent as she turned around to make brief eye contact before he proceeded to choke the life out of her. She fought back, gasping for air while swinging at his face with fruitless attempts to loosen his grip.

That was one of the few times I witnessed her fight back. She must have had enough, and so she mustered the strength to break free of his grip before running to the kitchen and grabbing the biggest knife in sight. My little sister, Pee Wee, and I cried as we watched in horror. *Would she gut his insides out this time?* We often trembled, sitting in those front row seats to our parents' constant routine, from the uncertainty of whether we'd be next. This time his narcotic rage must have subsided faster, as he took the knife from Tina before throwing it to the floor. Surprisingly, he let her off with an open-handed slap and a spit to the face before storming out again. As soon as that heavy door slammed, Tina ran over to calm us. She promised everything would be OK, but I wasn't convinced. Neither was I convinced that she believed things would be OK, either. Their fights were all too familiar to me. I knew he'd be back, and that they would fight again. Carlos had a tendency to blame Tina for his lack of self-control. "Ya mama made me do that to her," he'd say before apologizing to us

We had a couple of light moments, but nothing really changed. Even then, at four years old, I knew the problem was deeper than the glass pipe and the white powder they'd snort. Drugs were the catalyst for most of the fighting, but graver underlying issues existed as well. Carlos's insecurities, inability to lead, provide, protect, his knack for control, toxic masculinity, and piss-poor perception of manhood all showed up to fight.

I knew for certain that we gave Tina hope beyond the dictatorship of our home. As I recall, I *did* lock that door, only after several rehearsed drills with Tina.

Ouch! I felt a sharp pinch to my right arm as my classmate snapped me out of my reminiscent trance. Huh? "Girl, stand up. They're acknowledging our school," she whispered.

"Will the Tavis Smiley School of Communications please stand?" Cheers roared louder as everyone recognized that famous name. Tavis Smiley, a popular author, show host, media personality, and political analyst, had a partnership with my university at that time. I was grateful and thrilled to be part of the first graduating class from the Tavis Smiley School of Communications, and with honors. My eyes widened with hope and a tear solemnly fell, grazing my left cheek, as statistically this shouldn't have been possible. *Wow, girl, you did it! You are graduating from college!* It was a nearly unbelievable moment.

Realizing just how pivotal this particular year was, I began to reflect on my entire life leading to that point. I knew the coming year would hold blueprints and precursors for the future me. I knew where I came from and where I didn't want to be. A strong will to live burned on the inside of me; I knew there was far more to life than my past and what I had been exposed to. I was passionately determined to get out there and find it.

Let's define the makings of Dee. The year was 1984, a rather cool but pleasant spring morning when my life began at 3:05AM. I was born Rahkal Carla Danielle Shelton on a Thursday in May and promptly nicknamed "Dee." I was my mother's second child, although she wasn't much more than a child herself, still in her teens. She now had two additional mouths to feed besides her own. I imagine her feeling numb and hopeless. As a matter of fact, she told me she did, and she carried that hopelessness for quite some time before I arrived. Tina, my mother, a caramel brown-skinned, small but curvy-framed young woman, was the fifth child of twelve. Standing about 5-foot-3, there was a very distinct story hidden behind those almond-shaped eyes of hers. She had the rounded nose of her father, and a beautiful smile she occasionally flashed.

Her exterior was tough as cemented bricks, but internally, she was just a broken girl, begging and pleading to be liked, accepted, appreciated...even loved. Stained with the residue of uncertainty, bitterness, insecurities, and trauma from her childhood, Tina was a survivor: She just didn't know it yet. Her youth produced a seed of bitterness and resentment toward life at an early age. This resentment propelled a constant desire of flight and wanderlust.

She found safety in running away and avoiding reality. Like a track star exiting the blocks, Tina ran from her childhood—a true distortion possessing all the characteristics of a generational curse. Her parents separated after thirteen years and nine children. Tina recalls everything going downhill after her father, my grandpop, left their home. My grandma struggled to raise twelve children by herself on welfare in rough, inner-city Chicago in the 1970s. Having entered that marriage with three children of her own, Grandma was familiar with the struggles of single parenthood, but when my grandpop left, she found herself with a new level of difficulty, especially with now four times as many children. As a result, Tina was accustomed to going to bed hungry and living in abject poverty...and I'm talking P-O-V-E-R-T-Y. Dirty clothing, busted shoes, rats and roaches, filth, and most times no food or hot water. Yeah, that kind of poverty.

Grandma was employed most of the time but earned only pennies. She couldn't keep the utilities on, let alone feed or keep up with so many kids. Grandma did what she could and what she knew to do after Grandpop left. Like many single-parent families, living in poverty, children are left fending for themselves. Think about how challenging it is for any child to thrive academically or socially when they lack resources or have no idea where their next meal is coming from. Traumas associated with living in poverty is all too real, common, and have become sadly normalized. Longer-term implications are then etched into the survivor's psyche, daily decision making, and how they present themselves to the world. The effect of poverty isn't a sexy topic, or something discussed often—at least not from my experience.

I will say, one advantage of growing up in poverty is that it teaches resilience, innovation, resourcefulness, and provides unique compensatory life skills. If you can survive poverty, you can likely conquer anything.

My mother's experience subsequently impacted my own life. She recalls her childhood as a nightmare with occasional lighter moments of wakefulness. Those lighter times occurred before Grandpop left, and I could only imagine the humor and fun with so many personalities in the house. Twelve kids, pranking, laughing, fighting, playing with and enjoying each other. Tina's imagination and recollection of her childhood made the best stories, hands down. I loved hearing about fun times with her siblings. However, her nightmares were tough to hear but equally a part of her story. They helped shape my mother's being.

The nightmares started just after her ninth birthday, first with uncomfortable touches that slowly advanced to sexual assault from family and friends of family. Those memories and experiences specifically are what triggered her running. My mother had no clue just how precious she was, and that abuse and rape didn't define her. They were a part of her story but not her entire story. Because she wasn't aware of this truth, she internalized these nightmares, accepted blame, and adopted a victim mentality. Tina didn't know much about men, self-esteem, self-worth, self-respect, or how a woman should advocate for herself. Instead, she viewed life from a cracked lens and gathered most of her rearing from the streets.

Tina recalls Grandma being there physically but not mentally, socially, or emotionally. Grandma had her own life, trauma, and business to tend to. My grandmother was accustomed to an old school, Southern, passive slave-like, deaf-and-blind-to-reality mentality. I consider this mentality similar to the good ol' boys' mentality, where a system, culture, or set of behaviors exists, and the perpetrators are superior and accustomed to leaving things just the way they are to avoid exposure and accountability. Folks remain silent because no one wants to ruffle feathers or do the "heart" work associated with correcting behaviors and healing. In this climate, elephants roam freely, becoming decorative wallpaper.

Complacency, emotional desensitization, willing blindness, and flat-out avoidance leads to deeper generational issues. I know because I am a living example. I've spent the last five years of my life intentionally unpacking my baggage and healing. *Getting to the origin of the issue is the best way to uproot problems.* Therefore, sharing portions of my mother's and grandmother's stories helps to lay foundations and provide context. *Breaking the curses of generations can and must start with you!*

While my grandma's generation exhibited great strength, the lack of transparency and the absence of communication produced a greater weakness. Sadly, I've seen this before, thus leading me to conclude that these behaviors were not uncommon for Black women born in the earlier to mid-1900s. Ever hear of those cultures where older women are privy to or suspecting unspeakable things going on, but says and does nothing? Real courage and strength are demonstrated by speaking up.

Despite the issues that followed both my grandmother and mother into adulthood, they did what they could with what they had in order to survive, so I can't be mad at them.

My mother's good moments, although few and far between, are what helped her to push forward in life. She describes these moments as Grandpop's presence filled the home. She recalled my grandfather as being a strong provider, hard worker, and disciplinarian. I saw him as the same until my discovery of his domestic abuse, chauvinistic and adulterous tendencies while preaching from the pulpit.

It wouldn't be until I was in my twenties that he'd openly expose his own Southern childhood woes candidly with me. I interviewed all three — my grandpop, grandma, and Tina — before writing this book. Not only did I want their blessing to share, but I desired more understanding. I wanted to empathetically relate, strip their titles, and see them as humans.

My desire is to inspire change, dialogue, and reconciliation in the homes and hearts of others. I believe sharing my story can help achieve this.

I discovered that my grandfather's trauma included life as a black male growing up during Jim Crow in 1940's Mississippi. Grandpop dropped out of school in third grade, becoming a sharecropper who taught himself to read and write while avoiding the "blue-eyed devils." That's the name he gave white people after years of being emasculated, terrorized, and tormented. Just like his dad, he loved pretty women. In fact, he watched his own father get any woman he wanted. He also loved the fame that came from "preaching the Word." "One of my best sermons got me my first wife," he proudly stated to me. His background and mentality helped me understand why he wasn't there for my mother. Baggage from both my grandparents, their trauma, parenting, mentality, and emotional unavailability all contributed to Tina's desire to run. And there you have it; generational curses are developed and take root.

Tina ran and ran—to street life, which was a safe haven for her. She desired to be accepted, affirmed, and desperately wanted to be loved, and when she didn't get it, she turned to the street for answers. Furthermore, being in the streets required little to no judgment or responsibility. Tina was free to come and go and to do whatever she pleased.

She learned the technique of quick fixing to subdue pain. However, these quick fixes usually came with strings and severe consequences. By fourteen, she had dropped out of school and soon became pregnant with my brother Daniel, whose father left a fifteen-year-old Tina to care for Daniel alone. Shortly after, she ran right into the arms of my father—a drug-addicted man twelve years her senior. Upon meeting him, her quick fixes became far more detrimental.

Carlos, my father, certainly was a quick fix, possibly an older confidant. They met three years before I arrived, when Tina was sixteen and Carlos twenty-eight. He was well-versed in the Southside Chicago streets, and she was just a girl, broken and with no idea of what real love looked or felt like. She had no clue that her life would drastically be altered in just a few short years. Personally, I'm learning that we attract variations of what and where we are. After all, isn't a lack of identity and hurt the root of poor decision making?

Hanging out and running the streets together eventually led to an introduction to heroin and in no time, she switched from heroin to crack cocaine. My mother lived a double life while working to hide her new habit from family. She found herself addicted to two of the most powerful drugs in the country.

As her peers were preparing for prom and graduation, she sustained blackened eyes, busted lips, and pressure to get money to support their habit. Like many young girls in these types of situations, she felt trapped, complacent, and afraid. Her relationship with my father further validated her victim within and set the stage for my arrival.

My objective was to get here, and on May 10th, I did. My earliest memory is of an itching stomach marked with indentations from lying directly on a soiled piece of carpet in our cold and empty living room. My knees were bent and my feet waving in the air, my eyes glued to the television. I laid in my favorite spot watching *The Oprah Winfrey Show* on a small, thirteen-inch black-and-white television set that had pliers stuck to it because it was missing the bottom knob.

Our TV sat on a milk crate in a relatively large and empty room that only had a record player, a couple of records and a fireplace. There was no couch, curtains, or coffee table. I distinctly remember a big, bare window covered in plastic taking up the majority of the wall. I knew possibilities awaited out of that window and found myself drawn to it daily. I gazed out at street life: people milling about, fire trucks speeding, and the wind blowing hard enough to disturb our plastic covering. I would count the trucks in the post office's parking lot (there never seemed to be more than ten). Tina's raspy voice usually interrupted my thoughts, scolding, "Get away from that window 'fore you fall!" "Oh, Mama," I would reply.

Besides her voice, my earliest memories of Tina were her taking off her panties and placing them on me. Carefully, she took both hands and secured a little knot on the side of my hip to keep them from falling off. Four times too big, I wore them under my little skirt when company came over. I assume she didn't want anyone to think I was being molested or to have access to molesting me, the way she'd been. Obsessively, she asked if anyone touched my private parts and consistently warned me to never let it happen. I remember the fights, the name-calling, cursing, yelling, and the bruises inflicted by Carlos.

I remember the lighter flickers that not only lit the candles we used for lights, but also when they got high. Their faces would be partially lit from the flick of that little red lighter. Placing it directly underneath a spoon or soda can, their drugs were ready in no time. Nothing was done in secret, nor did they order me to leave the room. I assumed they thought I wouldn't remember, being so young, but my long-term memory is excellent and photographically, I remember everything. Two to three hits filled their lungs quickly. After reaching that last toe-curling hit, they'd blissfully fall back, almost simultaneously, into the abyss... stretched out, arms up, and without a care in the world, they sprawled across their stained and sheetless mattress that occupied the dark room.

If no pop or beer cans were available, they'd use Tina's ID card to separate perfectly even white lines of powder before rolling up a dollar bill to funnel the substance into their noses. Watching them fascinated me; I was very observant of everything. Tina's lifeless, apathetic appearance was certainly something I noted. Whenever Carlos was around, she behaved one of two ways, either robotic or antsy.

Two new additions were added to the family unit— another girl named Betty, who we referred to as Pee Wee, and another boy named Taylor. Because Pee Wee and I are just eleven months apart, I can't remember my life before her. I do vaguely remember the night Taylor arrived. We were forcefully rushed in the back seat of Carlos's yellow cab while Tina yelled in agony from the front seat, telling Carlos to hurry up because her water broke. Pee Wee and I shot each other confusing glances every time she cursed and yelled.

So, then there were six: Pee Wee, Daniel, Taylor, Tina, Carlos, and me. That was my family for at least a couple of years. During those years, I was very quiet but also precocious. Looking back, I believe my silence stemmed from variations of shame. Defective, helpless, and inferior would best describe how the four-year-old me felt at that time. Although I was precocious, I didn't have the words or tools to pinpoint those emotions. I just knew I felt out of place. I suspect my feelings derived from several sources. Maybe a result from the drugs fed to me while in Tina's womb, or perhaps my negativity stemmed from exposure to violence, not being affirmed or feeling loved.

As I remember it, I was always inquisitive and wanted to say or ask more but didn't. Clamming up was easier. It became my defense mechanism. I internalized and processed everything silently, which further ignited continual feelings of fear, dread, and sadness.

My embarrassment stemmed from our living conditions, sleeping under soiled carpets for blankets, living in dark spaces, taking cold wash-ups, and sharing panties with Tina. I knew that Carlos wasn't supposed to beat her like he did. The rage and fighting kept me fearfully on edge, afraid to get in trouble or make them angry. The overwhelming heartache that accompanied watching Mama take those beatings was unreal. I blamed myself at times, wishing I was bigger so I could help her.

Even as a kid, I knew we were in a bad situation. I knew, at an early age, that I had seen things I shouldn't have, so I became quiet. I figured that if you were quiet, people wouldn't know your secrets; they wouldn't be able to see through you and know that you had nothing. I thought that being quiet was the equivalent of being invisible.

The times I enjoyed visibility were when my grandpop or one of my aunts or uncles came to get us. I thoroughly enjoyed spending time away from our apartment with family and the cousins closest to my age. On the other hand, those happy moments away from home caused greater resentment when we returned. For example, my cousins' homes were always so clean. They had lights, plenty of food to eat and so many toys—lots of toys. Seemingly, they had everything, and each visit felt like a trip to Disney World.

When it was Grandpop's turn to pick us up, he'd cook us food and take us to church. As a preacher, Grandpop was very active in ministry. Everyone knew that Pop had a gift from God, so the family called him Prophet.

In the Bible, a prophet is a person who hears directly from God and has an ability to see and know things that others don't. As I got older, I learned just how gifted Grandpop was. He was able to look at a person and tell them very distinct and personal things about their lives. I witnessed that several times and was always amazed when they cried.

He and I share the same birthday, and he took a special liking to me. We always addressed him with the utmost respect. Tina taught us to respect all elders and to address them as "ma'am" and "sir." And to her, an elder was anyone older than us, even if just by a little bit. She learned that from him. As a matter of fact, Tina's strong will derived from his influence.

Despite the drugs and craziness at home, Tina was a good person with great potential. I believe she did the best she could with what she had at the time. My father, on the other hand, because he was older...I'm not too sure. Nevertheless, he gave me life, but also lasting misconceptions of what a man is and does, before he exited after my fifth birthday.

The vague, yet specific, memories of him are conflicting at best. I loved him because he's the first man I knew. He got us our first pet, a dirty little stray cat he had found in the alley. I named him Bubbles. Some nights, Bubbles went crazy clawing up my legs as they hung over the side of the bunkbed, he and Tina eventually managed to get for us. I cried, and Carlos doctored up my scratches with peroxide before telling me I would be fine. He showed me how to load a gun, too. Talking me through each step, he warned me, "Don't ever touch it, just watch and listen." I was fascinated by him and enjoyed having him around (when he wasn't angry).

I memorized his birthdate as well as my own. I knew his favorite cookies and sometimes helped Tina make his instant oatmeal. When he felt real good, he'd pick me up and toss me in the air, kissing me on the cheek when he caught me. I enjoyed those times but hated when he flipped. I assumed that was how people expressed love.

The happier moments with him were stored as mental photographs, images stashed in my mind and heart, using them to reconcile my future feelings in his absence.

My most cherished mental photograph associated with Carlos is of his sister, my Aunt Bertha, whom I loved dearly. Aunt Bertha's caramel-kissed skin radiated with beauty. She was absolutely breathtaking in her glamour, and always dressed to the nines. She owned purses, jewels, furs, and the softest leather gloves.

Sadly, she didn't have a single daughter with whom to share her wardrobe. Aunt Bertha had four sons, and the youngest, Lewis, was my favorite cousin. Lewis was closer to my brother Daniel's age, but a year younger. His brothers were a lot older than my siblings and me. Lewis was a chubby, extremely silly kid. Always in high spirits, he was very confident.

Over the years, I've grown to love Lewis' jovial nature, but growing up, I hated him at times. He frequently scared Pee Wee and me with a rubber Freddy Krueger mask.

He'd put it on and would jump out of the shadows yelling, "Roaaaar!"

That Freddy mask was just too real and reminiscent of the nightmares I had, not on Elm Street, but at home after seeing Freddy Krueger on the big screen. Only the good Lord knows why Tina and Carlos thought it was OK to take children to see a horror movie. Needless to say, we didn't last long beyond the opening credits. *Nightmare on Elm Street* was terrifying. I must have screamed nonstop at the top of my lungs at that burned-faced Krueger.

Upset, Carlos kept hitting me, instructing me to shut up. Luckily, we were forced to leave the theater after management came to quiet us a third time. I don't know how we afforded the movie tickets, but that buttery popcorn sure tasted good. I'll never forget that day.

Even though Lewis scared me sometimes, I liked hanging with him when we were at Aunt Bertha's. We went to visit mostly when Carlos needed something or needed her to watch us. Aunt Bertha's home was always warm and cozy, and there was always something cooking on the stove. She was far nicer and more tolerant of my brother Daniel than Carlos was. Aunt Bertha loved us all the same. Carlos, on the other hand, gave Daniel a hard time because he wasn't his child. I can't remember him ever being nice to Daniel, but we had all been trained to keep quiet about what happened at home.

At nine years old, Daniel knew what not to say at school if asked about his bruises. We were all told, "What happens in this house stays in this house," so when Aunt Bertha asked if we were OK, we always replied, "Yes, ma'am."

In spite of our assurances, she knew we weren't. Aunt Bertha was like a mother to Tina and always encouraged her to protect us. She told Tina to do fun things with me and Pee Wee.

When Carlos wasn't around, we did just that. Tina let us wear her lipstick, and when she cooked, we'd fight over who would get to lick the leftover cornbread batter from the spoon. She combed our hair and gave us baths. Fun moments with Mama were seldom, but cherished. We used to lie in our bunk beds, watching *Full House* episodes or listening to Tina's two favorite records. She was a Jody Watley and Too Short fan. Those were also the first two artist's songs I learned. We would sing along with Jody's "I'm Looking for a New Love" at the top of our lungs. Then Tina would ask us, "What y'all know about a new love?" and we would laugh.

On Halloween 1988, Tina painted our faces with red lipstick and darkened and enlarged our eyebrows. Pee Wee, Daniel, and I were transformed into three red devils and were ready to collect candy. We hit the streets of the neighborhood with our shopping bags.

After trick or treating, Carlos let us eat as much candy as we wanted that night. I remember bragging about getting the most Snickers to Daniel just before biting into a razor-laced piece of chocolate. The razor slashed my gums deeply, the piercing sensation causing my mouth to burn and fill with blood. Crying uncontrollably and choking on my blood, I feared I was going to die.

We rinsed my mouth for what felt like hours before Tina cradled me in her arms. Enjoying my mother's warmth and concern, I continued to cry as we rocked back and forth on the edge of our dirty bathtub until I fell asleep. That was the worst Halloween ever and one I'll never forget, because we moved shortly afterward.

Things were different the days following Halloween. I couldn't explain it, but I felt it. Tina seemed unusually disconnected. I honestly never judged her stony facial expressions or frail figure that stemmed from her drug use. I didn't focus on her bruises, untamed hair, or how we lived. To me, she was my shero, and I loved her no matter what. I knew she loved us, too.

And so, one particular night, I watched her watching us in between consciousness and coming down from a high. We were neatly tucked under a sheet and the living room carpet after crying ourselves to sleep. Earlier that day, she had promised us a White Castle kid's meal, but it didn't happen. She and Carlos either smoked up or lost the money and couldn't buy food. So, we were forced to go to bed early.

They always made us go to bed to quiet our hunger. I distinctly remember looking forward to those Castle burgers. I loved the bright lights, the castle-shaped building, and the french fries. Mmm, the sweet and savory taste of their strawberry shakes—my taste buds tingle just talking about it. But that night, I didn't taste anything but salty tears.

Although Mama was high, she was knowledgeable and seemed to have felt the hurt that she inadvertently inflicted on us. Tina later described that day as a very different experience. Watching us that particular night was harder for her than most. She and Carlos sat across from us, and she described Carlos as having had a very foul odor seeping from his pores. It wasn't typical body odor, but something she had never smelled before. She said the best way she could describe it was smelling like death.

She watched us lie there while the smell of death pierced deep into her nasal cavities. Tina had an out-of-body experience seeing herself clearly. *What am I doing? What am I doing?* she asked herself over and over. She did smell death—and suddenly she knew that if she stayed, we would all eventually die.

That very moment marked a point of no return. Tina decided she had had enough. She knew that after six years of being in a dreadful space with Carlos, she had hit rock bottom. She had no friends, no close family relationship, and her children were in bad condition. Tina wanted to change, so she prayed, asking God to help her improve her life. She pleaded for help, and she knew the first step would be to leave Carlos, to put an end to the drugs, the violence, financial troubles, and abuse. My mother loved us dearly and decided to fight for our future.

For this, I am eternally thankful and now understand why we boarded that Greyhound bus, leaving Carlos. I can still see the tears in his eyes as he promised to come back and get us. He promised to send our things as well, but that would be the last time that I'd see him for over a decade. At the age of twenty-four, with an eighth-grade education and no money, self-esteem, support, or experience, Tina did what she did best. She had an opportunity to run, and she took it.

One cold November day, we all ran, taking a bus ride from Chicago to Columbus, Mississippi. Thanks to Tina's courageousness, 1989 was a turning point for all of us. She told Carlos we were going to visit her older brother, and the very next day, she stumbled across just enough money to gather bus tickets with the help of Aunt Bertha.

Despite the beatings, yelling, and control, in some weird way, I do believe Carlos loved Tina. He kissed us goodbye and told me specifically to wait a little while, promising me that we would all be together again. Just like that, we were gone.

Many notable releases occurred in 1989. The Sega Genesis hit the scene; Bobby Brown's "My Prerogative" hit the Top 100, and Public Enemy's "Fight the Power" was released as part of the soundtrack for Spike Lee's film *Do the Right Thing*. Those events helped shape 1989, and my move down south would help change my life forever.

Columbus, a city in Lowndes County, Mississippi, lies above the Tombigbee River. It's part of the area of northeast Mississippi called the Golden Triangle, consisting of

Columbus, West Point, and Starkville. We moved right into the midst of the Triangle, staying with Tina's older brother, who God used to assist us. My uncle supported us because he knew Chicago was too much for Tina to overcome without a change in environment. Tina agreed and figured the South had an easier pace. She believed that we could build a new start and identity there.

But living with my uncle only lasted a short while. He had four children of his own who just about matched us in age. Although the children lived with their mother, it became too congested when they came to visit him. Pee Wee and I slept in his bed with Tina. He, Daniel, and Taylor slept on his couch and love seat.

I did enjoy having more cousins and loved going to their house. In Mississippi, Tina smiled more, and she seemed happy. If she was happy, then so was I. Occasionally, she'd go out to party with our cousin's mom, my uncle's ex-wife, whom we called "Auntie" despite the divorce. Pee Wee and I enjoyed watching them get dressed to go out. We watched closely as they squeezed their nice figures into sexy black minidresses and high heels.

Our aunt's figure was a bit fuller than my mother's small but curvy 5-foot-3 frame. I didn't miss a beat watching them make up their faces under dim bathroom lighting. They topped off the show by spritzing Malibu perfume on their wrists, necks, and between their thighs. I knew that someday, Pee Wee and I would do the same routine when we were old enough to go out.

I felt much older and exposed to life than the other kids. Things seemed slower down south. They even talked slower. By then, I had already witnessed how to make crack pipes out of soda cans. I had already walked five and six blocks alone and knew how to safely cross wide intersections. I had also witnessed Daniel get robbed for his shoes, had picked up a loaded gun, and been shot at while being cradled in Carlos's arms. Yet, there I was, learning colors and how to count.

Adapting to the newness and being separated from Carlos was challenging for me. I waited for him to return like he said he would and found myself daydreaming about life in Chicago all the time. I daydreamed so much that I wasn't paying attention in class. Still very quiet and withdrawn, my silence provoked my teacher to give me more attention.

One day, she pulled me to her desk and smoothed out my hair. Determined to get me talking, and she managed to find my weakness. She tickled my sides, and I laughed and laughed. I quickly covered my mouth, realizing I was smiling. I'm not sure why, but I had a habit of covering my smile and not letting people see me laugh. She put her hands over mine and whispered, "It's OK to smile, and you've got a pretty one. You have to laugh at life anyway," before giving me a big hug. Smiling that day felt liberating.

That was the start of a breakthrough for me, and I wasn't the only one. Tina and my siblings seemed to have been advancing as well. And, despite my nonparticipation in class, I received a Student of the Month certificate. In that moment, I noticed that anything good related to school always seemed to make Tina happy. That discovery marked the birth of an ongoing battle with people pleasing, as it provided reward and acceptance.

Seeing her consistently happy, laughing, going out, and more lighthearted was wonderful. Tina was more attentive to us, and there were no signs of drug use. We could talk to her, and she'd respond differently. We ate much better, had clean clothes, and experienced what felt like more love from her. It seemed like we all were coming alive, and the move was a success. But as quickly as I liked my school and became comfortable, it was time to move, again. We were squeezed too tight in my uncle's one-bedroom shotgun house.

However, this time the move was pleasant. We were getting our own place. With government assistance, we moved into the Sandfield Housing Project. These were low-income apartments located on the east side of Columbus. Either way, we didn't know or care that they were the projects. This was our kingdom, the place we called home. It also meant that we didn't have to share a bed anymore. We moved into a three-bedroom palace—actually a townhouse—that was fully equipped with a bathtub, lights, and heat. It didn't get nearly as cold in Mississippi as it did in Chicago, but I liked having heat and warm water to bathe in. Tina, then twenty-five, and employed, was studying for her General Education Development (GED) diploma.

Because she worked hard to attain the GED, it became the most important thing that she preached to us. It was imperative that we get our GED. What she probably didn't realize was that she was setting the bar low, by conveying (however unintentionally) that she expected us to drop out of high school and have to get a GED later. It's hard to succeed when a ceiling has been put in place.

Tina worked nights at Church's Chicken and went to school during the day. She'd been clean from drugs for over a year, which elated me. Despite the thrill I felt over that, internally I still waited for Carlos. I wanted to ask Tina when he was coming back but didn't want to spoil her happiness or have her upset with me. So instead, I secretly continued to wait because I knew he would come. He *said* he would. I thought about how much he was missing out with Tina being so productive and looking so pretty these days. He was missing out on the awesome new life that we were building. I thought since things were better, if he showed up, then we could be a real family. Also, I wondered if he missed us.

While Tina went to school and worked, Daniel was in charge. Just ten years old at the time, Daniel could not cook to save his life. We ate experimental cakes made of flour, water, and salt that he'd bake in the oven. That was our alternative when we ran out of leftover chicken. Tina always brought home a box of Church's Chicken for us. We used to fight over the last biscuit, and I stole Tina's okra.

We found new ways to entertain ourselves because we were not allowed to have company or to play outside. That forced us to get creative while playing inside. There was this one game where we would do stupid challenges. We had this imaginary group that we all wanted to join called the "cool kids." If you passed a challenge, you became a cool kid; that's how the game went. So, one day Daniel told us we couldn't be part of the group if we didn't take the closet challenge. Eagerly, Pee Wee and I accepted the challenge. Everyone except Taylor got in the hallway closet and shut the door behind us. It was a hot Mississippi summer, and the temperature inside that closet felt greater than one hundred degrees. The object of the game was to see who could stay on the closet shelf the longest. We didn't realize the door would lock behind us and that we'd be stuck in the closet for hours. Taylor was too young to decipher the difference between a spoon or butter knife to help us break out.

In our desperation to break out, we pleaded with him to slide a knife under the door to pop the lock. Three-year-old Taylor kept sliding spoons under the door instead. He was no help at all, and I was convinced we were going to suffocate and die. The phone began to ring, and we knew it was Tina calling to check on us as she always did. No one answered that day.

As a result, she had to leave work early and she broke the back window to attend to us. We heard her beating and beating on the front door in the minutes before glass shattered. I have no clue why she didn't have her key with her. Taylor had cried himself to sleep on the couch by then, and he couldn't open the door, anyway. We repeatedly yelled in unison, "We in the closet," as she called our names. Moments later, the door opened, and Daniel jumped out first, buck naked because he had removed his clothes in an effort to stay cool. I can still see Tina's confused expression when she looked at him.

What a stupid game, to think we could be a part of a nonexistent "cool kids" group. Daniel had the dumbest ideas, but he was the oldest, so we went along.

After Tina calmed down, we were instructed to go take a nap, and Daniel got a spanking, as usual. I never had an issue with her policy: The oldest got in trouble, and the younger ones would have to take a nap. However, to me, taking a nap was almost as bad as receiving a whooping. I *hated* taking naps.

We stayed in Sandfield a good little piece, and when second grade concluded, Carlos still hadn't shown up. I began to get angry and wondered why I didn't hear from him or have a dad. I recall really longing for him around the time Tina made a new guy friend, a man with a shiny black Jheri curl, pickup truck, and two sons. Giving her famous speech, she made sure we knew not to let any of them touch us. I suspected the guy with the curl was her boyfriend, but I was too young to know what that really meant aside from the few things I'd seen on TV.

My friends down the street always talked about what they did with their boyfriends. Tina didn't like me and Pee Wee playing with them. She often referred to them as being "fast." I didn't know exactly what that meant, but I knew it wasn't good. Tina and another neighbor would sit on the porch drinking for hours, talking about other "fast girls and they mamas" in the area. When I would hang around them and listen, she'd tell me to stay out of grown folks' business. I often thought, *How did girls get "fast,"* and, *Was Tina "fast"?*

Was I *"fast?"* Tina had a way of indirectly addressing topics without going into detail.

Speaking of fast, the seasons were always changing, seemingly quickly. I knew the next year was approaching soon because everyone had Christmas lights up except us. We didn't celebrate Christmas, and I didn't know why or how to explain it when other kids asked what I was getting. It didn't bother me until I got to the third grade. I remember wanting to fight a girl for telling everyone I didn't celebrate Christmas because I was weird and Jewish. Well, it was true that we didn't observe Christmas, and I was so embarrassed. But I didn't understand why that meant I had to be Jewish or weird. When the kids would ask me what being Jewish meant, I couldn't answer. I felt rejected and stupid that I didn't know how to explain it. They would taunt me by bragging about the nice gifts they got and how pretty their tree was.

My religious background and foundation is an interesting one, to say the least. In short, after Grandpop left, my grandma started attending a black Hebrew temple that followed strict Jewish customs. Making it her place of worship, she raised Tina and her other children to follow its teachings. Thirty years later, I recognize that temple was nothing but a cult and responsible for much of my family's hurt and downfall. I'll discuss the temple a bit later in this book.

But back in the day, the only good thing about not celebrating Christmas was that it gave Tina a bit of financial relief because she didn't have to buy gifts. Besides, she barely made anything frying chicken for a living with four kids. Tax time was our Christmas because of the extra money she'd get. Even though the rules of the temple stated we weren't supposed to celebrate birthdays or non-Jewish holidays either, Tina kind of bent that rule. She always made the best cakes and let us pick the flavor of ice cream for our special day.

I remember getting a pen pal around that time. The school set it up through some program for less fortunate kids. The pen pals wrote and sent toys. My pen pal was an older white lady named Drew. We wrote back and forth a few times, and she was scheduled to come and meet me in person. I was extremely eager for this, and I wanted to look my best to meet her. So, I borrowed Tina's red sweater for the special occasion. The sweater was much too big for me, and it was also dirty the day I snuck it out.

It complemented Tina's skin and made her look so pretty. I thought it would do the same for me, so right before school that day I took it and packed it in my backpack. After I walked a block or two up to the railroad tracks, I slipped it on. I practically swam in it.

By the time I reached the school, I noticed the sweater was not only badly stained, but it reeked of stale cigarette smoke as well. I was devastated, ashamed, and embarrassed. I began having a meltdown from feeling so stupid. I didn't want to meet Drew anymore. However, I reasoned with myself, I thought, *this white lady has been so nice and got you gifts. You have to see her.* I felt bad, too, because I was empty-handed. I couldn't get her anything in return.

My formative years were mentally and emotionally tough. The foundation for my developing personality was literally rooted in rejection, fear, insecurities, shame, sadness, and continual anxiety. Additionally, I was empathic and always bogged down with guilt and a desire to help, fix, and please others. I simply wanted to be loved, affirmed, accepted, and made to feel like I was OK. These were the crucial elements that I lacked as a child, both at home and at school. Oblivious at the time, I was straight up depressed and suffering from posttraumatic stress disorder as an eight-year-old. Life had shown me things that my eyes couldn't unsee. I know this now because I've unpacked those emotions.

By the time I met my pen pal, I had become prideful beyond belief and didn't know it, but it was there. I didn't feel good about accepting what I saw as charity. I knew my siblings and I were viewed differently from other kids. I'm not sure if they felt that way, but I did. Nothing I did felt good enough, and I never felt like I belonged. This created a chip on my shoulder, a chip that I traced to the first moment I met Drew. At that instant, I fostered an attitude that would hinder me from accepting help in the future.

Consequently, I developed a crazy need to prove myself. All I wanted was to appear and feel like a normal kid, with a father and a happy family. I wanted to celebrate Christmas. I didn't want to feel singled out, and I wanted to erase the bad stuff I saw and felt. I wanted to have "good" hair like the pretty girls, sleepovers like other kids, the latest toys, and other nice things. I wanted my own room and for Tina to own a car. It would have been nice to go on family outings, summer vacations, to join school teams, or play piano or participate in gymnastics.

It felt like we couldn't do anything and were always limited because of money. I learned early on exactly what "We ain't got it" meant. The sound of that made me angry at times. *Why don't we ever have anything,* I questioned myself. *When I get grown, I won't be like that. I'll be able to afford to do as I please,* I told myself. I knew there was more to life out there, even if I didn't know what "more" was. I just knew that I wanted it.

Eventually, I realized some of those "normal things" I wanted wouldn't happen. Later, I learned that normal wasn't real. I started to understand and accept that this was my life and would remain so until I grew old enough to change it.

I never told Drew how unhappy I was. Her letters were always very pleasant, and I enjoyed reading them. She truly changed my life in those few months. Shortly after the new year, I learned it was time for us to move again, and I had to break the news to Drew. I can't recall the circumstances of why we had to move this time. But being on the run had become Tina's trademark, and that was our life. As soon as we began to adapt, our lives were disrupted by yet another move. Instability became my normal. I learned quickly to detach.

CHAPTER TWO

Possum Town to Music City

In the spring of 1992, we packed up and moved to Nashville, Tennessee. Tina said we would have a fresh start and more support in Nashville. Her youngest and closest brother, my Uncle Roger, was attending college there. Uncle Roger and his roommate, Melvin, stumbled upon a big house for rent, and they needed more occupants.

We were closer to this uncle than our other one in Mississippi. Roger adored us, and we adored him. He had a genuine concern for our health and wellbeing ever since we left Chicago. I knew that because he always called and checked on us. It had been a while since I saw him.

When I did, I flashed back to my earlier Chicago years where there were plenty of faint yet distinct memories of him. He loved taking my siblings and me to museums, parks, and Pizza Hut. I'll never forget when he took us to see our second big-screen movie, A Land Before Time. After the movie, we ate all the cheese pizza our stomachs could hold. He got us the coolest dinosaur hand puppets to match the ones from the big screen.

My uncle was very bubbly, caring, and full of charisma; I always admired his confidence. Besides, I liked the thought of living in a big house with more family. It wasn't like I had many friends anyway, so moving wasn't really a big problem. I was just sad about leaving Drew; I knew we would lose touch.

Nashville had a faster pace than Columbus and offered better job opportunities for Tina. By then, she had earned her GED and enrolled in a community college. The house we moved into was down the street from prominent HBCUs in Nashville: Tennessee State University, Meharry Medical College, and Fisk University. Uncle Roger and his roommate were both students, one at Meharry and one at Fisk. Dwelling among two scholars and living near colleges was inspiring to me. Melvin, a 6-foot-1, light brown, extremely muscular, mild-mannered man, spoke in big words. He was older than my uncle and Tina. Melvin was more established and in med school.

The way he and my uncle spoke stood out the most. They had similar speech habits: minimal cursing, big words, and proper English. They sounded nothing like Tina.

My siblings and I liked Melvin so much that we started to call him Uncle Mel, and he took a liking to us as well. His thing was reading, and he always had a different book in his hand. Sometimes he had two or three books. Mel was notorious for quoting different literary geniuses and asking if I'd heard of them. With my head bowed in embarrassment, my answer was always no.

"Let's fix that," he said while encouraging me to read everything, and out loud. He got us our first library cards and gave us individual and personal reading support. This was the first time anyone helped us with learning or read to us. Basking in the euphoria produced by reading complete sentences, I felt unstoppable.

Mel helped us with homework and paid allowances for reading: a quarter for every page. I would have read for free but was determined to make the most money. Every Saturday, Pee Wee, Daniel, Taylor, and I piled in Mel's Volvo station wagon and headed to the library; it was a consistent and fun adventure that we all enjoyed. Spending uninterrupted hours picking out books, I never knew where to start. I'd take a whiff of the pages, read the blurb on the back and rub my fingers across the front cover. I made sure to select at least three books to get me through the week. Sometimes we'd stop for ice cream on the way home.

Tina wasn't too happy with the private reading time, and she always preached the same song to Pee Wee and me: "Don't let him touch you," dampening our happy moments. Her trauma wouldn't allow her to trust anyone. I never believed Uncle Mel would do such a thing, but we listened. She consistently projected her demons on us, causing me to not only fear but not trust men.

Mel bought our first bikes and taught us how to ride them, too. We'd gossip about his motives: "Uncle Mel is so nice because he likes Mama," we snickered. Laughing at their interactions, I would race to my bike the moment I finished my homework. Daniel and I took imaginary road trips to Chicago and back. Peddling fast and riding one block over to the stop sign, we'd say, "We back in Chicago." We would then ride to Jubilee Hall on the campus of Fisk University, leave our bikes outside, and go inside to view the historic photographs of the Jubilee singers and slaves. These were some of my fondest moments. I loved the camaraderie at the new space. We had a nice groove going...until the adults had issues. Before I knew it, Tina told us we were moving again.

I had already transferred schools three times and was still adjusting. I waited that year for Carlos, too, but he didn't show up. Fourth grade at a new school seemed similar to my last school. All the halls began to look alike and had the familiar smell of markers, popcorn, and sanitizer. I was a bit more social, but still spoke only rarely. Consistently, I made perfect grades, which caused tension between my siblings and me. For some reason, my siblings struggled with schoolwork and badly. It didn't help that Tina never helped with homework, and Uncle Mel was long gone by that time.

My brother and sister began teasing me, calling me the favorite, and "Miss Do No Wrong." It was then that I realized I was the black sheep of the family. I can't lie—being singled out hurt deeply, and the rejection was rough. But getting good grades also put me in a happy place; it was my way of feeling accomplished. My achievements made me feel like I was somebody. That developing chip on my shoulder was morphing into perfectionism, codependency, insecurity, and people-pleasing. I was extremely hard on myself and fixated on getting everything right and done perfectly. I longed to feel good and accepted. These were all characteristics and byproducts of my childhood trauma.

My siblings, on the other hand, were quite different. Daniel, being the oldest, had suffered and seen the worst of our rearing. At fifteen, Tina hadn't nurtured, encouraged, or shown her growing baby the love he needed. She was a kid herself with different priorities. Tina was closer to twenty by the time I came along, but the damage was already done.

Daniel began to act out in school. He was unpredictable and often displayed a sadness similar to mine. He certainly inherited Tina's running trait. Daniel was a golden brown, handsome fella with dark brown, distinctly puffy eyes that were bashful, matching his introverted personality. He had a wild imagination and loved to rap. Gifted for sure, Daniel was extraordinarily poetic. He was good with words but just too shy and socially awkward to put his full talent on display.

Chipped front teeth were part of his smile, dating back to our Chicago days. I remember the day Daniel chipped his teeth. Tina was washing Pee Wee's hair in the kitchen sink and instructed Daniel to take out the trash. He grabbed it, eager to go outside by himself, running out the door and down the stairs. His nine-year-old strength wasn't sufficient to push back the top flap, so he climbed on top of the dumpster (I couldn't tell you the logic behind that action). He yelled at the window for me to look at him standing tall on top of the dumpster. I looked out the window, waving frantically and saying, "Ooh, look at Daniel!"

Everyone came to look out the window and Tina yelled, "Boy, get yo' a** down!" As soon as she shouted that, he suddenly disappeared into the metal, hollow dumpster. We heard him screaming and crying two flights up. Tina rushed down to aid Daniel. Moments later, they both returned with Daniel's shirt covered in blood. And when he opened his mouth, parts of his two front teeth were missing. Dental insurance and getting them fixed...forget about it! So, those were his teeth for a long while. It eventually became my brother's signature look. He even made up rap songs about his teeth.

Daniel started running away from home and cutting classes. When caught by truancy officers, he'd create epic stories as to why he wasn't in school. I wish I had his nerve to lie to an officer. He was both convincing and manipulative. He even changed his report card grades at times. Other times, he brought home straight F's. Daniel's poor performance infuriated Tina, and the verbal abuse increased. She'd yell, "'F' stands for 'f*ck up.' Y'all know that, right?" before punching him in the chest. Tina cursed like a sailor.

Life felt like a seesaw. One minute we enjoyed a good home life, and then abruptly, things became bad. Tina's mood changes were extremely hard on us. I believe she started to punish herself because of Daniel's behavior. She was still young and presumably doing the best she could, but parenting solo became harder for her. Daniel was a teen now and needed guidance. We all needed a consistent male figure in our lives. Our uncles helped, but they could only do so much. I remember Tina would get mad when they tried to discipline us. "You can't tell anyone about they kids, especially if you don't have any," she'd say.

I remember watching the beatings my siblings got for their low grades. Our days of simple nap time were over, and everyone was held accountable except Taylor, who was still the baby and very spoiled, by the way. Taylor got whoopings, but we also felt he got away with more than the rest of us. My baby brother was very light-complexioned, animated, with cute cheeks and an adorable smile. We called him "waterhead" and "high yella." His buttery golden complexion complemented his perfectly shaped eyes and handsome face. Taylor was a true Gemini in every facet of his life. As the youngest of the four of us, he received just about anything he wanted. When he was very small, he used to wet the bed every night, and we'd tease him back in our Mississippi days. He'd give himself away, each morning by standing in front of the living room heater drying up that piss and smelling up the room.

He never told Tina, because he knew a backhand would go upside his head even at his young age. Taylor was also an avid booger eater, and that was the other thing we teased him about. We made up songs with lyrics calling him "pissy" and "booger eater." When I caught him digging in his nose, I asked, "What flavor was that one? Barbeque, or salt and sour?"

Tina coddled him, and in her eyes, he could never do wrong. However, she couldn't protect him from his own demons. As Taylor got older, life became more challenging for him, especially at school. He struggled with behavior problems and impulsivity, and he acted out. Teachers told Tina he seemed frustrated, violent, and short-fused. Tina did very little about this other than beating his butt, thus perpetuating more violence. The beatings didn't seem to faze him as much. He still found humor in things even when he knew he was going to get in trouble.

Taylor was actually quite the comedian but was also very smart. He just barely applied himself to his schoolwork. He had a temper, too, when he didn't get his way. His skinny frame made it hard for me to take him seriously when he got upset. I used to tell him to get out of my face and go gain weight. At dinnertime, he hardly ate and picked over everything on his plate. He'd be the last one to leave the table each night with veggies still on his plate. Taylor preferred a butt whooping over eating them.

Taylor and I grew close, although at times he was in his own little world and I'd be consumed in mine. In hindsight, I wish I had paid more attention to his needs growing up. I wish I'd observed him like he observed me. Pee Wee and I were close in age and he and Daniel were seven years apart. Therefore, being the youngest, he had to fit in where he could among us. As the years passed, I started to wonder what Taylor's deal was. I wondered if his short fuse was the consequence of our childhood trauma. I knew I couldn't be the only one with a constant internal battle.

Pee Wee had been my twin growing up. A few days shy of being one year apart, sharing the same birth month, with birthdays just days apart, for nearly one week out of the year we were the same age. Tina always purchased two of every shirt, doll, shoes, and even panties. Yep, Mama didn't waste any time nursing me before she conceived again.

Pee Wee, a pretty golden-complexioned, chubby kid with puppy eyes, had a beautiful smile and an infectious laugh. She had always been outspoken and the most dramatic, attention-loving one of us kids. She was the one with the audacity to run and hide under the bed when she knew she was in trouble. Which of course, only made Tina angry because she then had to drag her out from under the bed. I'd never been bold enough to try and hide from Tina. But that was my sister. She didn't give a crap and had no problem talking back to teachers, family, or anyone else she didn't agree with.

Pee Wee's impersonations and stories were the best. She had a funny way of dramatizing and animating the delivery of every story she told. She didn't take any stuff from anyone, but also had a heart of gold. Pee Wee was very loving and compassionate. I always envied her boisterousness growing up, wishing I could clown comfortably in front of people the way she did. She never had a problem embarrassing herself if it made people laugh, either. She had plenty of friends and, boy, was she domesticated and prissy, much more than me. She might have been the only third grader who loved to carry purses and acted like she was an adult and had some real business.

By nine years old, she knew exactly what she wanted to be when she grew up. Her answer was always consistent and simple. She wanted to be a nurse, wife, and mother. She wanted to have nine kids and a husband. We laughed every time she said that, but she meant every word. She was the one who followed Tina around the kitchen, taking notes while laying the foundation for her domestic future.

When we were younger, she and I fought like cats and dogs. Getting ready for school produced the most heated arguments. She got on my nerves growing up, being extra sensitive and dramatic. I didn't know it then, but she valued my opinions and really looked up to me. However, whenever Tina put me in charge, she teamed up with Taylor and they accused me of bossing them around. What can I say? I took my leadership role very seriously.

Truthfully, I had been the mischievous mastermind behind our schemes since we were about two or three years old. Most of my early rebellious planning stemmed from sheer curiosity. Pee Wee served as my accomplice and pawn. She was my muse and happy to oblige all my silly ideas. We would sit up in our shared little twin bed, having burp contests to pass the time. We'd burp until a loser was declared by whoever vomited first. I conducted these burping contests strategically at bedtime. Tina yelled, "Stop that nasty a** burping and take y'all a** to bed!" We'd laugh until we eventually fell asleep. Despite our annoyance with each other, she was my little sister, and I'd go to the moon and back for her.

Each of us had a unique quirk. I had always been the darkest in the family, and Tina called me "Blackie with the big ol' eyes." My deep-set eyes have always been my standout feature. I never thought my looks were anything special, and not receiving positive reinforcement and affirmations did nothing for my self-esteem. Tina loved to talk about how ugly I'd been as a baby. It didn't make me any never mind, plus I was as skinny as a broom and couldn't get a guy's attention for nothing, not that I wanted it.

Pee Wee, on the other hand, was naturally prissier, domestic, and girly. I was hardly the debutante. I preferred throwing a football, racing barefoot, and jumping out of trees. Despite my siblings' isolation by labeling me the favorite, I did notice a silent code that Tina and I shared. I felt it every time I thought I made her proud. Her "Blackie" was on an academic quest to please her. I brought home ribbons, made the honor roll, and won spelling bees. I noticed that made her happy, especially as my siblings were not so accomplished in school. This was my way to stand out.

Regardless of Tina's lack of help with my schoolwork, she regularly warned us not to come home with bad grades. If we did, she threateningly stated, "Yo' a** is grass, and I'm the lawnmower."

Just before moving, I reminisced about my days in Mississippi, when I picked plums and honeysuckle plants and threw rocks at the cows crossing railroad tracks. The Tennessee environment was a bit different than Mississippi. I didn't easily catch frogs or see cattle and random turtles. In the Tennessee air, I caught lightning bugs, rode my bike up hills, and experienced snow again. Speaking of snow, the season had changed again, and we moved to the east side of town, into a rough housing project, which eventually provided me with tougher skin as I slowly came out of my socially muted shell.

It's no wonder I couldn't make consistent childhood friends. By fourth grade, I attended my fourth school, and I would change schools six more times before high school graduation. That's one thing we all did well—adjust for a bit and then start all over.

Tina struggled to make ends meet, especially now that we were on our own. She found a couple of odd jobs, working as a housekeeper and as a supermarket cashier, sometimes juggling two jobs at a time. It was tough for her to find better work with minimal experience. Watching her struggle to pay the bills affected us deeply. She was always frustrated, short-fused, and had started to drink frequently. Consequently, I begin to battle with an apathetic attitude toward school, my peers, and life in general. At times, I felt as unpredictable as Tina.

She found different ways to cope with her life stressors of lacking stability, financial irresponsibility, and her lack of direction. The times that I caught her crying in her room, I would tell her, "It's going to be OK; I'm going to fix this and make our lives better when I grow up."

Foreshadowing the majority of my obstacles, I'd spend a lifetime overcoming them. I'd already navigated through separation anxiety, generalized anxiety, inadequacy, perfectionism, and depression, and now, at ten years old, I developed a fixer mentality, making others codependent on me. I became severely empathic, embodying stress caused by the problems of others. I had no boundaries and felt a supreme need to fix and rescue anyone hurting because I knew how it felt to hurt.

After all, it had only been five years since our move and Tina's drug-free sobriety. My mother was depressed as well, although functioning. She was very insecure, hurt, dwelling in the past, and struggling to recognize and establish her humanity. I could only imagine the negative self-talk and voices in her head. We didn't talk as a family, and she never addressed anything with us about our past, either. We just proceeded as if it never happened. We were all bleeding internally from the emotional scarring. The older we got, the silence and unaddressed hurt progressed, developing into resentment.

In many ways, we all harbored bitterness against Tina. My resentment confused me because, despite my bitterness, I loved her. Through it all, Tina never lost her resilience. She didn't even recognize her power or understand the magnitude of strength it takes to quit crack cocaine cold turkey. Tina never knew that I wanted to be just like her, the good and the bad. I wanted to be strong like her. I thought that anyone who had endured as much as she did had to be strong. She was so beautiful and smart. I admired and secretly loved everything about her.

My adolescent processing of my circumstances normalized even toxic characteristics as healthy. I didn't know the difference. What I did know was that getting good grades made Tina happy, so I worked hard to get them. I just wanted to make my mom happy, and I wished all my siblings felt the same. By fifth grade, I was a full-fledged people pleaser.

In the winter of 1993, we met a family who would restructure our foundational beliefs. Pastor J. Sumrall was a beautiful older woman with rich, even skin and beauty marks. She had a husband and three beautiful children, two daughters, and a son. One of her daughters was in high school, and the other was in her early twenties. Her son was the youngest. He had funny-colored green eyes and a high yellow complexion similar to Taylor's. Pee Wee and I admired the Sumralls tremendously...so much, that we pretended to be them around the house. Taylor would be Pastor Sumrall's son, and Pee Wee and I fought over which of us would be the high school daughter and who would be the young adult. They were both equally beautiful, but the older one was especially alluring to us because she was an adult. She was the proper one who was old enough to have a boyfriend. She dressed really fancy, her nails were always manicured, her hair shiny, and she wore a pinkish lip gloss.

Pastor Sumrall's daughter was the first person who told me I was beautiful. She always had the most positive, profound, and affirming things to say. Tina must have liked her, too, because she let us spend the night at their home. Prior to that, we were never allowed to stay at anyone's home overnight.

During our sleepovers, we'd stay up late watching her favorite movie, Beauty and the Beast. When she cried at specific parts of the movie, I cried, too. Pastor Sumrall's home became our weekend getaway, and we desperately needed a reprieve from our own unstable home life. The culture of their home was balanced, loving, and supportive. Their influence on our lives was vital, necessary, and a catalyst for my future. Their church became our church, and over the next couple of years, we were like one big, happy family.

Their services were held on Saturdays, just like our old temple in Chicago. I suppose I would describe Pastor

Sumrall's church as Pentecostal with a heavy Jewish influence. You were liable to see anything, from people speaking in tongues, running in circles, and violently shaking from the slaying of the "Holy Spirit." Customary Jewish holidays and feast days such as Passover, Yom Kippur, and Rosh Hashanah were also observed, just like at our old temple. But unlike the temple, our new church provided me with a sense of encouragement, community, love, and excitement to learn about God.

I guess, like most, I was more of a traditionalist, especially as a kid. I believe people tend to follow as adults whatever they were exposed to as children or grew up around like we did, although sometimes it can go the opposite way. For example, I've met plenty of preacher's kids who were off the chain and behaved in a fashion utterly opposite from their upbringing.

Tina taught us to pray every night, to say grace before eating, and she occasionally read the Bible to us. But that was the extent of our faith, besides our travels back to the temple in Chicago a couple of times a year for major Jewish holidays. Despite my lack of understanding of religion and spirituality, the temple and Pastor Sumrall's church were where my faith and introduction to God began. Attending the temple was very confusing as a ten-year-old. One moment Tina would speak badly about that place, yet in the next, she instructed us to go for religion's sake.

The temple was hostile, cold, violent, and legalistic. The temple pastor displayed all the characteristics of a narcissistic master manipulator, psychological warfare strategist, imposter, and criminal. You were likely to see anything there: fraudulent activity, homosexuality, "saints" beating their wives, adultery, child molestation, and a plethora of other egregious behaviors taking place while uttering the "secret name of Yahweh." At the time, I was too young to know the full extent, grave damage, and negative ramifications the temple would produce in my own life and the lives of my family. Right up to the present day, I'm still unpacking trauma and erroneous teachings from the temple.

Later in life, I learned the temple's role in my grandparents' split and how the place was perpetual chaos, hypocrisy, blasphemous, and an abomination to the characteristics and principles of God.

I had to attend in the interim because Tina, her siblings, and the rest of my maternal family had gone there. So, we kept the tradition. Yep, despite all the chaos and damage caused by the temple, people were afraid to leave. And if you left, you couldn't talk to your family anymore; you became an outcast. The pastor did an outstanding job of brainwashing, dividing, and conquering the minds of the congregation. Manipulation, fear, and guilt observed from the temple's culture tarnished my developing beliefs. I was taught that God would disown me if I strayed and didn't keep the faith and observe His holy holidays. These were all lies that I've worked hard to unlearn for years.

For anyone going through something similar or questioning God's authenticity and His love based on what a pastor says or does, please don't put your trust in huMAN. Fake pastors will get what's coming to them. The Bible says so, and revenge belongs to God; He's got you. Listen to your heart and gut: If something smells fishy and feels off, don't ignore it. Pay attention and ask God to reveal His truth to you. Also, remember that God is love, and anything and anyone displaying the opposite of love is a liar!

I thank God for Pastor Sumrall's welcoming, warm, and loving church culture, which I had to balance the temple's uneven teachings. The Sumrall daughters were also a big help to me. They reinforced that God loved me and assured me that He would never cut me off. I formed a strong bond with these two sisters. It was the oldest sister's influence in my life that planted seeds of assurance. Her affirmations had me believing I could be anything I wanted to be.

At Pastor Sumrall's church, I learned the books of the Bible, taught Sabbath school, and sang in the choir. I was determined to master anything new that got my attention. I wanted to be the best at everything. I looked forward to church, sitting with friends, and the cookies and juice served after worship. Church gave me a new purpose and escapism from home.

But neither church, God, Pastor Sumrall, nor the Holy Ghost helped prepare me for my first big fight. On my tenth birthday, I got jumped by five girls in the projects where we lived for no reason. I never understood why I never seemed to fit in. It wasn't a new thing, either. There was always someone who didn't like me, for whatever reason. The older I got, the faster I recognized it.

I was more of a quiet girl who some could have mistaken as being a pushover. However, I did possess sarcastic and smarty-pants undertones. Maybe they didn't like me because I unintentionally made them feel stupid. Who knows? I do know that the big showdown took place with our front porch being the main stage, which to my ten-year-old self felt as big as the MGM Grand in Vegas.

Mind you, we lived in one of the city's largest and roughest low-income public housing projects. So, when I say the MGM Grand, I meant that. Heck, it felt as if the fight was televised, too (in hindsight, I wonder if they had sold tickets). I was all dressed up in my new birthday outfit. The pink pants and matching pink-and-gray striped collared shirt, slightly cropped to expose a little of my stomach, made me feel fly. Excited to be in the double-digit club, I waited for Tina to get off work so she could bake my cake.

Local hood rats from the neighborhood knocked on my door and began yelling the moment I answered. The dialogue went something like this: "We heard that you been goin' 'round tellin' everybody we been eating all y'all's food at y'all's house."

As ridiculous as that sounds, they wanted to fight me for it. They had never set foot inside our apartment, and I never said anything remotely close to that about them. Since I was more articulate and rational, I wanted to talk about it first. But before I could utter a word or make sense of what was happening, I was grabbed off the porch and flung by my hair to the ground. My pink birthday pants tore as I hit the ground. Hovering over me like vultures, the five of them stomped, kicked, and punched me in my stomach. As I lay there receiving the blows, I learned what adrenaline meant. I felt no pain and, in slow motion, watched as each foot went into the air and then came down to collide with my stomach. The beating lasted for what felt like hours. My big brother, Daniel, grabbed a broom and hit one of the girls, which got all of them off me.

As soon as I was free, I jumped up and ran inside, grabbing the biggest knife I could find in the kitchen. I immediately had a flashback to the knife Tina had pulled on Carlos years before. I was furious and, in those quick seconds, reflected on the fact that it was my birthday, my new pants were dirty and torn, I was bleeding, and I was angry. Five years had passed, and Carlos still hadn't come back into my life. I'd been carrying so much anger and rage inside me, and now it had all bubbled to the surface.

Tasting the warm and salty blood from my dripping lip, I morphed into the ghetto version of Bruce Lee, but with a butcher knife instead of lethal hands. That's the last thing I remembered; I blacked out. I knew I intended to kill each girl who had stomped me. Later, I was told that I'd chased those girls all through the projects with that butcher knife. I ran after them until my chest burned, but they all hid from me. Not having caught any of them, I gave up the chase and walked home bleeding, crying, and feeling humiliated. I had just gotten jumped in front of my family's apartment on my birthday, and my new pink pants were ruined!

Neighbors, other kids, and adults simply watched me being attacked, yelling, "Kick her a**!" from the street, their porches, and out of their windows. Not a single adult intervened or came to my aid; they all just watched. That beat-down left a massive scar on my psyche, an epic blow to my self-confidence, and all but shattered my self-esteem. The kids talked about that fight for days.

As I recall the fury I felt that day, I'm very grateful I didn't catch any of those girls, or, I would be sitting in jail today, convicted of murder.

The years ahead changed me, and I started smelling myself, as the old folks would say. That's when I began testing my teacher and Tina's hand by occasionally talking back. I was frustrated and wanted them to know displeased I was. After my fight, I started getting in on the roasting sessions with the popular guys at school, and they roasted everyone! In school, talking about others could make a person popular, provided they were good at it and funny. We called it "roasting"—a skill or a sport where you basically picked people apart with truth, but humorously. Again, it was a skill. You had to be funny, and nothing was off-limits.

Being witty certainly helped my roasting debut. I had quick humor, and roasting became a protective shield. I mean, I'd watch my uncles do it from time to time, too. That generation called it the "dirty dozens" or "ranking." In Chicago, they called it "gunnin'." Either way, I'm convinced that universally, black people all know what it means to be roasted, gunned, ranked, or fried.

Daniel eventually dropped out of high school, and Tina sent him to the Job Corps to ensure he got a GED. It felt different not having Daniel around, as the program required him to stay on campus. In his absence, Tina depended on me to step up. I had already proven to be more responsible, anyway, by that time. She started a new job which paid a bit more, and we finally had health insurance. I remember because she talked about the job and her health insurance like it was a big deal. She worked for the government and managed to stay longer than any of her other jobs.

One good thing about Tina is that she took pride in herself and had no problem working two or three jobs if needed to stay afloat. Certainly, I inherited my work ethic from her but later learned to avoid working just to stay afloat.

Tina taught us to look presentable with the little we had. She taught us how to hand-wash our clothes, how to iron, and take care of our things, and she didn't allow us to leave the house without combing our hair and washing our faces. We had to make sure our shoes were clean as well. We either scrubbed them with an old toothbrush and a little water containing a few drops of bleach or put a coat of Vaseline on our dress shoes, so they appeared polished. Tina didn't play when it came to our appearance, no matter what we didn't have. She learned that from Grandpop.

During the weeks, Tina worked tirelessly, so we all looked forward to weekends. For reasons I'm not sure of, we stopped attending the Sumrall's church, but the daughters came to pick us up from time to time. Most weekends we spent home with Tina, ordering pizza and watching movies. We all piled into Mama's bed for our movie night. The one who laid right under Tina was both the luckiest and the warmest. Taylor often got that spot, while I wondered what it would be like if Carlos were with us. Every time my thoughts went to him, I tried to forget about it as quickly as it had popped up. Because by now, I knew he would never come, but another newness in my life did.

Uncle Mel reentered our lives, but this time more intimately. He and Tina started casually dating, and I was fine with it. Years seemed to zip by continuously, and all the sleepover and girl time conversations with the Sumrall daughters came in handy. Shortly after my twelfth birthday, I officially became a woman. So much happened those years: mentally, physically, and emotionally. I picked up a few new hobbies and would spend hours engrossed in activities I enjoyed: journaling, creating stories, dancing, and doing hair. I slowly started coming into my own.

That year, I wanted to audition for the dance team, and surprisingly, Tina allowed me to, despite lousy timing. Unbeknownst to us, she was about to get fired from her job. I spent hours making up eight-count dance routines every day after school. Pee Wee hated it but obliged my request to learn them with me. Auditions were held on a Thursday, and I danced to DJ Rob Base's "It Takes Two." Tina came to watch my audition as if she hadn't seen me prancing around the house all week. I spent the entire routine staring at her for approval. I wasn't a bit nervous and believed I did well. The high that accompanied doing something I loved was euphoric.

I can't recall fully having had the luxury of being a kid, of being carefree, or taking everyday comforts for granted. No, there was always dread and unease resting in my soul regarding Tina. I was thrilled to learn I had made the team, but my excitement was short-lived. Not only did Tina lose her job, but we were evicted and had to move in with a relative. Just before the move, Tina started drinking more, and our relationship became more strained. I suppose she sought refuge in her beloved Canadian Mist whisky. But like drugs, sex, or any other vice or substance, once the buzz or high wears off, we're still left with our glaring realities.

Pee Wee struggled the hardest to cope with Tina's drinking. After all, she had drunk her way into bouts of illness, car accidents, financial troubles, and a deeper rift between her and us. The alcohol made her angry and violent. When she drank, her verbal abuse worsened. I don't believe she realized how her drinking impacted us. Feeling hurt, discouraged, and emotionally bruised, Pee Wee decided to write a letter to Tina. The letter must have resonated because Tina checked into a rehab facility. She was too prideful to tell us exactly what happened. We just knew she disappeared a few weeks. Her time in rehab coincided with both Pee Wee's and my birthdays, so she wasn't there to make our cakes, a tradition we loved and looked forward to.

In her absence, our aunts cared for us, but I believe that was when Pee Wee lost respect for Tina, subconsciously giving up on the mother she wished she had. Their relationship would never be the same again, and my own relationship with Tina shifted drastically as a result. Shortly after making the dance team, I had to quit. We were moving, and I'd be changing schools yet again. I was heartbroken.

CHAPTER THREE

Devil on the Left

You are pa-the-tic, Carlos, you coward of a man. You messed up my life, my mother's life, and you left us! Those were some of the thoughts fumbling through my mind as I proceeded to close his imaginary casket. Carlos was officially dead to me, although still residing somewhere in Chicago (in all our visits to our hometown temple in the seven years since we moved away, we never saw him once).

Finally, I planned to eliminate every memory associated with him. It had been delusional for me to hold on so long. I had become callous and emotionally damaged by feelings of rejection, abandonment, and my father's absence. I was angry at myself for being in denial and hoping year in and year out that he would come to see us. Consequently, those emotional scars produced invisible seeds, which blossomed into heavier insecurities, a supreme desire to be loved that some may call "daddy issues."

So, what did I do? I searched for him and everything that I wanted from him among all the wrong people and in all the wrong places. As an adult, I thought because I had buried him decades before, that I was good…that in my mind, since he was dead, he didn't exist.

I couldn't have been more wrong, and it wasn't until life exposed this, placing all my baggage on a golden platter right in my lap. I guess I should've been able to assess my relationships with others—specifically, the opposite sex—to see these "issues." But I didn't, and never really gave it any deep, deep thought until I got married.

Marriage forced a deeper dive and a true raw assessment of all my relationships, previous partners, and people I've merely entertained and the motives behind each. From my teen years through my late twenties, I looked for people and things to validate me in attempts to feel good. I hung with questionable crowds and succumbed to peer pressure...you know, just going along to get along.

I discovered how my parents' absence, unresponsiveness to my needs, and emotional unavailability left me trying to fill my father-sized void with people and things that could never satisfy or fit. I thought I needed something to take the place of what I longed for all along from Carlos and Tina. I yearned for the love, affection, and attention that only emotionally whole parents could give. So, when I came up short, it made me more frustrated, confused, and sent me on the prowl searching once again.

Every negative thing that happened in my life up until that point (twelve years old) was my parents' fault, but I reconciled it as being my own. I thought *I* was the problem. I thought I was unlovable. These thoughts were a critical part of my foundation and consequently produced feelings of shame, guilt, fear, and inadequacy.

In my insecurity, I latched on to others and desperately needed to feel like everything was OK, like *I* was OK, and that whoever entered my life would never leave. I wanted to feel fully accepted and, most importantly, loved.

My journey to healing and reconciliation with my childhood trauma began shortly after my thirty-third birthday, three years before meeting my husband. Thank goodness, I started the work of tracking and tracing the roots of why, how, and who I am and of my beliefs and behaviors before meeting him.

But let me tell you, I am still discovering, still unpacking, and it has been one heck of an emotional journey. And I couldn't have imagined how my past, all the time I wasted with others — men specifically — would impact my future, but it has. For example, I developed unhealthy notions about sex, intimacy, how men were, and what relationships should be like. Regretfully, I accumulated partners who were shameful and detrimental, and hypocritical to my image as a mentor to young girls. I'd spend my thirties owning and unlearning my past and using it as a launch pad and platform to guide, support, and encourage others, specifically young women like yourselves.

The work has been therapeutic and rewarding, but still hard work. I've learned so much...and I'm still learning. I highly recommend that you do the same. Don't be afraid to identify your own toxicity and damaging behaviors. Trace the roots of your negative and/or self-destructive patterns and ask yourself where these habits stem from...then reconcile them!

Ladies, there is beauty in identifying the roots of trauma, as it allows for deconstruction at the core. Moreover, if you can track the origins of negative thoughts or behaviors, you'll have an opportunity to correct not only these, but the outcome. Think about it...we fight our inner child daily. And when a child doesn't have the capacity, knowledge, language, or tools to properly assess the trauma and toxicity around them, they'll likely internalize it in an effort to make sense of it. That is what I did, and I did it often. Now, at thirty-seven, I can protect my inner child and let her know she is lovable, valued, and more than enough.

We relocated to a quaint neighborhood, moving into a three-bedroom duplex that Mel had leased for us. He helped put money down to get Tina some wheels around that time and stuck around more consistently. The neighborhood was very suburban; we had neighbors who waved to us while watering their flowers or mowing their lawns. My new environment and the change of scenery introduced me to two of my favorite new vices: Boys, boys, boys, and the adrenaline that accompanied obtaining success were all I thought about. The thrill produced by success wasn't particularly new, but I was older now, so the stakes were greater. I understood that succeeding would be my ticket to a better life. At least, that is what I imagined. At any rate, the new crib, boys, and continued achievements didn't fix my less than desirable home life. It was still crappy, and the older I got, the worse it seemed to get.

As a temperamental teenager with raging hormones, I was certainly a ticking timebomb and angry at the world. My new school was a dump where I didn't know anyone, and I missed being on the dance team. Everyone had friends they'd known for years, and here I was, trying to fit in once again.

I heard about some epic parties thrown by a girl who got off the bus at the stop before me, but when I mentioned the party to Tina, her answer was no. So, I decided to sneak out of the house and attend the forbidden party. Like clockwork, Tina sat in front of the TV drinking whisky until she passed out.

My siblings and I liked to ask her for permission for things when she was drunk, because she tended to be agreeable to our requests. I asked again if I could go to the party, and in her half-asleep and drunken state, this time she said yes.

Dressed in denim overalls and tennis shoes, I eased out the front door, only yards away from the couch where Tina slumbered. I was excited to attend my first party solo. As a matter of fact, I was ready to show them who Dee truly was.

I heard the music's bass a block away; it actually vibrated against the windshields of parked cars. I knew the party would be lit. I'd heard that girl threw the best parties and had them pretty often. I figured she had to have the coolest parents ever. Little did I know at the time that she held those parties while her parents were away.

When I reached the front door, I walked in with my chin up, shoulders squared, and back straight, instantly recognizing at least two girls I'd spoken to before. The lights were dim, and the furniture was pushed against the walls. Master P's "Ghetto D" album blasted from the sound system. I spotted the boy I had a crush on across the room and made my way over to dance with him. Without hesitation and no questions asked, I started twerking, putting my best moves on him for what felt like an eternity. With every popping of my hip, dip in my back, and bounce to the beat, I felt free and desired—until the music abruptly stopped and the kitchen light came on, and I heard Tina's distinct raspy voice. "Dee! Dee, where yo' black a** at?" Before I could run for cover, she lunged into the corner where we were nestled. "What the f*ck you think you doin'?" she snarled before slapping the taste out of my mouth. She then proceeded to grab me by my collar and shove me out of the house.

Everyone followed us outside like a scene from the movie *Friday*. I heard them laughing hysterically until we were out of earshot. Tina threw a couple of more punches on the walk home before we made it into the house, continuing the verbal abuse. She poured herself another drink before collapsing on the couch again.

Crying hysterically, I stormed into the bathroom. I convinced myself that I would just run away if I couldn't find the courage to kill myself. I'd been humiliated in front of my crush and classmates, and from that day forward I truly despised my mother. I knew I would be the talk of the school for weeks, if not months. I hated being home. I hated everything about that place, and I hated how she acted when she drank. I hated how I felt about myself, and I hated life. I prayed that God would fix me and fix Tina as well. I prayed for someone I could talk to, someone who would understand me.

Therefore, I decided it was time for a boyfriend, and in the spring of 1998, I got one just before my fourteenth birthday. I met him back home in Chicago at the temple during Passover. It was a cold and snowy April, and the weather still hadn't broken. Pee Wee and I arrived just before sunset, the start of the sabbath and Passover. Entering the temple just in time, we covered our heads, as was the custom for women; and removed our shoes, the custom for all. We were greeted with "Shalom," meaning "peace" in Hebrew from the elders and a "Hey, girl, hey" from our cousins. They were always excited to see us when we came up. Despite living miles apart, we picked up where we left off each time.

We had a lot of family and friends who went to the temple, and the majority of our friends' parents had grown up with ours. It wasn't unusual for the congregation to have among it three or even four generations of a single-family.

That Passover, I noticed two new guys who were roughly our age. During the service, I asked my cousins PJ and Caty who they were. Caty, the younger sister, bearing brown skin, a beautiful smile, and a baby face, rolled her eyes at my question. She was hilariously sassy and flipped at the mouth, just like Pee Wee. Her sister, PJ, was my age and a bit more reserved like me. Caty was Taylor's age, three years younger but had the mouth and mannerisms of a forty-seven-year-old.

Annoyed, I snapped, "What the hell you rollin' your eyes for? Who are they?"

Caty responded with a smirk, "Yo' cousins, that's who. They finna be yo' cousins in an hour."

Pee Wee and I jointly exclaimed, "What?" I added, "Our cousins? By who?"

PJ explained, "By that woman your uncle is marrying tonight in service. Those are her nephews."

My heart sank. *Oh, shoot, they're about to be our cousins.* But then I thought, *But only on paper, and technically in-laws.*

His name was D'Mario Bass; I called him Mario for short. He had the most beautiful brown skin imaginable and the most captivating bedroom eyes. (Don't ask me what I knew about bedroom eyes at fourteen years old; I just knew he had them.) His demeanor was different from the boys in the hood, the bad boys I was usually attracted to. Mario seemed very charming and respectful, a gentleman. My attraction to him was mutual, because he tried hard to get my attention.

We spent the entire service catching glimpses of one another. I wondered how old he was, where he stayed and what was his favorite food. I wanted to get to know him. So, I devised a plan to make that happen.

Passover services usually ended the following morning. They were similar to watch night or shut-in service, where you stay overnight in the sanctuary. By daybreak, I begin petitioning to stay at our newly wedded uncle's house. I heard the boys were spending the night there, too. Surprisingly, our aunt who we were originally to stay with said yes, and we piled into our uncle's gray minivan and headed to the South Side. Mario was quite the comedian during the ride over, and I chuckled at all his jokes with my most "girlish" laugh.

I found myself completely out of my comfort zone; I'd never been this engaged or cared what a guy thought. However, I liked the foreign feeling and couldn't believe it was actually happening. This was the first time I'd truly been interested in a boy, and it was a big deal. More than anything, I felt he liked me, too.

I knew I wasn't the prettiest or even a real girly girl. I wasn't a large C cup; I didn't have long hair, round hips, or a big butt. I mean, I was the burp contest champ who wore Daniel's clothing and Taylor's shoes. I had hardly put on lip gloss before that evening.

When we reached my uncle's, the adults went to bed, and Mario and I sat and talked. We talked about everything from sports to the music we liked and our families, and we really hit it off. Eventually, I started to doze off, and each time I caught myself, and when I abruptly opened my eyes he'd still be right there, watching me. He told me he liked listening to me breathe and that I was beautiful, even as I slept.

Embarrassed and awkwardly clearing my throat, I sparked up more conversation about him to take the attention off myself. He had me so nervous that I was almost trembling. He noticed it, too. Before I knew it, he scooted his slim frame closer to me and whispered, "You can lay your head on my shoulder when you fall back asleep." I looked him in the eye to see if he really meant it, and he did.

I realized at that very moment that he would become my first boyfriend, and I would be his girlfriend.

We headed back to Nashville a few days later. I thought of Mario the entire drive, his dark brown skin, rich brown eyes, and those long lashes. I visualized his furry unibrow and the little mustache growing over his big smile. We had so much in common. He was really chill, laid back like me but also very witty. I liked everything about him, but most importantly, I liked the undivided attention he gave me.

When we arrived home, Tina told us she was sending us back the following month. She had arranged for us to spend the summer with our Aunt DeDe while she sorted out some things.

May came and went, and before I knew it, summer finally arrived in the city of Chicago, and so did we. I was excited about my first plane ride. Tina sat next to Taylor and Pee Wee. I sat across from them and managed to get the window seat. Admiring the clouds, I reflected on random prayers that I'd sent to God. I wondered if He really loved me, if He was listening to my prayers, and if things would ever get better for us.

Glancing at my siblings, I thought of Daniel and wished he could've traveled with us. With him still away at the Job Corps, it was starting to feel like he wasn't part of the family anymore. I redirected my attention to Tina, noticing her bold yet serene demeanor. She seemed confident yet hopeful. It had been nearly a decade since we moved away from Chicago. Tina may have visited a couple of times and we had definitely been back for visits, but we hadn't traveled together since we left. She appeared surer of herself this time, probably because she now had a GED, some college education, and had been eight years drug-free in spite of her struggle with alcohol. Observing my mother's demeanor provided a boost of hopefulness despite my conflicting feelings about her. She had no clue how I yearned and waited to have a better relationship with her someday.

My Aunt Bertha's was the first stop after we landed. She refused to lose contact after getting hold of our number, and she and Tina had kept in touch ever since. Aunt Bertha had always been big on family, something I'd appreciate about her later in my life. It had been years since we last saw her. She was still gorgeous and kind, the first thing she said was that she wanted to feed us and then take us to see Carlos. *Carlos.* Just the mere mention of his name made me revert to a five-year-old all over again, wanting to see my daddy. I had to remind my inner child that we buried him…but just in case Aunt Bertha arranged a reunion, I began rehearsing what I'd say if we saw him.

Tina and Aunt Bertha talked until their mouths dried out. I could tell they'd missed each other. The delicious aroma of seasoned food occupying pots on the stove brought back memories of her wonderful homecooked meals.

Now seventeen years old, my favorite cousin Lewis had grown out of his chubby childhood body. He was much taller and now sported facial hair. He reminded me of Al. B. Sure or Chris Brown, you know, the light, brown-skinned pretty boys with freshly lined haircuts? Lewis kept a brush in his back pocket in case his waves needed a touch-up. He wore chains around his neck and kept a bottle of cologne in his car's glove compartment. The brush and cologne were certainly light-skinned pretty boy accessories.

Standing back admiring each other, we flashed mutual smiles for what felt like forever, taking in how much we had changed. I still resented the Freddy Krueger terror he put me through as a child, but I loved my cousin dearly. It had been ages since we last saw each other. Lewis was entering his senior year in high school, and I'd be a freshman in the fall. I paid close attention, knowing that I'd meet guys like him. My cousin was fly, no doubt. He had a car and dressed real nice.

Tina and Taylor headed back South after a couple of days. Although we spent weekends with Lewis at Aunt Bertha's, Pee Wee and I stayed at Aunt DeDe's that summer. The first few days took some adjusting. DeDe, a part-time college student very dedicated to the temple, needed the house quiet, and weekends were booked for Sabbath. She didn't have children and ran her home like a military base. Our aunt was meticulous about everything, and initially it was challenging for us. She demanded we clean a specific way, we had to take timed showers and be mindful of our light usage.

As a grown woman, I understand the need to keep energy bills in check. But as teenagers, we thought she was crazy. In addition, the temple lifestyle was restricting and tedious. We had to follow a specific diet and were only allowed certain types of snacks in the house as well. She forbade us to listen to rap music, and we couldn't use the phone or have company. "Company" included family members. Aunt DeDe didn't trust too many people.

On the Sabbath, from sundown Friday until Saturday evening, we couldn't cook, shop, clean, iron, or watch TV. That meant Pee Wee and I couldn't enjoy weekends like we were accustomed to doing. Along with school and work, the temple was a big part of my aunt's identity and her life.

Despite all the adjusting, we knew she loved us and had really missed us. DeDe was very charismatic and kind but didn't play any games when it came to being respected. She was bold, fabulous, and confident. It seemed that all the Shelton women had that frankness about them. They were outspoken, independent, and strong black women…at least they met my perception of strength.

Growing up, I equated strength with pride, speaking up, and boisterousness. My scope and realm of exposure was limited, and what I and many other peers deemed as strength was actually weakness. It wasn't until I was maybe twenty-seven that I discovered just because a person is loud doesn't make them right or strong. I learned that foolish people tend to do the most talking. Furthermore, I learned that pride comes before the fall and that trying to garner all the credit and do everything solo is fruitless.

Summer was spent in the heart of the Westside's Humboldt Park community, where the Dominicans and Puerto Ricans stayed. The area was cultured, diverse, lively, and exciting. We shared a three-story building with other family members. Our grandma's sister lived one floor up, and PJ and Caty lived two floors up. Our second cousin lived on the top floor with his family.

With PJ and Caty around, I knew summer would be lit. We were a perfect blend of unique personalities balancing each other. PJ's eyes practically disappeared when she smiled, and she found humor in everything. She had the most contagious laugh I'd ever heard. We got a kick out of her reasoning and antics. She was certainly the mindless one of the group but had a heart of gold. There was never a dull moment with her around. PJ had developed way faster than the rest of us and had the biggest boobs. However, Pee Wee was still the looker and had the bubbliest personality. She had full hips and a nice booty since, like, fourth grade. Pee Wee was also the most feminine of our group. Her face and figure didn't stop her from being comical, and her impersonations and dramatic antics kept us entertained. Neither Pee Wee nor PJ's maturity level matched their womanly figures, and they both shared a silly naïveté.

I clicked the most with Caty, even though she was the youngest. We were both sharp, street smart, witty, and had hustling personalities. Caty even had a little booty on her. I hadn't gained any weight or developed anything new besides that growing chip on my shoulder.

Our favorite pastimes were watching or listening to hip-hop groups perform. Watching videos for hours, I came up with the bright idea that we should form a group. I had everyone sit in PJ and Caty's dining room, where I shared my idea.

Because we were into boys, I figured the group's name should a combination of how we described ourselves and the cute boys we saw—CBB, which stood for "cutie big booty." The girls all but exploded with excitement. "CBB! Aah, G! That's raw," PJ declared. CBB would also be our code for describing guys when adults were around. Everyone loved it, and collectively, we became CBB.

We needed new aliases and titles to match our movement. As founder and president, I took the name Rocky D. Pee Wee, our secretary, became Spicy B. Vice president, PJ, became Ms. P., and Caty, since she was the youngest at eleven, went by Baby J. I didn't quite know what type of group we were, but I loved the direction in which we were heading. That kickstarted what would later be my gift of mobilizing and organizing. I enjoyed coordinating and planning. I choreographed dances, secret handshakes and wrote rap lyrics and a theme song for us. So, I guess we were a rap group—a rap group that I took really seriously!

Obsessively, I tried to force everyone else to be as serious as I was. CBB gave me purpose and reignited my dreams of dancing. I looked forward to Saturday nights after temple. We stayed up late to watch *Showtime at the Apollo,* and I'd dream that someday we'd take the stage and perform as a group. Caty and PJ had the actual singing talent. I was stronger in writing lyrics, managing, and dancing. Poor Pee Wee couldn't rap, sing, or dance, but she was always down for whatever. We would talk of traveling to New York to perform on the legendary Apollo stage. Although it was fun to dream, deep down, I think we all knew it would never happen.

On Sundays, I woke the girls early and handed out paper and pens. We needed to perfect our craft as a group. We sat at the dining room table for what felt like hours, and I had everyone take a stab at writing their own verses. We also worked on our choreography. I made up dance routines from music videos, imagining I was a choreographer for Missy Elliott or Janet Jackson.

When we weren't writing, dancing, watching *Showtime at the Apollo,* or playing Nintendo, we relaxed on the building's front stoop. As we watched fancy cars on rims with tinted windows, listening to their busted sound systems, we'd yell, "CBB!" as random boys passing by.

Our summer thing was walking to the corner store, eating snow cones, double-dutching, and occasionally running through busted fire hydrants. When we got tired of those activities, we'd head over to the basketball court to watch pickup games. Like four little creeps, we camped out on the grass, drooling over shirtless guys with admirable abs playing ball. Summertime Chi was different from any other summer.

I loved the live atmosphere. I felt as if I'd wandered into a scene from Spike Lee's *Crooklyn* movie. There was always something happening and something to do. The second week of our stay, DeDe signed us up for summer camp at the local community college she attended. Aunt DeDe planned to work there part-time as a camp counselor. Camp widened my exposure to a variety of perspectives and people. We played softball, basketball, took African dance and did arts and crafts.

Kids up there were different from the kids down south. Kids up north seemed more confident and outspoken. They cursed a lot, moved faster, and were either gang-affiliated or had family who were.

Our routine became camp during the week, fun times at home in the evenings, and temple on the weekends. All that feminine energy surrounding me started rubbing off, because I found myself taking longer to get dressed and paying more attention to my appearance. Pee Wee, Aunt Bertha, PJ, Caty, and DeDe all looked so fabulous. So, the pressure was on, at least in my head. I was still quite the tomboy, but a cute one. I wanted to feel good about myself and give the guys at camp a show. Summer revealed just how boy crazy I was.

Meeting new guys all summer turned into a thing for us. I loved the attention and the feelings associated when someone showed interest in me. Each of us had camp baes or crushes. We weren't in real relationships; our camp baes were just someone to hang with and talk to. I know, I know, you're probably thinking, what happened to Mario? Mario was still around, and I considered him my actual boyfriend, but we hung primarily on the weekends.

During the week, I had my guy friends, but I was exclusive to Mario on the weekends. I loooved me some Mario! Being with him always felt easy and free. He was such a great listener, a sweet guy who always knew what to say. We could talk about anything, and I didn't feel the need to put on (if I did, he'd notice and comment on it). He knew me well and having similar childhood stories strengthened our bond.

Mario was different. While the guys at camp only talked about sex, he didn't. He never applied pressure, which I found refreshing, despite my own curiosities. Aside from the horndogs at camp, my introduction to sex was through music, inappropriate images, TV, and certainly my peers. Anyone else remembers dry humping in first or second grade? Come on, I couldn't have been the only one. I remember learning lots about sex from the "fast girls" who lived down the street from us back in Mississippi.

Then, at age twelve, I had a new teacher, and her name was Kimberly Denise Jones, AKA Lil' Kim. Don't ask how, but her debut "Hardcore" album stayed on repeat in my seventh-grade headphones. A year later, I graduated to learning not only what cunnilingus was, but experienced it. Lil' Kim's explicit lyrics about sex played religiously.

She was fabulous, fierce, hardcore (literally), and had the confidence of twenty women. After all, she did refer to herself as the *Queen B*. I looked up to her and wanted to be confident fly, and influential, just how I perceived her to be.

Her lyrics taught me that I could use sex to control, manipulate, and be powerful. They formed my foundational idea of sex.

Tina didn't give us a birds-and-bees talk. There were no warnings, education, messages, lessons, or anything. She didn't monitor what we watched or who we listened to. Her "don't let anyone touch you" speeches transformed into "don't bring no babies in this house," as we got older. That was the extent of her sex talk; it wasn't a priority to talk with and equip her daughters with knowledge. Maybe because Grandma didn't talk to her about sex, she didn't know how to talk to us about it. Besides, she was busy consuming her whisky.

We hadn't seen the Sumralls in years, so we had no other mentors. No one told me I should save myself for marriage. I had no clue of my value and that my body wasn't for sharing with any and everybody. I didn't know that there was a proper place and time for sex. Eventually, I learned the hard way that sex does *not* equal power, and that it doesn't make people like, love, or respect you, either. As a result, the misguided way I saw and understood sex cemented beliefs that it would take decades to undo.

Despite having early exposure to sex, I remained a virgin. I played the how-far-can-I-go-and-still-keep-my-virginity game out of curiosity. Parts of me wanted to see if Lil' Kim was right and if sex was all it was cracked up to be. However, I was scared to go all the way and fearful of getting pregnant. Sex was everywhere—as it is today—and between raging hormones, hypersexual music, and suggestive videos, it was *all* the boys talked about.

That was back in 1996, and of course now, in 2021, sexually explicit music is still the standard, plus there's Instagram and other social media outlets, producing earlier exposure and more misinformation.

I realized that if parents/aunts/mentors, etc., don't talk to young ladies about sex and all the possible repercussions it can bring, their friends, music, boyfriends, and their social media feeds will. I wish I had someone to teach me about sex before Lil' Kim did. Had I been educated and informed, the experimental cunnilingus would have never happened. Neither would that time with my friend's uncle…

I had a girlfriend who talked bad about me in the eighth grade because I hadn't been "fingered" yet. Fingering was the thing in eighth grade because most of us were still virgins. She wasn't, and she couldn't understand why I hadn't done it yet. She insisted on introducing me to her forty-three-year-old uncle who "taught all my other friends about sex." Yes, you read that right. I—just thirteen at the time—agreed for my classmate to introduce me to a forty-three-year-old man who "wanted me badly."

Now, I knew better and certainly wasn't comfortable with meeting him, but I believed her when she said it would be OK. She assured me that her uncle said it was best for young girls to be with experienced men rather than little boys. She assured me he had dated plenty of her friends before and that I should "woman up." Feeling curious and marveling at the idea of being wanted by a grown man, I agreed to go home with her after school one day. I didn't know what to expect, and I can't recall what I told Taylor and Pee Wee, but I didn't go straight home that day.

My friend's house was dim and old. She lived there with her uncle and grandmother. Her granny was in the room watching television with the door cracked. Her uncle greeted me by grabbing my waist as I walked in. There was no introduction (at least I don't recall one). Immediately, he proceeded to kiss my neck and play with my hair. He not only looked old as dirt, but I felt awkward as soon as I walked in. My friend stood there, just watching.

Locking eyes with her, I gave her my best "get-me-out-of-here" facial expression. She knew I didn't want to be there, even as she begged me to come. Tina's words, "don't let anyone touch you," began playing in my head. By then, it was far too late, because her uncle did more than touch me. He kissed my neck and felt me up. With every grope, I felt defenseless, stupid, and scared. I stood there letting it happen, not knowing what to do. I didn't want him or my friend to be too mad. I closed my eyes tightly. *Oh, God, why do I have to lose my virginity to this old man?*

Then I turned angry thoughts on myself. *You're so stupid; why did you even get on the bus with her? You're no real Queen B.* Several thoughts rapidly fired into my mind in quick succession. *What would Lil' Kim do? You know you can't tell Tina, right? Lord, please help me!* Then tears began welling up in my eyes as he fondled me. After a few moments of trembling, something came over me.

Out of nowhere, I got the confidence to jerk away from him, saying, "No! This isn't right. I don't like this. I need to go home!"

My "friend" instantly spoke up, telling me it was OK for me to stay, but I refused. I confidently repeated, "I want to go home. Take me home." By then, tears were running down my face, and I kept repeating, "Take me home!" louder and more insistently.

He angrily told my friend to go to her room before grabbing a set of keys and storming out. I followed him to a gray Oldsmobile Cutlass Supreme and hopped in the backseat, despite his instructions to sit in the front. The backseat felt cold as a hospice facility, and surges of guilt ran through my body. Only longing to be loved, I thought it was wonderful to have an older man want me. I liked the idea of being desired, but once things got started, I knew it had been a terrible mistake to go to her home.

He dropped me off two blocks from my house and told me never to mention what happened to anyone. I didn't intend on telling anyone, anyway. I was ashamed of myself and wanted to forget it...and eventually, I did.

The only place where I planned to share the details of what happened was in my diary. My diary was my space of comfort, where I could express my true thoughts. Writing stuff down was therapeutic; it helped me release my frustrations. What I loved most about journaling was that my writings never judged me. My diary held my deepest thoughts about everything, my deepest secrets, and desires. I did a great job of hiding it...at least I thought so. Therefore, I was surprised to open it one day and see that Tina had written a response to one of my entries. My face and chest burned with embarrassment and anger that she'd found my private diary and read it. My entry was a self-critical rant about what I perceived as my selfishness and not feeling pretty or good enough. This was her response:

Dearest Blackie, you are not selfish but actually very selfless, and you are beautiful. I appreciate your help around the house. Love, Mama.

Suddenly, my rage subsided into awe, followed by silent tears of joy. So much had happened in the last few days, and I felt overwhelmed. Tina's note moved me. She hardly ever complimented us. I can barely recall her ever expressing appreciation of us. Her written words energized me. I needed them and knowing what she thought of me provided a glimpse of hope.

Regrettably, Tina wouldn't be the last adult to read my diary without my prior permission. The other time occurred at the temple. It was a typical Sabbath service, and I was sitting off to myself in a pew, minding my business and journaling in my diary. Pee Wee and my cousins weren't too far away. At service, most of the teens sat together, laughing and whispering, typical teen stuff. There was no separate service for children; everyone attended the main service.

When kids got too loud, either a deacon or the pastor would stop the entire service and reprimanded them over the microphone to humiliate them.

As I sat in the corner writing, one of my older cousins, PJ and Caty's mom, who was a deaconess, came over and demanded that I hand over my diary. I quickly apologized, adding, "I'll put it away." I reached for my purse, but before I could put my diary away, my cousin snatched it out of my hand and proceeded to read it.

I pleaded, "Please don't; it's my personal diary. I promise to put it away if you give it back." She refused and continued reading...this time out loud. My face burned like fire, and I was sure she'd read about my experience with my friend's uncle.

Life as I knew it had ended. "Please give It back," I tearfully begged. She continued to read my most personal thoughts, and in a mocking tone. My own words were being used as a weapon of public torture.

Her behavior was typical of the temple's culture. Once more I asked her to return it to me. She cruelly replied, "Oh, let's all hear more of what you're talking about in your diary." Whimpering in pain at her heartless behavior, she snapped, "Shut up," and, determined to embarrass me further, continued to read.

Interrupting the service to reprimand me was more of a distraction than my silent journaling ever was. But she kept reading out loud and flipping pages while glaring at me. Her daughters and others sat and listened, spellbound.

When she stopped reading, I thought she would return my diary to me, but instead, she called her husband over and asked him to read from it. I began to sob with my head hanging low. Never in my life had I been so humiliated.

Finally, the reading stopped, but she kept it until the end of service and talked about me to anyone who would listen the whole day. Her husband, also speaking publicly, referred to me as slut and a whore. He told me I would get pregnant and that I wouldn't make anything of myself. Of course, I was still a virgin. What I found most perplexing was that a grown man, a leader in the church, thought it was OK to publicly shame a fourteen-year-old girl.

That evening, they declared that Pee Wee and I would no longer be allowed to set foot in their home, going a step further and informing us that they didn't even want us to speak to PJ and Caty again, in case my views negatively influenced their daughters.

Hearing a grown man and church leader call me a slut left profound emotional scarring on my psyche. I questioned myself for some time following that public shaming. Collectively, their words were like bullets, penetrating and wounding the inner parts of my esteem and soul. I was desperate to find my place in life, and I internalized those cruel words for years to come.

"Let's add more guilt and shame to the recurring negative self-talk," I imagined the devil saying. The shame that came from having my diary read aloud in front of an audience reminded me of my friend's uncle and that secret I'd been keeping. Once that memory had been triggered, I replayed and relived that forty-three-year-old man touching my body over and over again. I blamed myself for letting that happen and writing it down, now realizing what a poor idea it had been for me to write in my diary during church service. *Maybe they were right; maybe I* am a whore. After all, I'd let a grown man touch me intimately. The little confidence that I had begun to build started wavering.

I hated my cousin for instigating the incident instead of letting me off with a simple warning the way others were. I hated that DeDe didn't come to my defense. I felt she chose the temple's culture over protecting her niece.

Tina wasn't there, but she was furious when I called her and, between sobs, told her what happened. She cursed out both our cousin and her husband. The incident took most of the fun out of the rest of the summer, because Pee Wee and I were unable to associate with PJ and Caty. We literally had to walk past each other without speaking when crossing paths. I felt terrible being the cause of our estrangement. I could no longer speak to two of my favorite girl cousins, even though we stayed in the same building and attended camp together.

I shut down when the sabbath approached, and we would still have to attend the temple. The more I went, the more upset I became with God. I despised that place. Tina was right: That place was toxic, hurtful, and divisive. There was no accountability, and even her childhood abusers still attended.

That summer forever changed me on many levels: My growing internal battles with rejection, inadequacy, fluctuating confidence, and depression heightened by the experience with my friend's uncle. I became pretty good at "putting on" and pretending everything was OK, wearing a mask better at some times than others. However, deep down, it felt like a point of no return. The diary exchange sent me over the edge.

It felt like there was a thorn in my side sent to torment me. The thorn was disguised as anxiety, depression, and negative self-talk. At fourteen, I couldn't articulate what was happening, but I knew something had changed. I felt like a shell of a person, trying to obtain normalcy while navigating the best I could. I was so up and down.

The down moments occurred when the thorn pressed deeper in my flesh. When it pressed, it hindered me from being me. I began searching for something to fix it. My search developed into my own wanderlust. The void caused by my father's absence widened into a gigantic hole that couldn't be filled no matter what I put in there. Whenever the thorns pressed harder, my spirit shifted.

I'd like to call these thorny pressing moments the spirit of hopelessness (AKA the devil on the left). I hope I'm making sense. Just stay with me as I explain. My feelings of inadequacy and battle with depression stemmed from witnessing abuse and experiencing it myself, instability, parental abandonment, and lack of confidence. Still with me? OK, good.

This spirit of hopelessness made me feel trapped and stifled my ability to enjoy life. In turn, that hopelessness produced doubt, more fear, uncertainty, guilt, and hurt. Beneath the surface, I worried all the time. I desperately needed to reassure myself that I was OK and that everything was fine. My anxiety level was always high, and I usually felt unsafe. I tried to manage my anxiety through attempted perfectionism and control.

It was a suffocating way to live. When that spirit of hopelessness came, I stayed in the shadows and shut down. Muting my voice was easier than being disappointed by rejection. My battle with fear of rejection was also a direct reflection of childhood trauma. I habitually defeated myself before giving myself a chance to succeed at anything. I was on a treadmill of continuous, self-defeating behavior. I hated the feeling, and I recognized when it was starting. I just didn't know how to appropriate my feelings.

Of course, I'm now speaking from hindsight, as at that time there was no way to identify my problem. That's why I spoke about identifying negative behavioral roots and unpacking those bags as soon as you can.

Maybe you've experienced childhood fears, abuse, a lack of self-confidence, or have grappled with abandonment. Maybe you've been molested, humiliated, criticized and been called useless and/or a failure, or battled with anxiety or depression. Whatever your thorn is, there is hope, and if you're reading this, me highlighting these issues isn't coincidental. There is a purpose for your life, and your past does not, I repeat, does *not* define your future. You can rewrite your story and start fresh. Anything you don't like about yourself; you have the power to change it. Please know that you are unique and that the one who created you is with you. You are not alone!

Luckily, my "up" moments were powered by a different spirit, a complete opposite of hopelessness. These instances were easier to identify because not only did I feel peace, but I felt alive and hopeful. Up moments were accompanied by optimism, courage, and motivation, usually kicking in when I felt defeated for too long. I'll refer to this spirit as my "help"—an additional positive voice in my head. I know that sounds a little "off." I'm creative and weird at best, but I didn't think I was crazy with these conflicting feelings battling for territory in my heart and emotions.

The positive "help" voice was kind of like hearing someone say, "Something told me to do that." You know, like when you have a hunch about something? I know it may sound silly but follow me; I'm sure you've experienced this.

Furthermore, my grandma used to say, "Talking to yourself is OK. You're not crazy till you start answering yourself." So, at any rate, I knew I wasn't crazy.

My help was like my good conscience, the angel on my right shoulder, and my hopelessness was the bad part of my conscience, the devil on my left shoulder. My help placed hope and positive thoughts in my heart. You get what I'm saying? My help usually kicked any overriding pity parties and fear out of my head. Remember when I told that forty-three-year-old pervert that I needed to go *now* and said that it felt as if some unknown force had come over me? That was my help, and when my help arrived, it boosted my confidence. My help gave me the courage to believe in myself and turn my wondering into a certainty that there was more to discover in life.

This duality set me off on a quest to discover what life had in store. I wanted to break free and be more, to obtain and to do me. I wanted to be the inspired version of me. I desired to lead, speak up, make friends, organize, plan, dance freely, and step out of my comfort zone. On the flip side, I wasn't sure what my life would be and struggled with the painful memories of my past. However, I was determined to keep pushing. The conflicting up and down emotions and hormonal changes were a lot to process at that age. It was like a tug of war going on between a trusted advisor and an inner critic in my head. No one knew this but me.

The summer of '98 was ending, and I laid there on my stomach, listening to Nicole Ray's *Make It Hot* with my knees bent and my feet swinging in the air, singing lyrics to what had become my summer's anthem and the song I sang to myself while composing goodbye letters.

I decided to write letters to my guy friends at camp. Pee Wee and I had to go home early, so the handwritten notes had to suffice as my goodbye. I left PJ with about four handwritten notes to pass out after I went home. (Her mother had another talk with Tina after things calmed down, and she relented and occasionally let us spend time together when her husband wasn't around.) Each note said essentially the same thing, expressing how I enjoyed hanging with them over the summer. And, in true playa fashion, I ended each note with, "You got played. I have a real man, and his name is D'Mario Bass. You were just a summer fling."

With a devilish grin, PJ looked over my shoulder, laughing at every word I wrote. She couldn't wait to hand them out.

That summer couldn't have prepared me any better for my high school experience. I left Chicago more outspoken, creative, and assertive. Most importantly, deciphering and identifying conflicting emotions provided a stronger awareness than I had when summer began. I stood up to a grown man and his verbal abuse. Mario and I shared incredible moments, and I finally managed to be more social. Summer felt validating for my newly embraced womanhood. The ride back south didn't seem as long, either. I had vivid memories to keep me company.

CHAPTER FOUR

Love, Is That You?

Angel was one of Daniel's girlfriends who he met before enlisting in the military. She was a senior in high school and drove a gray Volvo. Thin and plain as a sheet of paper, she wasn't my brother's usual type. Angel was slightly taller than me, wore glasses and had a golden complexion. Socially awkward for sure, she was unusually quiet and shy, but articulate. It was her simplicity that I found appealing. Our different personalities were distinctively fascinating and incompatible at times. Curiosity to learn more about her consumed me.

Angel was black, but she didn't seem black at all. She wasn't like the black girls I knew from the hood, but more like the sheltered suburban ones, which she was. As a matter of fact, I had never met anyone like her. We were from two different walks of life, and we knew it. I had to translate every other slang word or phrase I used when talking to her. In return, she had to break down her vocabulary for me. We didn't listen to the same music, share the same jokes, or watch the same movies.

Angel attended one of the most prominent private schools in the city, and get this, she was one of just five blacks at her entire school—something I couldn't imagine. Her having attended the same school since kindergarten was mind-blowing for someone like me who moved practically every other year. She had things I dreamed of, like stability and a two-parent home.

Her parents were professors at prestigious universities and owned things that we only saw on TV. I appreciated her genuineness, and we became and stayed best friends, even after she and Daniel broke up. Honestly, I believe God sent her to me. We crossed paths for multiple reasons that we'd spend the next decade uncovering. But in that moment, our world was equally exciting to her. She was always very pleasant and helpful with whatever chores or homework we had. In turn, I taught her how to dance, braid hair, and innovative ways to kill roaches. Lord knows, we had so many of those. She said she'd never seen a roach prior to meeting us.

The overwhelming disparities between our lives and Angel's uncovered more of my own insecurities. My life's discontent grew deeper watching hers. It wasn't jealousy but more of an awakening to just how differently we lived. It seemed like she had everything, and anything she didn't have, her parents had access to.

Pushing 70 mph on the expressway, we rode that little Volvo to the ground, and I loved it! We went to see friends, to the mall, and simply took joyrides. We actually needed each other that year. She was my college model, and like a hawk, I watched her entire process. She excelled exceptionally well, landing full rides to just about every school she applied to. Angel represented the only tangible, positive example of high school success for me.

She served as my unofficial academic advisor and helped me conquer freshman year. Watching her process solidified my own college desires. Furthermore, our family gave her confidence and the kind of comfort one derives from being around people of similar ethnicity. She confessed that she was afraid of less affluent blacks prior to meeting us, and that interacting with us inspired her to attend a historically black college.

I, too, wanted to attend a historically black college or university (HBCU). But my desire stemmed from watching *The Cosby Show* and *A Different World*. I loved seeing progressive black people on television. As a matter of fact, Denise Huxtable's character and her college experience was something I wanted to emulate.

I couldn't wait to graduate and leave for college. I had no idea how I'd pay for it, but I had no doubt I would get a college education. That's all I thought about. At times, I vowed never to return home, but in the same breath, my heart ached at the thought of leaving Taylor and Pee Wee.

Frustrations at home were pretty consistent; I hardly wanted to be there. Tina's behaviors and choices were still a catalyst for my disdain and search for love in all the wrong places. And one of the people whom I loved dearly was leaving for the military. Tina thought it best that Daniel join the military after the Job Corps so he could do something "good" with his life (it wasn't presented as an option). Despite our differences growing up, Daniel had become my very best friend. I had a deep love for my brother and sympathy as well. We had been through so much together and had seen a lot as well. This time, his leaving felt more like he was being taken away.

For me, his departure was no different than having to move again just after getting acclimated to a new school. Sadly, I had become so accustomed to instability and people leaving my life that it was hard to truly be happy and to trust that people would stay. The hurt of his leaving for military service made me angrier at Tina. Because of her, my best friend was leaving me.

Daniel and I made up dances together, played Monopoly every day, laughed, sang, and hung out all the time. Although he wasn't really into sports as much as me, we still had our fun, and now it was time for him to leave my life and he'd be gone almost as long as I'd known him.

Everyone attended Daniel's epic going-away cookout. Aunt Bertha and my cousin Lewis even drove down from Chicago. It was a bittersweet moment for all of us. Now an eighteen-year-old man, Daniel was making his solo debut into a cold world with heavy childhood baggage in hand. I monitored every facial expression, hand gesture, and look in his eyes that day. I knew I would be the next to leave, so I wanted to see how he handled it.

Angel had her own adventures ahead as she prepared to leave for college. Daniel was heading to basic training, Angel to Atlanta, and I entered my sophomore year of high school.

I often wore midriff shirts that summer. By then, my hips had started to fill out a tad more. I even grew a little booty in the back that I was proud of. I looked nice and for once, felt good about my appearance. Dancing in a few talent shows that year, I became more social and actually gained a little popularity. My skillful wit and ability to roast people never failed me, and I switched up my crew a bit. Class clowns and athletes were my go-to. I was a full-bred hustler, making a couple of dollars by letting the guys copy my schoolwork.

It became apparent that the fellas didn't look at or treat me like the other girls. Their easy disclosure of everything right in front of me as they talked trash and exchanged male banter made me feel like one of the guys. I was cool with it and took the opportunity to learn from the opposite sex.

"Fingering" was a thing of the past; sophomore year was all about hitting home runs, aka "that action." That's all the boys talked about…that and how big the girls' butts were. While sex and boys were on my brain, too, a third thought regularly emerged. I became laser-focused on going away to college. I reconciled in my mind that college would be my ticket out of the hood and the life I despised. Living vicariously through Angel's stories, college was heavy on my radar. We wrote each other all the time while she was away, and it provided escapism from Tina's drinking.

Her Canadian Mist bottles drowned my thoughts as they began to pile up everywhere. She didn't even have the decency to throw them away. We found whisky bottles under her bed, under the couch, in the couch cushions, in the bathroom and kitchen. I found her constant drinking unsettling, and when she passed out for the night, I'd sneak out of the house.

Most of those times were spent with a guy friend who lived across the street. His parents were very strict religious fanatics. He hated his home life as well and needed an escape as much as I did. He was always a gentleman and never judged or disrespected me. He told me I was beautiful every time we met. I needed to hear those words, and I loved it when he said them. For me, beautiful was equivalent to love and so much more than the physical.

Hanging with him reminded me of time spent with Mario up in Chicago, and I valued every moment. Every week, we met on the side of his house, closer to the backyard, in case our parents discovered we were missing. Lying in the grass, looking up at the moonlight, we talked for hours, sharing our secrets and laughing. Occasionally, I'd recline with my head on his lap and wish he loved me and could take care of me. He was a great listener, although sometimes he'd interrupt me mid-sentence and say, "You're so beautiful, Dee." Hearing him utter those words elevated my heartbeat. I'd exhale, losing my train of thought. "Love, is that you?" I'd ask under my breath.

We never stayed out beyond 2 or 3 AM, and each time the hours flew by. We'd sneak back into our respective bedroom windows, mindful that we had to get up for school in a few hours. No one ever knew about our weekly late-night meetups. Those moments were magical and incredibly special for me. He was my outlet, unofficial therapist, and friend. Our relationship was purely platonic. He never behaved inappropriately, which I appreciated. Besides, I was saving myself for Mario.

Mario and his brother moved to live with their pops right outside of Nashville, only twenty minutes from my house, which allowed us the opportunity to see each other a bit more. Still being a virgin at the start of his junior year finally got to Mario. He started sounding like the guys at school, talking about nothing but sex. I rationalized that maybe it *was* time to go to the next level. After all, we loved each other and had vowed to share that moment together. I can't lie, my curiosity started nagging at me; I did want to know firsthand what "doing it" was all about.

Angel coached me on what to expect during the ride over to Mario's. She was in town for fall break and agreed to drive me over. Mario had the place to himself, and we both were nervous, afraid of conceiving a baby. So, I suggested prayer beforehand. Leading the prayer, I said, "Dear God, please don't let me get pregnant. I really love Mario, but I don't want to be a teen mom. Protect us and guide us. Amen." Hilarious, right? Well, not really hilarious, but looking back it's pretty funny, knowing that I prayed asking God for help to fornicate.

After turning out the lights, we awkwardly struggled to get comfortable, eventually doing the do. After just a few moments, a loud knock sounded at the door. Angel had come to warn us that Mario's dad had returned home. I darted for the living room and settled on the couch and Mario ran into the bathroom, just seconds before his dad walked in with two large pizzas. "Y'all hungry?"

LOVE, IS THAT YOU?

Losing my virginity wasn't as hyped as I thought it'd be. It turned out to be the only time Mario and I had sex. I broke it off shortly after because I didn't like the idea of being in a committed relationship with someone I hardly saw. Neither one of us drove, and we attended different schools. It was hard, but I didn't want to cheat on him.

The breakup wasn't really bad. I mean, Mario wasn't exactly happy about it, but we knew we were connected for life through family. Besides, I couldn't help thinking that Mario was too nice for me. I wasn't sure if a damaged girl like myself deserved a great guy like him. Sounds crazy, right? Well, those were my teenage thoughts. But you'd be surprised by the number of women (and sometimes men) who run away from or push away wonderful people because they're uncomfortable with how they see themselves. Don't do that, please don't. If you're struggling with similar thoughts, know this: There is no one—and I mean that, *no one*—"too good" for you. It's impossible! We can be incompatible with people, but there is no such thing as being better than or too good for another human.

During my sophomore year, I entered a phase where I preferred the bad guy, the drug dealer/D-boy/hood dude. I liked the guy with tattoos, sagging pants, braids, and/or gold teeth. They were more exciting to me. Even though I appreciated Mario's intelligence, he didn't have an edge about him. My ideal man as a fifteen-year-old would've been a combination of intellectual and thug.

The more I hung with the fellas and bumped my Lil' Kim tapes and other venomous music, the more desensitized I became toward values and, most importantly, sex. I had no respect for my body or anyone else's. After losing my virginity, I adopted a flawed philosophy that was equally as complicated and conflicting as the angel and devil on my shoulders. On one hand, I liked the attention and affection that accompany sex. I figured if sex meant guys would like and appreciate me, maybe it wasn't so bad.

Sex provided a false sense of fulfilled desires for attention and to be loved. Consequently, it would be the means by which I'd attempt to find love and get attention. The instant gratification it produced developed fake feelings of satisfaction.

I am deeply convinced that this may be the case for many of you, teens and adults alike. You know the saying: women use sex to get love and men use love to get sex? The truth is that sex will never be emotionally fulfilling because it doesn't produce real love. True love and fulfillment come first from God, and then from within. Additionally, true desire and appreciation is built over time and through genuine relationships and connections.

On the other hand, sex felt good, but my emotions remained detached from the physical act. I didn't see anything wrong with doing what made me feel good at that time in my life. Maybe some of you feel the same? Maybe you don't think there's anything wrong with doing what makes you feel good. Listen, I'm not here to judge or be the morality police, but I will say I've learned that just because something feels good doesn't mean you should do it, freely and willy-nilly.

For me, sex produced the opposite of the love I sought and indulging in what made me feel good encouraged a greater disconnection of my emotions from the act of sex. This was my defense mechanism strategy to avoid feeling played or hurt. It all still ended the same way, and my strategy was a smokescreen, an apathetic tough exterior used to protect myself. I didn't want to be viewed like those other girls the guys talked about. Those girls used sex to find love, thinking that sleeping with a guy would make them stay and like them more or be their boyfriends. Those girls were delusional. Sex didn't make anyone like anyone more. I knew it because I heard the guys talk.

And despite my hearing the fellas talk and knowing what time it was, I, too, was deluding myself in the times I had sex in hopes of finding love. I think I sometimes actually resented being a girl. I didn't appreciate the vulnerabilities associated with femininity. I saw women as soft, emotional, and weak…and I never wanted to be weak. So, I refused to let a man have me in my feelings or lure anything away from me. The Queen Bee wasn't weak, and she played men on *her* terms. I wanted to be like her!

Deep down, I knew I wasn't wired like Lil' Kim and as a matter of fact, I was an empath who cared about everything and everyone. I hated that about myself. I also hated that I so desperately wanted approval, acceptance, and love, but didn't know how to obtain it. My emotionally detached perspective was about owning my power and having fun while my attached viewpoint used sex to find love. I was conflicted, and because I didn't know how to operate within my conflicting chaos, I played both sides: indulging in sex in hopes of finding love yet being emotionally detached from it.

Enduring the regular growing pains of a fifteen-year-old, I had different groups of friends and met and fell for several different guys that year. If the guys were too nice, I didn't like them. If they were too stupid, I couldn't talk to them. My clique of female friends was just as tough as the guys. Occasionally, I ran with the project girls, the hood rats who fought, smoked weed, got suspended, wore Jordans, and kept their hair done. My identity was all over the place. I wasn't nearly as rowdy as they were, but they provided a break from testosterone town.

Neither crowd did their schoolwork nor took their academics seriously, which was also my conflict of interest. They were obsessed with trivial things, like how many girls they smashed (the guys) or who they wanted to fight (the girls). My only other option was to hang with the cheerleaders, majorettes, and pretty girls. I had no intention of hanging with that crowd.

When I wasn't with either clique of friends, I was with my new boyfriend. He was a street dude with gold teeth and gold jewelry. He sagged his pants, wore white tees, the latest tennis shoes, and The Cash Money Millionaires were taking over for the 99 and the 2000s. I didn't find him attractive like that, but the flashy stuff held real appeal for me. He was a sweet guy, but I dated him because he looked like he "had money." And girls, I liked guys with money.

We kicked it at his house, went on a couple of dates, and I even met his mother. Of course, Tina knew nothing about this. Mel didn't even know, and he was my chauffeur, driving me around on weekends. "Always have a decoy and a plan in place," was my motto.

Aside from my gold tooth boyfriend, I had a huge crush on our star linebacker, who happened to be graduating that year. Yes, I had both a boyfriend *and* a crush—don't judge me. My crush had me all types of nervous, and I never believed in love at first sight until I saw him. He literally *zapped* all the cool out of my system. I would have traded my Jordans in and wore dresses and heels every day for him.

I couldn't even think straight whenever I saw him. Now, I knew I had nothing on the pretty girls who flocked to his locker every morning, but he was still my crush. Everything about his swag was really gritty and Midwest or East Coast.

Standing about 6-foot-1, he played killer defense for our football team. His name was usually mentioned in the daily morning announcements and constantly published in the local papers. We had homeroom together, and I made it my business to never be late. I found myself staring at him every morning and doing everything I could think of to get his attention. Secretly, I loved the chase and challenge of *not* having him.

Having a crush was fun, but my boyfriend at the time had most of my attention until the inevitable happened. Not only did he publicly dump me, but he played me, and really bad. He dropped me for a freshman, and I found out in the worst way.

The day I found out was pretty typical. I stalked my crush, went to class, hung with my guys, and went to lunch. At lunch there was this cheerleader girl within earshot exaggeratingly talking about her boyfriend. She was one of those really prissy, lighter-complexioned girls with long hair who dressed really cute.

She mentioned my man's name in her conversation, saying how they stayed up late talking on the phone. He was the only boy at school with that name. I quickly realized the conversation was intentionally staged for me to hear, and my face fumed like hot coals. I wanted to beat the breaks off of her for trying me, but I played it cool. She and her friends were definitely the catty, snobbish, mean girl type. I didn't take well to her kind and wasn't a fan of people purposefully being messy, either.

After hearing the conversation, I got up and walked over to my man's table. Can you believe that those heffas had the nerve to follow me, snickering and chatting? I asked my boyfriend, "What is this, this *girl* talking about?"

He stood up and announced, "I don't go with you no more and I don't answer to you, either. It's over. This is my new girl." He placed his arm around her shoulder as she looked me up and down. She laughed, and they walked off.

My face burned with embarrassment, my chest tightened up, and I felt tears welling in my eyes. But I refused to cry in front of everyone in the cafeteria. Embarrassment quickly turned to fury; I was so mad that I didn't know what to do. So, I said "bet" and walked off with a puffed-up chest. Humiliation gave way to anger at that public exchange. *He's dead to me.*

My head embraced my desk during the rest of my classes, my method of cooling off. I kept my head down, not wanting anyone to see me. Then, just before last period, I spotted my crush at his locker solo, and a glimmer of hope rose in me. I stuck out my chest and confidently walked up to him. "Hey, can I sign your yearbook?" To my happy surprise, he replied, "Sure, I'll go to the car and get it. Meet me here after this period," flashing his gorgeous smile.

I could hardly believe that he not only agreed but invited me to his locker. Watching the clock intently, I made the plan to leave my class just before the bell rang. I pretended to need to use the restroom, so my teacher excused me early. I needed to get a head start to his locker. I hoped my ex would walk past and see me at his locker, and I wanted to appear totally unbothered by the public dumping of just hours earlier. I also had to figure out what I was going to write in my crush's yearbook, ultimately deciding to just draw a heart with my number next to it.

I reached his locker just as the bell rang. There were usually people packed at his locker, but that day it was a ghost town. As a matter of fact, he never showed up, but my ex and his new girl walked by, scoffing at me. Realizing I'd been played twice in the same day, I decided to leave. The afternoon announcements ended—the class that ended was the final one of the day—and I almost missed my bus waiting for him.

Sprinting like a track star, I chased after my bus as it left the school's parking lot. I knew better than to miss my bus because Tina wasn't going to pick me up. Running for the bus was social suicide because the drivers didn't always stop. Thank goodness, my bus driver did stop. I climbed on the bus, gasping for air, my face burning with humiliation. *You'd better not cry, either!* I warned myself. I felt like everyone on the bus knew what had happened to me that day.

Spotting Pee Wee, I grabbed the seat next to her. She looked at me and asked, "What's your problem?" I sarcastically replied, "Nothing."

The walk home from the bus stop felt like the longest block ever. Pee Wee knew I didn't feel like talking and that something was wrong, so she cut out fast, zooming ahead of me. With every step closer to home, I imagined Tina being inside waiting to embrace me. I envisioned homemade cookies resting on the table with a note reading *Dee, you're beautiful and you are more than enough. I love you more than any guy ever could.*

Upon walking inside, I saw the house was dark. There was no note, instead, there lay a drunken Tina, irate that the lights had been shut off again. I stumbled to my bedroom, crawled between the sheets, and cried myself to sleep.

CHAPTER FIVE

Chi-City

Learning to read the writings on the wall and telling time became second nature for me. My Granny always advised, "Don't stay too long and wear out your welcome." Tina must have taken that literally. With all the moving we did, it was hard to feel welcomed anywhere. Despite reading time well, I didn't see the next bombshell coming.

"We're moving back to Chicago," Tina announced.

Wait. What?! Chicago? Why are we moving out of state? It's more expensive, and I'm sure you don't have a plan. Didn't we leave because of your drug addiction? You already drink like a fish. This can't be a good idea," were the thoughts dancing in my head.

I was sick of it, sick of starting over, meeting new people and being new myself. Flashing a toothless smile, I figured she needed my buy-in and support. So, I responded, "Well, there's nothing in Tennessee, anyway. There are more opportunities in Chicago. Change and starting over is always good." Validating what I thought she wanted to hear gave me a bit of hope. And in true Tina fashion, she broke the news at the eleventh hour.

We were so behind on mortgage that Mel needed to move in to save the home from foreclosure. Also, a week before my sixteenth birthday, I had plans that didn't factor in a move. I planned to take my rebellion up a notch. The goal for sweet sixteen was to completely "do me." I was fed up with being responsible and diplomatic around the house. After all, I made it beyond the magic age of fifteen without getting pregnant. I thought I was doing very well—honor student, doing chores, helping my siblings, coming home on time, and being a respectful child. Because I never gave Tina problems, I felt entitled to a reward. My personality rapidly shifted at that age. A switch was flipped, and that chip on my shoulder turned into a boulder. *Where's my credit and incentives for such big accomplishments*, I had the audacity to think.

I planned to get a job, save some money and move out until college. I wanted to move to Arizona and get into modeling. It seemed like models relished in as much attention as they wanted. They partied and got paid to look fabulous. *Yes, models live the best lives*, I thought. Well, the only modeling I'd be doing for the time being was role modeling—playing the role of head housekeeper and serving as a positive influence on my siblings.

We abandoned our home and moved in with my aunt, her kids and Grandma, again. I landed my first job, a salesclerk at an accessory shop in the mall. Commuting via public transportation, always arriving on time, contributing at home financially, and finally getting a nose piercing made me feel as if I'd gained a bit of independence. Independence felt good, knowing that I could buy little things for myself and my siblings. No matter how small the contribution, I felt empowered. Maybe sixteen wasn't so bad after all, although our moving date was quickly approaching. My first taste of rebellion consisted of lifting a sixty-five-dollar designer dress from Macy's, just to see if I'd get away with it (I did). The blue polo-collared dress was super stylish and something I knew I could never afford.

Admiring my brown frame in the dressing room's mirror, I pressed that soft cotton against my skin. I visualized myself as one of the "it" girls from TV. *I belong in a dress like this*, I thought. But only the pretty girls in school wore brand-name clothing, not girls like me. Taking a deep breath, I stepped into the dress, zipped it up, and zipped out. No one stopped or noticed me. I wore the dress the remainder of the day, still high from my shoplifting rush. I felt fantastic at having gotten away with it until my help appeared, the inner voice flooding my conscience. "You're too good to be stealing," it said to me. Instantly looking up at the air conditioning unit between customers, I murmured, "Sorry, God." I was instantly convicted and decided stealing wasn't for me.

My little blue dress garnered the frat guy's attention working the pager kiosk across from my store. I saw him from time to time and we'd briefly speak, but he was very friendly that day. Dark complexioned with a shaved head, decent looking but nothing super special, he was older than me. I identified him as a college student from his fraternity jacket. I'd learned about fraternities through Angel's letters, in which she warned me to avoid frat guys when I got to college. He smiled and waved me over. I knew it was the dress that made me look feminine. After all, it fit my small frame just right.

Nervously approaching the kiosk, I greeted, "Hey." He asked my name and what time I went on break. He said he wanted to show me something. I asked what, but he said it was a surprise.

"Wait, how old are you?" I asked.

He replied, "I'm twenty-three."

"Well, I'm sixteen." I wasn't sure if he knew how young I was, but his response told me he didn't care.

"OK," he said.

"Cool. I'll come back on my lunch."

"Yes, please do."

Sashaying away wearing a huge grin, I silently prayed, *Thank you, God. I wonder what the surprise is.* Beaming with pride, I felt great to have gained the attention of a college man.

Time couldn't have moved any slower that day…maybe because I looked at the clock every three minutes. I kept wondering what surprise he had for me. Maybe he was going to hook me up with one of those pagers from his stand…

When my break time finally arrived, I practically ran to his booth, slowing down before he saw me. I didn't want to seem thirsty, so, I played it cool. Slightly out of breath, I asked for the surprise. He quickly shut down his booth and responded, "Follow me."

I followed him out of the mall and to his car. Nervous, I asked, "Where are we going?"

"Get in. The surprise is at my place."

My heart dropped suddenly from a blend of fear and curiosity. He'd put me on the spot; I had no time to prepare. I thought, *Dee, you're sixteen now, and you need to grow up, so get in.*

We arrived at his place in about five minutes. He took me by the hand and led me into his bathroom, sitting me on the vanity. My eyes bulged out of my head when he removed his shirt and started unfastening his pants. As naive as it seems, I was caught completely off guard. Everything went completely over my head until that moment. As he lifted my dress, I coughed and asked, "Umm, is this the surprise?"

"Yes. Haven't you done this before?"

Desperate to not appear lame, childish, or inexperienced, I loftily replied, "Yeah, of course. I do this all the time."

He proceeded to kiss on my neck while his hands roamed over my body. I felt a knot in my throat, and tears began welling in my eyes. Honestly, I was afraid and uncomfortable. I didn't even know his last name. Eventually my tears graduated to full-fledged sobs.

He pulled back and demanded, "Get down. What's your problem?" Possibly feeling ashamed of himself, he raised his voice at me. I felt like a child getting in trouble, in addition to feeling foolish for getting into a car with a stranger. I hopped off the vanity and adjusted my dress. Upon catching a glimpse of the nearest clock, I announced, "Oh my God, I have to get back to work!"

Seeing how much time had lapsed made me fearful that I'd lose my job. I felt terrible, like I'd disappointed him, and I had disappointed myself. The spirit of hopelessness, aka the devil on the left, appeared, and negative self-talk accompanied my tears on the ride back to work.

I wondered why I couldn't think of anything to say instead of just crying. *You're sixteen and crying like a baby. Stop it! You knew what he wanted. That's what they* all *want,* I chastised myself. Then my thoughts would wrestle, and I'd counter, *But I thought he had a real surprise for me...*

Upset and disappointed, I internalized that disastrous encounter as being my fault. It felt like another instance where I allowed my longing to be desired and curiosity to take over, not knowing what to expect. Getting in the car was foolish, but I liked the thought of a college man having a surprise for me. At the same time, I didn't like to feel played, pressured, or at the mercy of someone else. *It's time to get off the fence,* I thought. I vowed that would be my last time helpless and at the mercy of a man.

OK, my intention for sharing that story is to highlight a couple of things. Moreover, my desire is to create teachable reflective moments and learning opportunities that I believe could benefit some of you. For me, that experience:

1. Created a resolve of not wanting to be at the mercy of a man

2. Affirmed my notion that men only wanted sex, thus creating a deeper disrespect for them
3. Gaslighted me into thinking I did something wrong
4. Perfectly illustrated how I used to stifle my own voice

Remember, this book is about empowering you to rewrite your own story, reflect on poor personal behaviors, but most importantly, to help you learn from my mistakes. So, I'll share what I wish someone shared with me after that experience. Listen to me *closely:* You are not obligated to do any*thing* with any*one*. Your body is yours, and it's special, beautiful, and loved by the God who created you. He loves you daily, and that's far more valuable and important than any man or boy on this earth. Be smart and always ask questions up front. If you don't feel satisfied with the answers, don't trust it…and don't feel bad or punish yourself for saying no. You don't owe anyone anything.

Remember, "no" is a complete sentence. Please don't beat yourself up too long. We all make mistakes and have lapses in judgment at times. Keep it moving and aim to avoid making the same mistake twice; be better next time! Lastly, if you're under eighteen and some guy over eighteen is trying to holler at you, he's too old; men over eighteen trying to have sex with younger girls is considered statutory rape in most states.

I hope these words are helpful for any woman, girl, or teen who has found herself in a sticky situation in which she's afraid to say no or doesn't know how to get out of. Unfortunately, we live in a male-dominated, egotistical rape culture that easily punishes and blames victims for "wearing that," being there, or texting back.

Ladies, I want you to know that regardless of where you are, what you wore, or what message you sent, that still doesn't give anyone the right to assault or initiate anything with you. Not giving consent means NO, and be sure to say no, loud and often. Use your voice and be smart, even if it's not a decision that will make you popular.

After the mall incident, I started stealing Tina's cigarettes and secretly smoking. I'd sneak bottles from my aunt's six-packs as well. Both habits disgusted me, but I did it anyway. I figured that since adults drank and smoked to relieve stress, they'll help me."

As the trusted oldest and most responsible, I practically got away with murder. Both my aunt and Tina worked nights, making it easier to devise sophisticated schemes and sneak company over. Neither of them suspected my rebellion. Besides, Grandma never left her room. I used code names and clever questions as methods to inquire about their work schedules without being obvious. Code Red indicated both adults would be working that evening. Code Blue meant only one of them was going to work. Getting the color codes to Pee Wee and my cousin was easy. The challenging part was creating non-obvious conversations to pinpoint when they would be returning home. My scheme went on for weeks until that one time we almost got caught.

It was the end of summer and our last week in Tennessee. Tina came home early, and there were at least three guys upstairs. She barged in the room, calling my name. Luckily, I'd had the presence of mind to unscrew all the light bulbs, which saved us big time. My guy was literally beside me, Pee Wee and our cousin had their guys near them and on the floor. Tina said, "Dee, what y'all doing?" as she repeatedly flipped the light switch.

"Nothing. Just talking," I innocently replied. I knew she suspected something was up but couldn't put her finger on it.

Just before closing the door, she stated, "Come downstairs when you get a minute and look at this cake my coworkers got me."

"OK, I'll be right down."

Once her foot hit that last step, baritone voices began whispering. "Aww, sh*t. How we suppose to get out?"

I screwed the lightbulb back in and answered, "Y'all better get to jumping." Quickly, I adjusted the room and coordinated the jump plan. I told my cousin and Pee Wee, "Make it fast and efficient while I stall Tina. Don't use no sheets to climb down, either. Y'all ain't white, and this ain't the movies." Running down the stairs, I met Tina in the kitchen with a fake smile. "Yum, this cake looks delish. That was real nice of them," I said. Tina went on and on about work that night while cutting her cake. I pretended to listen, but my thoughts were with the girls upstairs.

Because Tina kept talking, I figured she needed me. I froze when I noticed a pair of legs dangling outside the kitchen window. *Damn it. Jump, already!* Thinking quickly, I snatched the cake off the table and suggested, "Oh, let's show Grandma!" and practically raced to bust open Grandma's bedroom door.

Tina followed, exclaiming, "What the hell is your problem?" She snatched the cake back and returned to the kitchen, placing it back on the table. As she turned to retrieve a plate from the cabinet, I saw another set of dangling legs. This jump wasn't smooth at all. We both heard a loud thump. Once more, I froze. *Oh shoot, somebody landed on the air conditioner.*

"What the hell was that?" Tina said, turning around.

"I'll go see," I quickly answered. I ran to the front door, getting there just in time to see the last guy limp away. I blew my guy a kiss, and just like that, they vanished into the night.

Tina asked if I was ready for the journey north, but I saw in her eyes that she wanted my approval on the move. I knew it was hard for her not to have it together. It had to be challenging to have three children old enough to see her learning curves, and all her failures, in real-time. Her pride made it tougher than it needed to be. Tina had actually done well that summer.

She had even put down the bottle a few months before moving in with my grandma. Maybe that was her motivation, but either way it had been months since I saw her drink. I loved my mother and had a deep sympathy for her. I understood that alcohol and her former drug use were a means of escape, but only exacerbated her problems. I liked the sober Tina a lot—she was warm, funny, and caring.

That night she seemed free talking to me, and I understood, even at sixteen, how much my opinion and support meant to her. I enjoyed those rare moments to chat with my mother. I enjoyed knowing she cared about me and what I thought. That moment in the kitchen reminded me of when I first got my period. She took me to Burger King, and we got milkshakes. While sipping those thick strawberry shakes, she said, "You a woman now, Dee." Moments like those were rare, but they meant everything to me. I wholeheartedly wanted to please her. I wanted to make her proud.

Grabbing a slice of cake, I looked Tina in the eye and very optimistically stated, "I think Chicago is a great idea." She smiled with relief and gave me a warm hug.

Boarding the Greyhound headed for Chicago was reminiscent of eleven years prior, minus Daniel. We had come full circle; we left Tennessee with only a couple of trash bags full of clothes. We moved into Aunt DeDe's one-bedroom apartment. Pee Wee and I already knew the drill, the neighborhood, and house rules. We shared DeDe's queen-sized bed with her. Tina and Taylor slept on the living room couch and a pallet, respectively. It was a tight fit, but functional. The hot water didn't work, so we had to boil water for cleaning and bathing, which was fine until winter and the Blizzard of 2000 hit. But we Sheltons are accustomed to making something out of nothing and, most importantly, surviving.

Being back in the city reminded me of how different Chicago is from the south. Quite a bit of time had elapsed since the falling out with PJ and Caty's mom, and by then even her husband had mellowed, so we were permitted to hang with our cousins like old times. Our first few weeks were dedicated to applying for government assistance, food stamps, housing, and Medicaid. We had to get physicals, plus we needed uniforms for school. Uniforms were new to us; we'd never worn them previously. I didn't have many expectations for either school or the move. Trying my best to be fluid, I vowed to just go with the flow.

Any contempt held from my previous school paled in comparison to the Chicago public schools. We were in the heart of the West Side of Chicago but felt like we'd been cast in the 1989 drama *Lean On Me*. (Younger readers might need to Google that movie.)

Luckily, previous summers in the city and attending camp there prepared me for the public school's culture. Only this time, things were different. The ending of summer wouldn't save us, and I knew attending school in Chicago would be life-altering. Depending on the community, a large portion of Chicago public schools were ranked low academically, heavily gang-infested, and flat out dangerous. Our cousins shared horror stories of shootings and kids being thrown out of windows, brutal lunch brawls, you name it.

Farragut Career Academy, a well-known basketball school and home to notable alumni Kevin Garnett and Ronnie Fields, was where we enrolled...with the help of another relative's address. Tina accompanied us on public transit with us our first day. Public transit was an entertaining adventure within itself. You were liable to see anything on city buses and trains. Kids swearing like adults, people arguing, crackheads under the influence slumped over, and people having fistfights, all in a two-block radius.

Upon arriving, I took a deep sigh before walking through the metal detectors. *First time for everything,* I thought. We were greeted by security, who asked us for our names. He handed us nametags and directed us to the main office. Tina explained to the counselors that we had just relocated and needed help. Sucking my teeth, I stood there, upset and embarrassed by our truth. *I'm too old for this. How can we be in the same predicament as when we left?* I felt humiliated, but also in need of everything they could offer.

The nice lady in the office signed us up for the "KG Scholarship." "It usually takes a while to qualify, but I'll get you started. What's y'all sizes?"

Disappearing into a rear closet, she quickly returned with new shoes, socks, coats, and uniforms. Tina thanked the lady profusely with tears in her eyes before getting our schedules and leaving for the day. Navigating to and from school would now be up to us. I enjoyed challenges, so I knew commuting would be fun. Chicago already seemed to be just the speed of adventure I'd been searching for.

My reinvention began very quickly. I did our hair nicely that night and ensured our uniforms were pressed to perfection. I added a colored shirt under my uniform top because I wanted a pop of color to help me stand out.

The next morning, we sat close to each other during the bus ride to school. I surveyed every street sign we crossed, absorbing the environment and not wanting to miss a thing. I felt Pee Wee's nerves, so I made conversation with some other teens to break the ice. She was typically the more outspoken of us, but it seemed like our roles reversed now that we were back in Chicago. I was usually quieter, the strategic mastermind, but morphed into quite a people person.

I saw other teens in similar uniforms, and one person's ID card read "Farragut." Pee Wee noticed it, too, and announced, "He go to our school."

The boy turned around and questioned, "Where y'all from?"

Not knowing he meant which neighborhood, we both answered, "Tennessee."

A girl overheard us and laughed out loud before saying, "Oh sh*t, they new."

It took everything in my power not to ask what that was supposed to mean. I didn't want the situation to turn unnecessarily confrontational, but I also didn't want to laugh at us again.

So, trying to be friendly, I asked, "What grade y'all in?" When they told us they were sophomores, I immediately retorted, "Oh, y'all underclassmen."

The girl then snapped back, "What you is?"

"Do you mean what grade am I in?" I corrected her. Before she could answer, I added, "I'm a junior."

"Oh, OK." Then she got quiet.

I smiled on the inside, thinking, *This is going to be too easy.*

We walked behind them after getting off the bus, letting them lead the way to school. "Y'all sistas?" one of the girls asked.

One of the boys shouted, "Naw, dumb b*tch, they just look alike," which made everyone erupt in laughter.

Pee Wee and I were both alarmed by his disrespect. Playing it cool, I replied, "Yeah, we sisters," then reversed the conversation by asking her questions. As a newbie, I wanted to make sure I set the tone for future encounters. These kids used terrible grammar and slang we had never heard of. I had no intention of talking like them. I knew Pee Wee and I already had leverage as the new girls. Being from another state made our popularity advance even more. However, in time that eventually backfired.

The security guards knew we were new and told us to be careful. We got our ID cards and had to split up, go our separate ways. My thoughts were with my sister, I knew I would be fine. We'd barely taken a few steps in opposite directions when we heard security yelling over their walkies and saw everyone running. Girls were screaming, "The GDs into it with the Kings."

I was thinking, *Who did what?* The Gangster Disciples, also known as the GDs, had a standing feud with The Latin Kings, and they brawled that morning. The fight was pretty brutal, resulting in a stabbing and an arrest.

Arriving at my first class, I was interrogated with over 20 questions. Kids kept staring and seemed fascinated about having a new student. "Where you from?" was the primary inquiry. All the moving we did made that a hard question to answer. I was born in Chicago and partially raised between Chicago and Mississippi but lived in Tennessee equally as long as the other places. For simplicity's sake I just said, "I'm from Tennessee."

As lunchtime approached, I didn't yet have a strategy of who I'd sit with. At my old school, I was used to hanging with the guys and athletes. Like any school, the lunchroom was most important. My lunch happened to be early, right after third period. Walking into the cafeteria, I grabbed my tray and surveyed the segregated tables.

The Hispanics were on one side and the blacks on the other. Slowly, I walked toward the black side. The first table I passed was full of guys whose long legs stretched out on their sides made me assume they played basketball. The next table was occupied by a bunch of girls who could have been mistaken for guys...they looked rough, like they loved to fight. *Keep going, Dee.*

Socially awkward-looking girls sat at the next table. *They must not have pretty or popular girls here,* I thought because I didn't see a table for them. Not that I would have sat there anyway; I was simply curious. I kept walking before hearing a voice say, "What up, Tennessee?"

I looked in the direction of the voice and saw the guy from the bus that morning. So that's where I decided to sit. He sat with two other guys who looked appealing. I asked everyone's name and where they stayed.

I only did that because it seemed to be the important thing to know. It also helped me get familiar with neighborhoods. I needed to know what was going on at all times. It was vital for me to stay ahead. Some of the guys were in my same grade, and others gangbanged, meaning they were gang affiliated. Little did I know, I parked at the gangbanger's table.

One of the guys, in particular, had a nice vibe about him. He had a magnetic energy, and he made me feel most comfortable. He was very light skin, what we called high yellow, he stood about 5-foot-10, and they called him AJ. The moment we locked eyes; I was drawn to him. It wasn't so much a romantic attraction as it was a gravitational connection.

I heard one of the other guys call him White Lord and figured he belonged to the Vice Lord gang. It was fascinating to be seated between a Vice Lord (VL) and a GD that were cool. At that time, I didn't realize that all gangs weren't beefing. Capitalizing on the moment, I asked, "So the GDs and the Kings got into it today, hmm?" I intended to use what I'd heard earlier to appear knowledgeable.

"Yeah, and they stabbed Lil' homie eleven times, too," AJ informed me.

My eyes widened at that news. *Yo, they're flippin' crazy here.* Part of it was scary, but also exciting. It felt like I was starring in my own movie. It was definitely a change of pace, but also real life.

AJ interrupted my thoughts, "So, what you claim?"

I responded, "I'm neutral, and we don't bang like that down south."

"Good," he said. "I got you. Let me break it down to you, then."

He sat there schooling me on the tiniest details and intricacies of street jargon, money talk, drug lingo, what colors to wear and which to avoid. Over time, I learned about the types of Vice Lords, different gang colors, symbols, and handshakes. As he said he would, AJ had me and Pee Wee's backs.

His lunch table became my table moving forward, and we became really close, and he looked out for us every day. He walked us to the bus stop and told me to always know who I was messing with: "You always need to know what block people are from and where they stay in case something jumps off." He always talked about something jumping off. I didn't know what that meant, but I wanted to be prepared.

Coincidentally, AJ lived across the street from our older cousin, the cousin whose address we used to attend Farragut. AJ aka White Lord was well respected, and no one messed with him. He was cool with the athletes, hood girls, and other gang members, and fearlessly walked us from the bus stop to our cousin's house, where we'd sit until DeDe picked us up. The neighborhood we commuted through to get home was relatively rough. I learned something new daily from AJ.

The schoolwork wasn't challenging at all, but I respectfully paid attention in class. One day at lunch, AJ told me, "Avoid those ugly bi*ches at that table behind you. They some haters."

I laughed and said, "Really? Hating on who?"

"They already hating on you and yo' sister. Be careful," he warned. "You finer than a muthaf*cka, and them bi*ches will try to disfigure yo' face. So just be careful."

Dang, is it really that serious? My thoughts quickly shifted to AJ's compliment. I played it cool. "I'm good. I know how to handle 'em."

"OK, just be careful," he repeated before we parted ways.

Walking away, I smiled to myself at his description of me. *Finer than a muthaf*cka, humph.* I had no clue that AJ had been peeping me. He'd assumed a big brother role, so that's how I viewed him. He was also a street dude, so I couldn't imagine him macking a girl, anyway.

Eventually, we were assigned art class together, and so was Pee Wee. That was my first time having a class with my sister, and the three of us had a blast every day. Pee Wee was adapting well in her other classes.

Prior to the move, I didn't worry about her much, but became very protective that year. The thought of girls intentionally trying to disfigure another girl's face was pretty insane to me. I wanted to be smart, but I wasn't afraid to fight if I needed to. I was used to girls primarily fighting over guys, not out of sheer jealousy of another girl's looks. Speaking of guys, I didn't want any problems with another girl's boyfriend or crush, so I stayed low-key.

Guys in Chicago looked different than guys down south, anyway. The early 2000's was the Ginuwine "The Bachelor" pretty-boy era. Guys looked metrosexual and they wore twists, coiled curls, and even perms. It seemed like everyone at school was going for the pretty-boy look. Personally, I happened to find braids, locs, and Afrocentric appearances more appealing at that time in my life, but I must admit, those guys had swag that outweighed appearances any day. Chicagoans possess a natural confidence and assertiveness about themselves. What you saw is what you got, with minimal bull crap...except for the slick fast talkers who were full of crap.

Me and Pee Wee kept ourselves up: hair, new shoes, and nails done. This caused our names to circulate more consistently throughout the school. We became very popular and referred to as "those Tennessee girls." I intentionally kept my circle tight and gave very little information about myself. I was cool with a few girls, but the majority of my friends were guys. I made friends with the Mexicans and Puerto Ricans as well. They provided me with smoke and had access to any drug you could dream up. Drugs weren't my thing, but smoking weed was. For whatever reason, we didn't consider weed to be drugs.

Hanging with new influences, I started smoking here and there with AJ and others. Prior to Farragut, I never smoked anything other than cigarettes. Never did I imagine I'd be purchasing weed and skipping classes. I know times have changed tremendously but buying and smoking weed in those days was illegal and taboo.

At least, I kept my grades up, I rationalized. Classwork was too easy, and my academic prowess kept me in the "good kid" zone. I kept up a great rapport with teachers and even the security staff. I was so cool with security that one of the guards would forge hall passes for me and let me in the back door whenever I was late for school.

The notoriety slowly transformed into serious hate, and for the first time, I got more attention than Pee Wee. I wasn't used to that type of attention, but maybe it was because I was the upperclassman. No doubt, my fellow students found my mystique intriguing and admired my ability to be super cool and drama-free, unlike some of the other chicks. I was neither loud nor very quiet. I spoke when I wanted to add my two cents on occasion. I participated in class and didn't set out to try too hard, but to just be myself. I enjoyed the new space I created.

In time, I started hanging with a few guys for kicks but stayed clear of upperclassman athletes. They had too many groupies, and they talked too much. I didn't need any more enemies. I also didn't want a boyfriend. I liked the idea of being noncommittal and flexible. I knew a relationship would devalue my ability to be free. I understood that people desire what they can't have. Exclusivity was my goal and I decided to run my own game, milking my new persona. I had gained a lot of confidence and learned a lot about myself those early months back in Chicago.

Maybe guys just enjoyed being around pretty girls. Then again, maybe they liked me for me. Hanging with different guys would help discover the answer. The sight of me with my guy friends kept my audience guessing. I enjoyed watching my peers try to figure out which boy I was really interested in. In actuality, I wasn't interested in *any* of the guys I hung with. I had my eye on someone else...

He was a freshman on the junior varsity football team — handsome with beautiful golden-brown skin matching his light brown eyes. He wore long braids that draped his broad shoulders and muscular physique. Humoring myself, I got a kick out of staring at the freshman table in the cafeteria. I knew he knew who I was but was obviously too shy to approach me. So, I decided to approach him. "You try'na cut out at lunch and smoke with me?" I asked. He looked up, his expression looking like he'd seen a ghost, but quickly recovered and was happy to oblige.

We snuck out the side door at lunchtime, out of range of the school cameras. One of my Mexican friends had taught me how to sneak out and time the rotating surveillance cameras. It wasn't like the security guards did their jobs, anyway. Many of them were focused on trying to impress the students.

We ran down 24th Street toward Cermak and hopped on the bus. I was following his lead, although I'd been the one to initiate leaving school. He suggested his place and I agreed, but he failed to tell me that he lived in the Rockwell Housing Projects. I had heard about them and other projects such as Cabrini-Green, Robert Taylor, Ida B Wells, and Stateway Gardens. I also heard how dangerous it was there.

The commute mesmerized me. That part of the West Side looked like a third-world country. People stood on every corner, selling drugs, drinking, fighting. Crackheads leaned, listened to music, and danced in the middle of the day. Impoverished and frolicking in ignorance, they seemed peaceful, as if they had no worries. Leaving school with a stranger and having no clue of where I was going was foolish, but it excited me. We spoke minimally until reaching his place. We were greeted by his sister and two toddlers upon entering. She looked roughly two years older than me. The kids were about two to three years old. I made eye contact with her and kept going. She didn't even ask why he was home from school.

The room we entered was filthy, with two dirty mattresses laying side by side on the floor with no sheets. "Is this your room?" I asked. "No, this is my uncle's room." He closed the door, we rolled up and just like that, I emotionally disconnected.

Quickly getting dressed, I rushed out past his sister, leaving the apartment solo. As soon as the air hit my face, my heart started to beat fast, and my conscience kicked in. *What are you doing? Have you considered what will happen if the school calls Tina? Dee, you must do better. You won't find love this way.*

I felt myself starting to panic. I hadn't previously considered the possibility of the school calling home. Frantic, I ran, looking for a bus and the route we'd taken to get here. I forgot which bus we took and got on the wrong bus. After ten minutes of going in the wrong direction, I hopped off the bus.

I asked a random lady for the time and knew I needed to get back to school and fast. I remembered AJ showing me how to identify unmarked cabs (which are today's Ubers & Lyfts). Back then, we called them gypsy cabs. They were very dangerous, especially for a sixteen-year-old girl. Unvetted, unscreened drivers cruised the streets, looking for passengers illegally. It was like hopping in a car with a complete stranger.

I saw two black gypsies parked. Taking my chances, I walked up to one, "I need to get to Farragut on Twenty-fourth and Christiana."

"Get in!" He got me there, and I gave him the five-dollar bill I had on me before hopping out. Lord knows, there must have been angels with me that day. I could've been kidnapped, raped, and never gotten back to school. These were things I simply hadn't considered when I left school.

To this day, I am grateful that driver was legit. Things could've gone really bad, and I knew better, but went with what I wanted to do, what made me "feel good."

Arriving back at school by the end of the day, I met up with Pee Wee and AJ walking toward the bus stop. They both asked where I had been. I quickly changed the subject but met AJ's eyes and he nodded and quietly said, "I *told* you to be careful out there." I shot him a smirk; he knew me so well.

Those hater girls at school started teasing again, but this time they started bothering Pee Wee. I was able to keep my composure when it came to myself, but not my sister. Pee Wee and I got into the biggest fight we'd ever had the week after AJ's confession and a secret party with cousins and our CBB group.

I had been planning a shindig for the girls at our older cousin's place for a couple of weeks. After begging Tina to spend the night with our cousin after school one Friday, PJ and Caty got dropped off to meet us. CBB was back together, like in previous summers.

Our older cousin was twenty-three at the time, super fabulous, and quite the socialite. She was the cousin everyone loved: outspoken, down to earth, and fun to be around.

Big Cuz called herself hipping us to the game about men. "Honey, he has to drive the big boy trucks. And he must be able to pay bills and furnish your apartment. If a man can't take care of you, you don't need to be giving him no coochie," she advised.

Her coaching was useless and inappropriate for our ages, but certainly helped shape my growing perspective of men. She was boisterous with an ego to match, and she liked material things. Her influence on our lives was the golden standard. Like many older, cool cousins, she shot us a bone from time to time when we hung out. That night she let us use her crib for the shindig. She had plans with her friends, so we technically had the space to ourselves. She was the decoy.

We sat around helping and watching her get ready. Lil' Kim's second album "Notorious Kim" blasted while we sipped on cheap champagne. Golden Champale was her drink, and she let us partake with her that night. Her only instructions were, "Y'all bet not have no lil' niggas running all through my mama's house." With all the game she had, you would have thought that she would've lived in a condo on Lake Michigan, but she still stayed with her mom.

We promptly agreed, "Yes, we won't have anyone over." She wasn't gone ten minutes before AJ and his friend came over and suggested we walk to the liquor store. I told the girls I'd be back. Although a teenager, AJ had a hookup at the corner liquor store. We got a fifth of blue gin, which we called "blue beast" back in the day, then headed back to Pee Wee and my cousins. En route, AJ stopped abruptly and backed me against the wall. "I want you to be my girl," he declared.

I didn't know what to say. *This isn't supposed to happen.* AJ was my friend, and I wanted to keep it that way. I trusted, respected, and appreciated him. At the same time, a part of me wanted to open up and tell him everything. I wanted him to know how much I secretly struggled with feeling rejected and how I truly didn't believe I was lovable. When he tried to kiss me, I turned my head. "Let's just drink and enjoy the night," I suggested, despite having feelings for him, too.

He looked me in my eye and answered, "Yeah, OK. Cool, Dee. Enjoy the night. Mmm. Let's enjoy the night, then."

I felt him simmering, but he played it cool and didn't let me see him sweat.

Gin would be my first alcoholic beverage other than beer and malt. PJ, Caty, Pee Wee, AJ, his friends and I all sat outside, drinking and smoking weed. Pee Wee and Caty kept choking. I had already learned to do shotguns and pass smoke through my nose and hands to others.

After our third blunt and the last of the Seagram's, Big Cuz pulled up. She must have been tipsy herself, because she didn't say anything about the guys or the weed. We helped her up the stairs and to her bed. "Don't be out too much later," she stammered before going to sleep. We hung another hour, and the guys left. That night went down in history as one of my most memorable high school moments. And I couldn't stop thinking about AJ's confession. The same week, before our big fight, I met another person who would change my life.

Darius stood about 5-foot-10. He was a skinny little something, and I wasn't a fan of skinny guys. But he had the most gorgeous dark skin, dimples, and curly eyelashes under those terribly thick glasses. I was pretty sure I'd seen him before around the neighborhood, but didn't realize we went to the same school. He stocked groceries at the local market up the street. Caty, PJ, Pee Wee and I used to walk to that market all the time. I smiled at him but never really said anything. He smiled back but never said anything, either. Darius dressed pretty fly and had that pretty boy, smooth operator swagger I liked so much.

Zipping between classes one day, we accidentally bumped into each other pretty hard. "Excuse you. What's your name?" I asked.

"Darius."

"OK, cool, Darius, but you need to watch where you going next time." I chuckled and walked off.

He was my type, for sure, but wasn't under the radar enough for me. We ended up running into each other again later that same day. That time he asked for my number, and I responded, "Nah, give me yours." He wrote it on a little sheet of paper that I stashed in my back pocket. I probably should've made him wait a few days, but I called him that night.

DeDe was working overnight, so I knew I'd have full use of the phone. That call turned into us talking for hours. He was so easy to talk to and funny. We hit it off, but in a different type of way. He had something unique about him that I couldn't identify. I placed him in the friend zone, where I figured he would be more valuable. I also knew I wouldn't be the only one who found him attractive at school. The brotha was fine, had a job, and dressed nice. I figured he had girls interested, anyway.

Speaking of girls, the taunting and bullying at school escalated to obscenities hurled at us during class changes. Literally, walking down the halls and minding my business,

I'd hear a remark like, "Those Tennessee b*tches think they cute. They won't be cute for long, though."

One girl chanting that wasn't a big concern, but it became problematic when multiple girls started saying it. I knew that a good number of those girls carried razor blades under their tongues as weapons. They bragged about slashing people's faces. I have no idea why they ramped things up, but it persisted.

The day that Pee Wee came to me crying, I had had enough. I planned to kick someone's tail and went searching for the culprit. To be safe, I reached out to one of my homegirls and my Mexican friends for backup in case I got jumped, and they agreed to jump in with me. I was tired of the abuse and flippant insults.

The cheerleader who was picking on my sister had French class with me. I'd let her jabs go unchecked for too long, and it was time for there to be some consequences. So, I instructed Pee Wee to skip class that period and meet me outside of my French class. We posted up against the wall and waited for the girl to turn the corner. Like clockwork, she came down the stairs, loud and rambunctious, her usual. She saw us posted against the wall and stated, "Oh, y'all about to jump me, huh?"

I retorted, "Nah, we ain't about to jump you. We go'n take turns beating yo' a** instead. I'm tired of you talkin' all that sh*t." I rushed her with my fist before landing a solid punch straight in her eye socket.

We had drawn a massive crowd by then, and her friends came out of nowhere and pulled me off of her. As one of the girls grabbed me, she and Pee Wee started fighting. They were on the ground punching and going at it for a minute. I managed to pull away and, full of adrenaline, started stomping her.

It was definitely an out-of-body experience. I would never consciously stomp anyone or condone initiating a fight, but I do believe it's important to protect yourself. Could I have handled it much better? Absolutely, but my sixteen-year-old self was full of anger and tired of being bullied. The fight felt like it lasted for hours before security separated us. Pee Wee broke away from the officers and ran back to get in a couple more blows. We were escorted to the office, then let go to our next period. Mine happened to be lunch. Although we didn't have cell phones back then, word traveled fast. I was still amped up and ready for whoever else wanted some.

As soon as I hit the cafeteria, AJ grabbed me. "Y'all finally shut them hoes up, huh?" Before I could get a sentence out, this girl from another table, a cousin of the girl we fought, started talking stuff and threatening me.

"Run up so you can get banged like yo' cousin just did," I hurled at her, still with a wad of her cousin's hair in my hand. As I threw the hair in her direction, I noticed I was bleeding. I looked down and saw two perfectly slanted razor cuts through both my shirts and felt a cut behind my left ear.

One of them cut me and actually tried to slash my face. Feeling the blood behind my ear, I jumped across the table and took my best swing at the cousin before AJ grabbed me and security rushed me out of the cafeteria. They escorted me to the office, and DeDe got to the school in no time. Since this was our first offense, they decided not to suspend us, but we had to leave for the rest of the day.

That fight was only the beginning, things got worse, both at school and at home.

Others wanted to fight us, and the threats increased. It wasn't safe for us at all. I never messed with anyone, and I was exhausted by it all. In addition to school stress, home felt claustrophobic, with five people staying in a one-bedroom apartment. Tina and Aunt DeDe occasionally bumped heads, making the atmosphere more contentious. We were half a year in and desperately needing our own space, but with the expensive cost of living in Chicago, Tina had difficulty finding a place.

I needed a new escape, so I hung out with an older guy I had met in the laundromat to pass the time. He used the classic gift-giving technique in efforts to bait me. Taking my cousin's advice and "spending their money" helped me to ask less of Tina. I felt terrible, wanting things I knew she couldn't afford. So, every new pair of shoes that he bought for me, I hid. Neither Tina nor DeDe ever noticed.

Receiving gifts and spending time with him provided satisfaction, but only temporarily. What I appreciated most was that he *listened* to me. However, my personal feelings of frustration, wanderlust, and apathy remained. There was no gift he could buy to silence my pain.

The more time we spent together, the more I learned about the power and technique of manipulation. Furthermore, the trauma of my middle school experience with that forty-three-year-old still lingered. I was bitter toward older men who had a sexual interest in younger girls. I saw them as repulsive perverts who deserved to be played. I wasn't naive to what he wanted and actually adopted a "play him" mentality, since he was trying to play me.

Chicago was making me cold and turning me into a different beast. I didn't feel bad for using him, either, and quickly learned to control the situation. I used my appeal to garner things I wanted while refusing to give up anything I *didn't* want.

When I wasn't entertaining my older friend, I kicked it with Darius or made drug runs with my other homies from Farragut. I'd pretend to be at PJ and Caty's, but I would sneak out the side gate and hop in the car with a friend from school. We drove over to the barber shop on Chicago Avenue near Pulaski to make a few sales. As he yelled, "Rocks, rocks, blow, blow!" from the front seat, I saw people gather around, quick and would think, *This is how it's done. Hmm, maybe this is an opportunity.*

I sat there, dazed and reflecting on school and life, and wondered if the future I'd visualized the year prior was even still a reality. College was the furthest thing from my mind while in Chicago. I was becoming someone else, but in my heart, I wanted better. Oftentimes, I wondered if things would get better or if this would be my life forever. Darius didn't believe it would be. He could always be counted on to hype me up. I never met a soul who believed in me like he did. He was like my extra calm conscience. Darius listened well and repeatedly told me I would one day be someone… and I believed him every time he mentioned it.

Well, it was moving time again, but for all of us. My aunt moved further north to a larger space and fortunately, we moved into our own spot. Just before the move AJ went missing. He got into a fight one day at school but never returned after his suspension. I must have called his house a thousand times, to no avail. That would be the last I'd see or hear from him for years.

We relocated to a Puerto Rican neighborhood and transferred to a predominantly Spanish-speaking school. Most of my teachers refused to teach in English, making it difficult for me to keep up. Aside from making a few friends, I was extremely disengaged the entire time. I did avoid getting too attached or vested in the new space. I was getting older and uncertain if my life would ever become stable. *We'll probably move again.* So, I was just there, existing. I did keep in contact with a few other friends from my previous school.

Our new place was a small but functional two-bedroom apartment with a basement. Pee Wee and I took the basement. Taylor and Tina had their own room. Being removed from DeDe's strict house rules, Tina resumed drinking again. The alcohol use shifted our home's dynamic. Pee Wee and Taylor seemed just as irritated with this as I was.

Trying my best to stay away from home as much as possible, I spent weekends at Aunt Bertha and Lewis's place. This was always a treat. Pee Wee and I spent afternoons either hanging at the mall or at my friends' during the school week. Whatever we did, we found reasons to avoid going home until we had to. I also found refuge in dancing again and was excited to land my first choreography gig with a local boy singing group. I stumbled across the opportunity through a friend's mom who knew their manager.

The boys were managed by their dad, who happened to live five minutes away from us. I spent hours after school creating routines, taking the opportunity seriously. The dad/manager was always pleasant and really cool, the type of dad I'd always wanted. He, too, was very serious about business…and other things. Enthralled by my passion for dancing, I was oblivious to how his eyes lingered on me inappropriately. While Tina warned me to be careful around him, she did let me continue the job. *I got this. I know more about men than you do,* I thought. The older I got, her words usually went in one ear and out the other.

The alcoholism caused my admiration for her to waver. It was hard to respect her. I was still upset by her life choices and non-attempts to rectify, the damage she caused in our relationship. Besides, my meetups with the manager were strictly about dancing, something that I took very seriously.

The group was booked to perform at one of the city's largest back-to-school parades and we were deep into rehearsals. Everything was going great; having something of my own provided a glimmer of hope for my future. One day I walked over to practice, and strangely, only the dad/manager was home. He said the boys would be there soon and instructed me to proceed with the routines for him. Watching me dance in the middle of his living room, he reclined further on his sofa. "Again," he insisted. He had me do the same routine over and over. The boys still hadn't shown up, and eventually, I inquired, "Where are the guys?"

He admitted the boys were away, and the room got silent. Realizing what was happening, my chest caved in with the burning sensations of hurt and frustration. I stopped dancing and looked him in the eye. He got up and approached me until he was close enough to grab my arm. He flat out asked to have sex with me.

My heart dropped, I felt both stupid and enraged. All this time, he cared nothing about my passion for dancing. He had no intention of taking me seriously, respecting me or my future. I looked at him and spoke earnestly. "You're too old for me. You're thirty-seven, and I'm sixteen. I'm not interested. All I wanted to do was dance."

Now massaging my arm, he said, "But you're about to be seventeen, so it's OK."

I started for the door, and he grabbed both my arms, asking what I wanted. "I can buy you clothes or shoes; just name it."

"I wanted to dance," I yelled before jerking away and storming out, crying. He followed me, pleading, "Please don't mention this to anyone."

Hysterical, I took off running full speed and kept it up the entire way home. All the unwanted predatory advances from men had me fearful, ashamed, and questioning my purpose in life. I hit an ultimate low, and the devil on my left chose that moment to appear.

The words spoken by my cousin's husband years prior resurfaced. *Maybe I am a whore and only good for sex, because these men keep approaching me. Maybe he was right, and I'll never amount to anything;* my thoughts persisted. My tears flowed heavier because I'd let my guard down, trusted him, and just hadn't seen that coming.

Entering through the back door, I avoided everyone and lay in my bed crying for what felt like hours. Reflecting on the guys, I had been with and life, all felt worthless. Despite my attempts to emotionally disconnect, I still felt powerless. Spiraling down into a darker headspace, pained from my father's rejection as the root of my problems with males, I wondered if I would ever truly be loved or respected.

It was the loud music of the Rainbow Roller Rink that got me out of my funk. I had been in shutdown mode longer than I ever had. Tina let Pee Wee and me take the bus up north to the skating rink every other Saturday. Rainbow was *the* spot for teens on the weekends. PJ, Caty, and other cousins and friends from both schools met us there. Despite Rainbow being a skating rink, none of us really knew how to skate…but we didn't go there to skate.

At 11 PM, the skates came off, lights dimmed, and it turned into a juke session. Dancing to the latest tracks, house music, and hip-hop songs, we battled against other girls and each other. Those nights were magic, every time I was with PJ and Caty it felt like CBB was back in action. Popping our booties, feet working, getting boys' numbers, laughing, and dropping it low was just what the doctor ordered.

When we weren't at Rainbow, we went to the temple and stayed the night at DeDe's with PJ and Caty. Sleepovers with our cousins were still very classic. Whether we danced, rapped, pranked one another, or just did nothing, we enjoyed each other's presence.

Of all our nights of piling in one bed, sharing couches, making pallets, and epic sleepover proportions, none of them could measure up to the greatest sleepover of all time!

It was a Saturday, and DeDe worked an overnight shift, leaving us with keys to the castle and no adult supervision.

She had just gotten new couches delivered earlier that afternoon and was adamant about us not sitting on them. We promised we wouldn't and that we would be responsible... but before she pulled off from the curb, I was already on the phone inviting people over. I reached out to a friend who worked at the fish spot in the same shopping center where Darius worked. I told him I had the crib to myself with my cousins and we were hungry and wanted something to drink. Asking what we wanted, I named the first thing that I heard in a rap song. "Bring us some Grey Goose and pineapple, and bring your friend, too."

The only alcoholic drink I'd ever had was the gin with AJ months before. The guys showed up in no time with the drinks plus food. The new QB's Finest album, "Oochie Wally" blasted on repeat. Our evening turned into an impromptu house party, and we broke in the new couches nicely. The night was young, and we didn't have a care in the world besides ensuring no food or drink was spilled on the furniture.

Just like lightweights, both PJ and Pee Wee got drunk instantly. I must admit they were a funny combo together, drunk hilarious! Seeing them stumbling, talking crap to each other while under the influence, had us erupting in laughter until our sides ached. I learned what liquid courage meant as Pee Wee popped off at PJ. Things started to get out of hand, so I had to end the party. We walked the girls to the guest room for the evening and the fellas to the door.

Caty and I cleaned meticulously, walking all trash outside to the alley, so DeDe wouldn't know we had outside food and drink. We managed to get everything all tidy but panicked at the sound of dry heaving and gagging in the next room.

Pee Wee and PJ both started vomiting all over the sheets and the room reeked of alcohol. Simultaneously, Caty and I looked at the clock. "Oh, sh*t." It was nearly 4 AM. DeDe was getting off work in an hour, and we didn't have a washer and dryer. *Think quickly,* I told myself before dragging Pee Wee to the tub and PJ to the toilet. "Caty, go grab the sheets, we go'n hand wash them," I ordered. After cleaning up our sisters, I ran a little water in the tub before adding detergent and both sheets. Our hands ached from squeezing, wringing, and scrubbing Grey Goose and vomit from the linen. We ended up using a hair dryer to dry the sheets. The physical labor exhausted us.

We managed to get everything back in place, spray the couches, and make the beds mere moments before DeDe walked in. Caty and I hit the light, hopped in bed, and pretended to be asleep when DeDe checked on us, whispering, "Never again," the moment she closed the door behind her. Needless to say, Pee Wee and PJ both had terrible hangovers the next day. That would be our very last wild run with our cousins.

Moving time came before we knew it; we were abruptly getting evicted because our landlord decided to sell the property. So, we were heading back to Tennessee. Because I continued to be emotionally disconnected from life, I didn't care about moving that time. Actually, I was kind of relieved by the news and ready to get back to some sense of normalcy. Chicago was life-altering, and the time there changed me significantly. I felt as if I rebelled quite enough. Pee Wee, on the other hand, had had enough of the instability of living with Tina. She decided that moving out was her best action, and approaching sixteen years old provided an opportune time. She planned to live with another relative once we arrived back in Tennessee and finish high school there.

The only thing exciting about my last semester of school in Chicago was being asked to prom. It was less than a month away, and so was my seventeenth birthday. Since we were moving and I was turning seventeen, I knew Tina would let me go. My homegirl and I went dress shopping at the mall every day after school. One day, in particular, I ran into a very familiar face at the JC Penney counter. We stared at each other for a bit before I spoke.

"Wow, it's been a really long time."

"Dee from summer camp? Man, you look good."

I was thinking the exact same thing, but he got the words out first. He was one of my camp boyfriends from previous summers. We stayed connected a few years after camp but lost touch. We hugged and chatted a bit before I asked, "Why'd you stop writing?"

He explained that after I left town, he hooked up with another girl. "I understand. Let's exchange numbers. It's so good to see you," I replied while discreetly sizing him up. He was still fine.

We talked later that night and the next couple of nights. Catching up eventually turned into skipping school to spend time with each other.

My day of reckoning began like any ordinary day. Tina's work commute usually consisted of three buses over two hours. Everything was timed to perfection, and I wasn't worried—after all, I had gotten away with my schemes for years. But I had no idea Tina would leave work early that day. I planned to have him gone before Taylor, and Pee Wee got home from school, so no one would know I'd had company.

That morning, I pretended to be sick and instructed my siblings to leave for school without me. I just wanted to see him and genuinely hoped for some innocent one-on-one time. The smooth sounds of R Kelly's "TP2.com" played softly in the background while we played spades and sipped our Capri Suns. We laughed and talked for hours before the long-eyed gazes, and our teenage hormones put us in Taylor's bunk bed. A couple of moments into it, I heard pounding at the door. Rushing to the front, I took a moment to be grateful that I'd locked the inside lock. *Who the hell is this, anyway?*

I quietly tiptoed to the door. Tilting my head close to the peephole, I closed one eye to get a better look. *Sh*t! It's Tina. What's she doing here so early?*

Angrily, she beat on the door, "Pee Wee, open the damn door now." I backed away on tiptoe, then raced to the back. "You gotta go!" I told my guest.

He stumbled while grabbing his shoes and jeans, but managed to put them on before running out the back gate, never to be seen or heard from again. Thinking fast, I quickly hopped in the shower, so I'd have a valid excuse for not answering the door. Splashing sufficient water on my chest and face to look authentic, I wrapped a towel around me and then went to open the front door for a disturbingly calm Tina. She came in and politely asked, "What took you so long, and what are you doing home from school?"

As she questioned me, she opened the coat closet and then surveyed the living room. I fought back my rising panic. *What the hell is she looking for? She must know someone was here. But how?* In the meantime, I had to answer her question. "I didn't feel well, so I stayed home. I was in the shower and didn't hear you knocking until I got out."

"Oh, yeah? So, who was in my house?" Her tone—as well as her words—told me she didn't believe me for a second. Then she walked to a chair and picked up a Pelle Pelle shirt from it, then looked at the spade score sheet, upon which I'd written a heading with both our names. I was busted. R Kelly was still singing "Feelin' On Yo Booty" in the background as if he were describing what had gone on in Tina's absence. Was it just my imagination, or did he sing the word *booty* more vigorously?

I swallowed hard. *Yo, of all my years of mastermind material, I am finally caught.*

The hard backhanded slap to my face snapped me back into reality. Tina yelled, "Go look in the mirror at your f*cking neck!"

I did as she said, stared at my reflection in the living room mirror and saw that my first hickey had been planted in the center of my collar. She then announced, "You ain't goin' to nobody's prom," before walking off and slamming her bedroom door.

Paralyzed in deep thought, I stood in the same spot. Honestly, I was numb and confused by unfamiliar emotions. I didn't feel bad or upset, actually, I felt hurt more than anything. And then I realized why: My heart was broken from disappointing Tina.

Finally, I had managed to garner her attention, and I realized that was what I wanted all along: I wanted to know that my mother cared. Understanding that she thought highly of me, I didn't want to destroy that. So, I stood there mentally rehearsing the apology that I drafted in my head. I knew I let her down when she opened the door to discover Pee Wee wasn't on the inside.

Eventually, she stepped out of her room to grab something from the kitchen. I followed her there, looked her in the eye, and said, "I want to apologize, not because I got caught, but because I know I let you down. I am very sorry." Then I asked what I could do to make her feel better and trust me again.

She answered, "Girl, I'm very proud of you. You made it further than I ever did. You are smart, ambitious, and beautiful." Every syllable she uttered produced uncontrollable tears from me. Her words were exactly what I'd been searching for. I longed for her approval.

She went on, "I want you to go off to college and to be better than me. I don't want you to get pregnant and throw your life away as I did. I've been screwed, counted out, and messed up over and over in my life. I don't want you to go through this. These boys out here will f*ck you, but don't *give* a f*ck about you. They only want what's between your legs. I love you and don't want to see you mess up your life! I want you to go higher."

By the time she stopped talking, I was sobbing so hard that my body shook uncontrollably. She grabbed me, pulled me closer and held me until I stopped crying. The love I felt from my mother that day was more fulfilling than any of the guys I'd been with, hands down.

Our breakthrough came the day before my seventeenth birthday and turned out to be the most humbling gift ever. I forgot all about telling my date that I couldn't attend the prom after all. I didn't even care about the prom anymore.

My siblings headed back to Tennessee with relatives. And Tina and I stuck around to pack up belongings, tie up loose ends, and prepare for the move. I was relieved and very excited to be heading back to my old school.

My remaining time in Chicago was spent hanging at the skating rink and hanging with my cousin Lewis or with Darius, attending concerts and meeting some of my favorite artists.

July 14, 2001, ironically my father's birthday, would be the day that I not only met my favorite artist at the time, Sean "Diddy" Combs, but saw Carlos for the first time in over a decade. Everyone who knew me knew that I was obsessed with Diddy and The Bad Boy family. A dream of mine—to meet him—came true. Aunt Bertha set it up as a surprise for me—not only with that meeting but seeing Carlos, too.

Aunt Bertha casually announced while driving through Hyde Park, "We found Carlos. We're going to see him." I felt ambushed. *This wasn't in the plan!* Aunt Bertha pulled over at the corner of 53rd Street, and there he was: A frail, brown-skinned man, selling Street Wise papers, a local publication distributed by the homeless and drug addicts. I stood there looking at him, uncertain of what to say.

Aunt Bertha nudged me. "That's your father, Dee. Speak. Don't be rude." I wasn't bitter toward him, but I couldn't help thinking, *He knows how to speak, too.* Breaking the tension, I got out of the car, went over to him, and gave him a hug.

He must have been high because he was fidgety and unable to stand still. I looked closely at his eyes to see if I saw a resemblance between us. I didn't, but Taylor was Carlos's twin. Maybe I didn't want to see a resemblance. After all these years, I thought I'd feel something, but I didn't. There he was, finally, right before my eyes, with no clue of how painful my life had been because of him. I thought about asking where he'd been, but for once, I was at a loss for words. I just couldn't think of anything to say to him. I felt sorry seeing him like that, selling those papers.

His face, demeanor, and too-thin frame confirmed that he was still using. Finally, I uttered the simple phrase, "Happy birthday."

He thanked me and told me to tell Pee Wee and Taylor he said "Hi." I responded, "Sure, I'll pass the message," got back in the car, and we drove off.

We were moving back into Mel's. He came up and rented a truck to help us move our things. During the ride, I received devastating news. The date was August 25, 2001, and the radio had just announced that my dancing hero and R&B idol, Aaliyah Haughton, had died in a plane crash. I cried all the way to Tennessee. I had just watched her on my favorite music video show, *106th & Park,* the day before. I couldn't believe she was gone.

We arrived at our old neighborhood the following day. Things looked the exact same, but I was a completely changed girl.

CHAPTER SIX

I'm Neva Coming Back!

In my seventeen years of living, I'd never been faced with so much pressure. Life as I knew it was about to completely change forever. Relocating back south felt like an identity crisis. While I returned far more confident, decisive, and determined, I had to readjust my new perspective to correspond to a calmer, more quaint way of living. There wasn't a need to be constantly ready and on guard or to watch my back as much. There also wasn't a need to protect Pee Wee. She had been doing very well living with one of our other aunts.

One of the first orders of business for me was to get a job ASAP. I wanted to save for college and help Tina as much as possible. Senior year was all about being laser-focused on getting into college and making something of myself.

Some of the pressures I felt were self-inflicted, stemming from being the first to graduate and my struggle with perfectionism. I wanted to get things right, set a great example for younger kids, and be successful. But I was uptight, rigid, and overly hard on myself. Chicago had flipped a switch in me and provided a healthy amount of the hunger, exposure, and grit needed to prepare for life ahead.

My new mindset made the difference, and I now saw things through a more pragmatic lens. I didn't need much validation that year, either. I walked boldly into the lunchroom, confident and comfortable sitting by myself. I did miss my guys, though, and occasionally sat with them. Picking up just like old times, we roasted everyone and cracked jokes. We roasted people from head to toe, but it was all good fun; no bullying occurred. My lingo had changed, and I hipped the guys to a couple of Chicago terms, and they started using them, too.

My style had changed as well. Having a job kept me fresh in the latest sports jerseys, shoes, and boots, and I also kept my nails done that year. Occasionally, I switched things up and went for a more feminine look, wearing bodysuits and tight jeans. I had gained a little weight over the year and filled out more. My legs had gotten toned, my curves more pronounced. I wasn't the Skinny Minnie that I was used to being. I finally began to blossom. Tina and my aunts noticed… and so did the guys at school. I happily embraced the shift in my appearance. Don't get it twisted. I didn't take the girly-girl thing too far. I was still a cute tomboy and managed to avoid looking like those lip-gloss girls I despised. Lip-gloss girls wore lots of lip gloss, had perfect hair, and dressed in designer clothing, girly and cute. They wore French-tip manicures and mascara and discussed fashion, boys, and other stuff I wasn't interested in. Most of the lip-gloss girls were materialistic, mean girls, and overly dramatic. They were the middle-class, privileged chicks that didn't know they were spoiled.

I was cordial to the lip-gloss girls, but I didn't hang with 'em. Because I was cool with their boyfriends and crushes, we had a conflict of interest by default. I wouldn't have fit into their circle, anyway. I was too real, uneasily impressed, and too rough around the edges. My life-inflicted trauma wouldn't allow me the patience, trust, or confidence to try to fit in, anyway. However, the only thing worth envying about them was the fact that many of them were daddy's girls.

I'M NEVA COMING BACK!

My homegirl, who picked me up for school each morning, blasted lip-gloss girl music on repeat during the ride in. A diehard Destiny's Child fan, we kept that "Survivor" album on repeat. I preferred to listen to LOX or DMX, but I went along, and sounding like drowning kittens as we wailed in unison, we sang our hearts out.

Barely putting the car in park, we raced into first period, typically late but just in time for morning announcements. My schedule was sweet that semester. I had a free period and a bunch of classes with friends. Balancing my job while keeping my grades up, I even managed to pick up a boyfriend, a guy I met before the move back to Chicago. We had kept in touch the entire time I was away.

I calmed down significantly after my come-to-Jesus talk with Tina. So, I was a one-man woman focused on life after graduation. My boyfriend's presence helped me retain my focus and kept me out of trouble as well. His name was Devin, and he stood about six feet tall with Hershey-brown skin. Devin had big, beautiful brown eyes and long braided hair. He happened to play basketball for my school's rival team.

Devin was close friends with most of the guys I ran with at school. We started as platonic friends until he decided to mess things up by asking me out. We were better suited as friends, but I liked the idea of being his girl. Dating him was like the best of both worlds because even though he was my boyfriend, he was still like one of the guys. We hung out at the mall, went to the movies, and cracked jokes all the time, including roasting each other. Devin liked my style and how low maintenance I was. We had lots in common, as he aspired to rap, and rapping was one of my favorite pastimes. Devin liked everything about my swag, and I liked the fact that we attended separate schools.

We trusted each other, so attending different schools wasn't a problem…until his best friend transferred to my school. Jalil Peterson was his name, and he conveniently joined my fourth-period ACT Prep class. The first time I laid eyes on Jalil, I thought, *which heaven did God drop him from?* He had me at first glance. I needed to know who he was, like ASAP.

I asked my guys, subtly, wanting to remain cool but not obvious. The only problem I had hanging with the guys was that I couldn't express my interest in other guys to them. He was much shorter than Devin, but had a nice physique, with full lips and perfect teeth. I was in love…and then I learned that he and Devin were close friends.

Jalil became a massive distraction, and making matters worse, his schedule got changed and he was also assigned to my first period. That was the same period I shared with my guys, where we all hung in the back of the room, laughing and clowning with each other. Jalil joined our roasting squad. He fit in well and knew most of the guys anyway. He and I hit it off well, too, although I couldn't focus nor keep my cool or edge around him. Jalil was down to earth, and I knew if nothing more, we'd be great friends. My only problems with him were his distracting looks…and his girlfriend.

He happened to be dating one of the prissiest lip-gloss girls ever. She was, like, the queen lip-gloss girl of our senior class. She was beautiful, no doubt, and seemed nice enough, but when I learned they were an item, I wasn't a fan. Comparing myself to her became a habit for me. I envied everything about her, and I wasn't usually the jealous type. However, I couldn't help the way I felt at seeing them. It wasn't even her; she wasn't my problem. I think I envied what they had.

I kept cool, never treated her differently, never acted petty or even came at him. Internally, I simmered the times we spoke in passing. High school was tough, and I really didn't have time to be sucked into those teenage complexities.

My thoughts needed to remain on my future and how I'd respond to the million-dollar "What's next after graduation?" question so frequently asked of me. I had my heart set on experiencing the rich history and cultures of an HBCU, I just wasn't sure which one yet.

My bike riding visits as a kid to Fisk University's Jubilee Hall were still etched in my memories. I had relatives that were HBCU alum, and on Friday mornings, I'd wake up early and listen to the *Tom Joyner Morning Show*. They broadcast live from different HBCUs around the country. The momentum was there, and I felt unstoppable going through senior year. I just had to decide what to major in.

Because I loved music, movies, and sports, I figured I would do something with either radio, TV, or communications. "Maybe I'll be a filmmaker, sports reporter, or radio personality," I reasoned. Yep. I set my heart on media and spent free time practicing my radio and sports reporting voice.

Despite the excitement of the process, I began to feel overwhelmed. So, I decided to simplify things by applying to only five HBCU schools (all out of state). I made a promise to myself to attend whoever said yes first. Checking the mail every day, I hoped it would be Clark Atlanta, but the idea of being accepted by any one of my choices excited me. Actually, all the moving we did prepared me for my move to college.

Senior year was going well until the morning Jalil stopped me dead in my tracks. "I really have to tell you something," he announced. I hoped he planned to tell me he thought my custom senior shirt was fly. We were in the midst of a spirit week, where all the seniors wore personalized T-shirts. Instead, he said, "I hate to be the bearer of bad news, but Devin doesn't want to be with you anymore."

Confused, I looked at him, hoping he was joking and couldn't tell I was having heart palpitations. "What did you say?"

"He wanted me to tell you. He's breaking up with you." I felt my face instantly get hot. I saw red and couldn't believe what I was hearing. Tears started building up, and those familiar feelings of rejection began to set in again. Most importantly, my pride was hurt, y'all, and I was embarrassed.

I stood there, trying to absorb this bombshell. *Did Devin really dump me and deliver the news through my crush? What the heck is going on?*

Finally, I choked out, "Why? He couldn't tell me this himself?" My mind raced. Devin and I literally just stayed up talking on the phone until 2 AM that same morning, and he didn't say a thing about breaking up. He was my roasting partner, my man, and my friend. And he was supposed to be my prom date, but that was out of the question now. "Oh, my goodness, and prom is right around the corner," I lamented. It was actually months away, but I couldn't bear the thought of not having a date.

My brain processed what it all meant, and before I knew it, I was crying uncontrollably in that hall, staining my shirt with tears and feelings. I'd just gotten dumped in my senior year. I knew the guys would roast me for crying, but I was hurt and felt betrayed.

Jalil wrapped his arms around me, hugging me securely. "It will be OK. Let's get you cleaned up." We walked to the restroom, and he brought me a roll of tissue. After thanking him, I entered my next class, dazed and with red and soggy eyes. I sat in the corner with my head down. My classmates saw me as a tough, funny, and cool girl, so to see me distraught was a big deal. People took turns asking me what happened, and several lip-gloss girls came over to rub my back and tell me it would be OK. I didn't want to talk to anyone. I knew the rumors would spread soon, and I couldn't wait to get home to call Devin. We usually talked every day after school if I wasn't working. But he didn't answer my calls that day, nor did he call me. I must've called his house twenty times.

Like a coward, he avoided me, and not having closure was rough. After all, he was the one who'd asked for a relationship. For that reason, I felt he owed me a response, but I wouldn't hear from him for months. The heartbreak was excruciating, but I decided to stay busy working more hours and spending time with Taylor. The breakup gave me additional fuel to focus on college. I couldn't wait to leave and now wanted to go far, far away.

Christmas break provided a much-needed breather. I was able to get both my homegirl and Jalil jobs at the store where I worked. Working with friends made my job more fun and helped me get over my breakup. Jalil was surprisingly supportive, and we found ourselves becoming real friends. Before we knew it, we started talking on the phone every day and spent more time together. Jalil met Tina and Taylor, and Tina even allowed us to hang. She had no issue with him coming over after school and doing homework with me.

As much as I fought it, we had real chemistry. We started falling in love. The closer we grew, the more complicated my feelings became. We kept our growing relationship secret at school so his girl and our homeboys wouldn't catch wind of it, and more importantly, Devin. Despite Devin's breaking up with me, Jalil getting involved with me violated all types of guy codes. We didn't intend to get so close, at least I didn't. I just enjoyed crushing on him. Him delivering the breakup news is what fostered us.

Jalil juggling a girlfriend and maintaining a relationship with me drove me crazy. Comparing myself to his girlfriend's beautiful long, shiny black hair and amazing body wasn't good for my self-esteem at all. She appeared perfect; she smelled great, owned nice things, and even drove a luxury car. I imagined her to be a beloved daddy's girl from an affluent family.

Because she was so great, I wondered what he saw in me. Playing the high school side chick role wasn't for me. "You can't do this," I told myself daily before school. Working hard not to be moody with Jalil around our friends was challenging. I hated pretending that we didn't talk all the time and that I didn't care. We were together, but we weren't official.

After another couple of weeks, I finally broke it off with Jalil and got back focused on the months facing me. *You're going far away to college soon, and he can stay here with her*, I told myself. I just needed a prom date, and to stay focused the remaining months of high school.

One of my buddies agreed to escort me to the prom, so that was one less thing to worry about. At least two months had passed, and I still hadn't heard from Devin. I knew just how to fix that.

Our school's basketball team was set to play his team in the coming weeks. I requested that day off from work and invited Pee Wee to attend the game with me. My cousins from Mississippi and Angel happened to be visiting town that day as well, so I had an entourage attend. Mixing things up a bit, I wore the sexiest, smallest clothes I could find to that game. It was freezing out and too cold to be wearing tank tops, but I wanted to show Devin what he was missing.

My girls and I strutted in that gym, looking like an R&B singing group. Devin and I somehow made eye contact the moment I stepped in, although from a distance. His team was warming up and stretching on the court. I was high up in the bleachers and making my way closer to the court. Since it was a home game, I assumed he anticipated me coming.

If looks could kill, he would have fallen over with ball in hand. I intentionally sat courtside, only two rows up from the action. I slowly removed my borrowed black fur coat, revealing my backless tank top and tight pants. I must have gone to the restroom and concession at least a dozen times in an effort to be seen.

My plan worked; Devin looked at me during timeouts, fouls, and from the bench. Other guys looked at me, too. I must've gotten five numbers that night. To my delight, Devin saw all the attention I was drawing.

As I suspected he would, Devin called me later that night to apologize. I let him know how much he hurt me and how I thought he was better than his behavior before hanging up in his face.

On March 18, 2002, the decision was made. I arrived home from school to find that Tina had left a piece of mail on my bed. I knew it was an acceptance letter. The moment felt surreal, and I reminded myself of the promise I had made, to attend whatever school said yes first. Grabbing the letter from my bed, I saw Texas Southern University (in Houston, Texas) in the return address section. I ripped it open and initially only read the first sentence before rushing to tell Tina. I practically screamed, "Texas! Oh my God, I am moving to Houston, Texas! Mama, what you think?"

She calmly answered, "Go. You deserve this opportunity. I want you to be everything you desire." Her calmness surprised me until it hit me. I'd have to leave her, Pee Wee, and Taylor behind, and that would be tough. I was the official sidekick, the unofficial second parent, and the responsible rock of the family. Tina had been on another streak of progress around that time. It had been at least five or six months since I'd seen her take a drink. She'd go through long spells of sobriety and my senior year was one of them. I was grateful for that, as my compassion for my mother had grown ever since our conversation in Chicago.

As I got older, I realized she didn't have it all together and struggled badly. I saw her junk. She was used to quick fixes and indulging in clandestine vices and probably never felt that she had truly lived for herself. Yet, she desired to feel alive; her inner child wanted to be healed and loved. We were similar in that way, and my frustration stemmed from her inability to give me what I desired. Tina was a massive puzzle with so many complexities and being me, I was determined to help solve it. Granted, she made selfish and poor decisions, mismanaged her money, and wasn't always present for us, but she was still my mother. She was flawed and fighting demons the best way she knew how. Tina was human, like the rest of us. The most inspiring thing about my mother was her resilience. Throughout all the moving we did, she still had the strength and the courage to start again and again. Tina never gave up, and she was a hard worker. Even when she lost jobs, she always found new ones and worked multiple ones when needed. Her philosophies and behaviors were untraditional, but this was the thinking that made her, her.

In some ways, I saw her as bold and courageous. I didn't know it at the time, but Tina had a help conscience, too. Her personal help gave her the strength to quit crack and heroin cold turkey. Her help probably saved our lives by providing us with an escape during our move south. Tina was my mama, and even amid my love-hate emotions for her, I loved her. I was proud of her for what she had overcome. She was proud of me as well, and truly stepped up during my senior year. You would have thought that she was the one graduating; she was so engaged with my process.

My senior year of high school was by far the best year we'd had together. She spoke highly of me every chance she got. On days that I overslept and needed a ride to school, Tina happily got up to bring me. We grabbed breakfast during the ride every time. Those moments were special for me. They provided an opportunity for us to bond. She never knew it, but sometimes, I'd purposely move slowly, oversleep, or miss my bus just to ride with her. I loved hearing her "this is your senior year" lecture: "Dee, these last few months are very important, so you keep pushing. I'm proud of you and want the best for you in college," she'd say. Her words gave me additional fuel to keep going. I needed to hear them from her, and often. Knowing she cared and that she believed in me was valuable, but hearing it was priceless. I felt unstoppable, purposeful, and empowered that year.

Prom was held on Saturday, April 13, 2002. I only agreed to wear heels because my Aunt DeDe asked me to. I planned to wear Jordans, but the heels were a nice touch. Tina invited everyone over to see me off to prom. Locking eyes with Tina as she did my makeup, I wondered what was going through her mind. *Is she living vicariously through me? Is she scared? Did she mess up my eyebrows?* My dress was a shimmering champagne color. The clingy material made the most of my curves. My hair was pinned up ever so perfectly over a side bang. I felt beautiful and wished I could have bottled up those feelings forever.

My date pulled up in a newer model luxury Cadillac, the color an exact match to my dress, a plus we hadn't planned. We made our rounds, took a few pictures, and ate a bit. Finding the other fellas, we high-fived and dapped each other up. They had never seen me all dolled up in makeup and heels. I could tell by their silent stares that they approved. We mingled, laughed, and roasted each other until their dates dragged them away from me.

As much as I loved to dance, I didn't dance that night. I preferred to stand in all my glory, feeling gorgeous and taking it all in. The only problem that night was Tina's curfew. Everyone else had hotel rooms and no curfew, but I did. But I wasn't tripping too bad; it's not like I had a boyfriend. But before heading home, my date and I stopped by the guys' hotel room, blazed up, sipped on some drinks, and then swung by White Castle before he brought me home. That was prom.

The rest of senior year was a breeze. Taylor and I developed a very strong bond that year, and our connection blossomed. It was dope seeing my little brother getting older. He followed me around that year, paying close attention to everything I did. Watching me with deep admiration and intrigue, it was obvious he still believed that "Dee can do anything." We were tight as skinny jeans. We hooped together and watched and played football, too. It was important for me to be a positive example for him, especially in Daniel's absence. I had stepped into that big brother role years prior.

It had been some time since we heard from Daniel. It had become apparent that he had no intention of reaching out. I thought, "Who goes away and don't contact family?" It hurt Taylor, and it certainly hurt me. Daniel and I used to write each other when he first left, but the communication stopped abruptly. All we knew was that he was deployed somewhere in Germany.

On graduation day, I was moments away from making history for my future legacy and my family. I promised myself I wouldn't cry, because I knew Tina would be crying enough tears for both of us.

My row stood and climbed the stairs to the stage, where my counselor whispered, "Those are a lot of supporters," adding, "Wow, you have a long name." I looked over at my family and smiled. Principal Bruce shook my hand; the photo was snapped, and he said, "Congratulations." As I exited the stage, DeDe threw down a dozen roses from her seat. With a big smile, I caught them.

Graduation was one of the most memorable days of my life. We went to dinner afterward, and the money and gifts showered in from loved ones. Angel's gift stood out the most—her family purchased my plane ticket to Texas. I looked at her with tears in my eyes, confiding, "I didn't know how I was going to get there and I'm afraid to leave."

"You don't have to go by yourself," she smiled. Angel's parents purchased her a ticket to accompany me.

CHAPTER SEVEN

Texas Southern University

Hot and humid, I could smell the heat seeping through the revolving doors adjacent to the baggage claim. Angel and I landed in Houston on Saturday, August 17, 2002. Dressed in my favorite blue jean skirt, yellow tank top and a pair of retro Jordans, sporty but cute was my aim. I'd pinned up my hair in a side ponytail, tightly secured with half a bottle of *Pump It Up* holding spray and couldn't nobody tell me nothing. Honey, I was ready to take on freshman year!

I eagerly walked up to the luggage carousel, reached for my first bag and silently announced, "Yo, I'm here, in Texas." I felt my energy: electric, ready, and curious. I had a plan to reinvent myself almost immediately, this time for the better. I arrived focused on growth into womanhood and my future.

As I grabbed my second bag, someone's voice interrupted my thoughts. "Aye, y'all go to TSU?" Caught off guard, I looked to Angel. She flashed me a reassuring smile before responding, "She does," and pointing in my direction.

So, I answered with a slight nod of approval, "Yeah, I go to TSU," before heading to the exit.

"Man, it's so hooot!" Angel and I exclaimed at the same time, chuckling at our timing. We waited near the curb for my cousin to arrive. Weeks before leaving, Grandma connected me with relatives who live there. They were cousins of cousins or something like that, probably my granny's second cousins or so. Either way, I was delighted to learn I had family there, no matter how distant.

A black truck pulled over and a slim, tall guy wearing glasses, roughly my age, hopped out. "Hey, cuz. I'm Keith. How was the flight?" he said with a warm smile while popping the trunk. "Hi, Keith," I answered. "I'm Dee, and this is my best friend, Angel. The flight was cool. Thanks for picking us up."

My eyes were glued to the window during the ride to meet my other relatives. Houston looked totally different than Nashville or Chicago. The city was spacious—everything seemed so spread out—and the expressways were super-wide. It also had a retro vibe, as if we were stuck in the 90s. I smiled because I liked it.

We arrived at his family's place in no time. I was a little nervous but followed him to the front door with my chin up. A beautiful, middle-aged, brown-skinned woman came to the door to greet us. Her smile and tight hug eased every nerve in my body. "Well, look at you, looking just like TSU already," she observed before inviting us in.

I had no clue what that meant, but I said, "Thank you," and followed her inside. We sat at the dining room table and talked a while, going over just how we were related. She was Keith's mom, and they were my grandma's aunts, cousins, or something like that; I don't remember the exact connection.

"Take them 'round the corner to meet everybody," she instructed Keith. We followed him back to the truck, hopped in and drove off.

We rode just minutes down the street, where I met his mother's sisters and dad. Everyone was so warm and friendly. One cousin in particular—an older lady, nearly my grandma's age—took a special interest in me. "Girl, what you plan on studying?" she asked.

"I want to study television and media," I responded. She told me about the campus radio station where she volunteered annually and promised to put me in touch with staff there. I gratefully thanked her. By now I couldn't wait to get over to the campus. Angel and I said our goodbyes and we headed out.

Bruce Hall would be the place I called home over the next couple of years. While waiting to get registered and checked in, Angel and I people watched, told jokes, and listened to random conversations. There were two people handling registration, a beautiful dark-skinned girl with amazingly smooth coal-black hair and a pleasant smile, and a lady dressed in African garb who talked really fast. I didn't miss anything and observed everything. The culture was enticing, the people fluid, free-spirited, and welcoming. I felt great about being there, it already felt so right...and I hadn't even met my roommate or made it to my room yet.

Captivated by a pearly white set of teeth before me, I tapped the guy in front of me to make small talk. He gave me a friendly smile that nearly blinded me with its brightness, making me curious about whether those were really his teeth or implants. His name was Curtis, and he was from Virginia. We talked about our majors and career plans. Because we hit it off so well, we planned to connect later. He was moving into the dorm across the street from mine and became my first friend at college.

Angel stood back like a proud parent and watched me engage with others. She schooled me on all the nuances to look out for. She talked about shuttle buses, parties, roommate tips, and, most importantly, freedom. We talked about college guys, specifically fraternity dudes. "In college, you're grown, and nobody cares what you do or who you talk to," she informed me. I listened intently to whatever she had to share and eagerly awaited my own journey.

My roommate hadn't arrived yet, so I got first dibs on picking my bed and closet. Placing my things down, I opened the restroom door and saw from the toiletries my suitemates had checked in. They must have left because their room was empty. So, Angel and I decided to take a walk around the campus instead. We talked about her post-graduation plans, and she schooled me on other things to anticipate.

The campus was well manicured and *breathtaking!* This was the first time I'd ever seen palm trees, other than on television. A brick road, reminding me of *The Wizard of Oz*, laid in the center of campus...but these bricks were painted in school colors: maroon and gray with images of Tigger, the school's tiger mascot.

We spotted the boys' dorms in no time. Laughing at TSU's non-co-ed policy, Angel bragged, "At least Spelman let us have guys over."

"But y'all still have curfew," I pointed out. TSU certainly wasn't having it, and the fine was $150 per person if the non-co-ed policy was violated. "Oh well," I added, "I didn't come here for that, anyway. I'm here to focus first on my education. I take it very seriously, you know?"

She chuckled. "Yes, I know, Dee." Within the next minute, a tall, gorgeous guy with an athletic build approached us. Angel and I both looked up at him, taking in the chiseled arms peering through his sleeveless blue Greek shirt. "Y'all comin' to our party, right?" he queried.

"Yes," we replied in unison. I nudged her, and after clearing her throat, she corrected, "I mean no; she is, though."

"Cool!" He handed us a couple of flyers to a pajama party before walking on. Angel read the flyer, then looked at the excited expression on my face. "Um-hmm. Focused on your education, all right." We both laughed and continued walking the paw-printed brick road in the center of campus until it was time for Angel to leave for her hotel. She planned to come back in the morning one last time before heading to the airport. She had her own college tour and was scouting grad programs. And she mentioned possibly moving down the following year.

I changed clothes before heading over to the cafeteria. Just like high school, where to sit while eating was still a big decision to make. I knew college was different, but I also knew that who I sat with would reflect on me. I carefully surveyed the room as I got my tray. I was hoping to run into some of the people I'd met at check-in because I didn't want to sit by myself. Passing the athlete's table, I thought, *Dang, these are real men.* I noticed the football players first, as identifiable by their broad shoulders and thick necks as they were by the TSU football shorts they wore. I found them a bit intimidating. *No, ma'am, you're not sitting there.*

Then I saw the baseball table. These guys were smaller than the football guys, but also very fit. The majority of them wore quarter-length-sleeved TSU baseball tees. I met the eyes of a few of them but kept walking. I noticed two slim, dark-skinned guys sitting together at a table. I was drawn to the one with a piercing in his upper ear cartilage. He wore a TSU track shirt and had puka shells around his neck. Our eye contact lasted for what felt like hours. He eventually looked away and continued talking with his friend. That was all the challenge I needed. *She's baaack,* I thought. Was this love at first sight? I put him at the top of my need-to-know list.

Don't judge me. I mean, I've always been drawn to handsome men, but these first few hours at college truly confirmed just how boy crazy I really was. I loved everything about the masculine form God had created. After our prolonged eye contact, I had to gather thoughts, taking a deep breath and heading toward a corner table. *"You're in timeout,"* I thought. But before I could sit down, I was stopped by a light-skinned girl with glasses. "Don't you live in Bruce

Hall?" she loudly questioned, in the strangest accent I'd ever heard. Immediately my eyes focused on her lime-green tongue ring. It kept hitting her teeth as she talked in a way, I found distracting. I wanted to say, "Take it down a notch!" But instead, I politely responded, "Yes. I live in Bruce. Where you from?"

"Funky Town." Laughing uncomfortably, I high-fived her before saying, "Funky *what*?"

"Come on, guh, sit wit' us. Funky Town is Forth Worth, Texas." I followed the strange girl over to a table occupied by several other people. Standing with my tray, I introduced myself. I had just put down my tray and was about to sit when someone said, "Hey, Dee!" I turned and was greeted with a tight hug from a familiar face.

"Curtis from Virginia, right?" I said.

"Yep."

I quickly picked up my tray "Funky Town, I'll catch you later, OK?" I said over my shoulder before walking off with my buddy from Virginia. We sat at a nearby table, laughing at everything Ms. Funky Town had to say. "Thank you for rescuing me," I said with a sigh. He and I talked about our lives, families, and what we wanted to get out of college. We sat there for over an hour before leaving to explore the campus. Curtis was mad cool, caring, and easy going. He laughed at my sarcastic wit and felt like family already. I had a hunch that we would be close friends. Our bonding was both platonic and organic. We sat on a bench on the grounds and talked beyond nightfall until I said we should get back to our respective dorms before they were locked.

My roommate still hadn't arrived, so I sat in silence, recapping the day. In the quiet, my help came to visit. "You're going to do amazing things in Texas. You will succeed here." It had been a while since my help visited me, and I was doing better at managing my emotions, and the moment felt surreal. Smiling as I fantasized about taking over the media industry after graduation, Taylor, Pee Wee and Tina entered my thoughts next. I wondered what they were doing.

Then I got tired of being alone. *Where the heck is my roommate? Let me get out of this room and be social.* I figured I'd first check to see if my suitemates had arrived. A beautiful dark-skinned girl answered my knock on the door. I heard yet another strange accent and asked her where she was from. She chuckled and replied, "N'awlins."

"Come on, N.O.," I said, "let's go meet the floor. First, we should prop our doors open." She obliged, then followed me as I started knocking on everyone's door.

Funky Town heard the commotion, opened her door and asked, "What ch'all doin' out heah?" in her heavy accent.

"Come on, Funky Town. We're having a party," I announced.

The ladies on the floor seemed just as eager as I was to explore. They seemed cool and bubbly, and were friendly, too. I've never been big on hanging with females, but it was my first night at school. I hoped to make a splash, and the idea of making girlfriends was kinda exciting. I proposed that we all pile into a single room to chat as a way to break the ice. The girls who participated sat in as large a circle as the little room could hold. We went around the room with everyone giving their name, where they were from, and their major, and then we proceeded to play the question game. Boy, boys, boys were the topic of discussion most of the night. We laughed together; some even cried when conversations turned personal.

The diversity in personalities, accents, and perspectives made our meetup all the more interesting. The group was a variety of personalities: prissy, dingy, ratchet, down to earth and hilarious. I observed everything and noticed some of the ladies were already cliqued up. They looked at each other and or tapped each other while others talked, as if conveying silent messages. Not shy to call them out, I asked how they knew each other.

Some had come down with friends from high school and others came solo, like me. "What is everyone wearing to the Labor Day Classic?" I inquired. The Labor Day Classic was the first football game of the season, a longstanding tradition at TSU. I'd seen a flyer posted in the lobby about it and planned to attend. One of the girls native to the area reported that it was a really big deal. She also informed us that P. Diddy was that year's special halftime guest. After seeing Diddy, the previous summer and as a die-hard fan, I was sold on attending.

"Ah, let's do a fashion show to find our outfits!" I suggested, taking a leadership role. The room erupted at the idea. Excited, everyone jumped up to rush to their closets. Funky Town pulled her speaker to the door, becoming DJ for the night. Fortunately, I'd bought a few more girly outfits before arriving. Lord knows, I didn't have much else appropriate for the occasion. Still, I pulled out my Jordans and Air Force Ones, just in case. We all eyed each other's clothing and were swapping garments.

I noticed one door on the floor remained closed, so I decided to knock and invite the occupant to join the fun. A gorgeous, brown-skinned girl with beautiful eyes and a warm smile answered. Roughly the same height and size as me, she had big boobs that matched her bubbly personality. "Hiiii," she answered, sounding like a true Valley girl. Intrigued, even before introducing myself, I asked where she was from.

"The Bay Area."

"Where's that?"

"Oakland, California," she answered.

"Well, I'm Danielle, but you can call me Dee." My eyes went to an older woman sitting in the room. "Is that your mom?" Her mom stood and answered as she approached. "Yes, it is; I'm Mrs. Willis, and this is my daughter, Ophelia."

She invited me in, and I noticed that her bed was on the other side of a room divider. I looked at it for a moment and then turned to Ophelia and started telling her about the fashion show we were having. I told her she was welcome to join us.

"Maybe later; I need to unpack."

"Well, I'm in 311 and the fashion show is in the hall. Just follow the music," I said as I waved goodbye. I paused at the door. "Hope to see you later, Ophelia. It was nice to meet you, Mrs. Willis." I pondered the encounter as I walked off toward the music. *Hmm, she seemed cool, but what's up with that room divider? She must be a little standoffish.*

That night I let my guard down, setting aside my tough, street exterior to make real friends. Intentional vulnerability was new for me. Despite my ability to lead and spearhead activities, I felt self-conscious. I hoped the girls liked me, and I wanted everyone to get along well.

After the fashion show, we piled back into another room to finish talking, and Ophelia joined us. I observed her closely as she sat back, listening to different stories with a smirk on her face. There was something about her that I couldn't put my finger on, but I found it intriguing.

The loud banter prompted our resident assistant (RA) to stop by. She introduced herself and warned us to keep it down—by now it was after midnight. The RA seemed real pleasant as she went over the rules again. She alluded to—without outright saying it—a policy that if she didn't see anything, she didn't know anything, while reminding us about the non-co-ed policy. "Have a great night, ladies," she smiled before heading out. As the hour became later, we all returned to our respective rooms. I was still wide awake, and my roommate still hadn't come. So, I went by Ophelia's room. "Those girls are crazy," I announced.

"I wasn't telling them sh*t; I don't know them like that," she responded emphatically.

I laughed. "I knew we were thinking the same thing." I told her good night before going back to my room for good.

The next day, I threw on a cute NYC T-shirt, some Timberlands, and a pair of shorts before hitting the cafeteria (which we called the café). Yes, it was still hot, but I wanted to wear my Tims. As soon as I entered the café, I locked eyes with my dark-skinned track star crush. Seeing him first thing in the morning, I just knew the day would be great. I plastered on a friendly smile to break up what had become an awkwardly long gaze. He smiled back, and I knew it wouldn't be too long before we officially met. Before settling in a seat, I was approached by a dark-skinned football player with a platinum grill in his mouth. He had a very thick accent that I couldn't place, which made it really difficult to understand him. "Wha'chu doing afta dis?" he asked. Looking in the direction of the football players' table, I answered, "I'm playing football; what about you?" I figured I was being set up because his teammates were looking on with broad grins on their faces.

He laughed and told me that was real cute. I asked where he was from. He sounded a bit like New Orleans with an even thicker accent. "I'm from Miami," he answered, then without hesitation asked if he could call me. I was a bit taken aback by his request and didn't want to write down my number in front of everyone. But when my eyes settled on his massive biceps, clearly visible in his muscle shirt, I had second thoughts. *Mm mmm, he looks older and he's definitely trouble."* I slyly looked at where my track star had been sitting—I didn't want him to see me talking to Mr. Miami.

Luckily for me, he'd already left. With one last glance at the football table once more, I made up my mind. "Sure." Why not? He was handsome and seemed cool.

The morning of freshman orientation, I got up early and knocked on everyone's door, suggesting that we stick together. We named ourselves B3, which stood for "Bruce Hall, third floor." Although I'd suggested that we stick together, I knew in the back of my mind that our clique probably wouldn't last. Angel shared with me that girls fight, fall off, split, and that some wouldn't return for the next semester. She explained that was just how college relationships went. Making real girlfriends was a first for me, so I planned to enjoy and live in the moment while we had it. We were B3 and ready to take on college.

The week flew by, and in that time, I started class, finally met my roommate, waved at my track crush, got my first tattoo, and prepared for the Labor Day Classic and the Phi Beta Sigma pajama party that I'd been invited to while exploring the campus with Angel. That was only the first two weeks, I had so much more to look forward to.

My roommate looked nothing like I imagined—not that I had much to go by, anyway. Her name was Devita B. Devita was a light-complexioned, busty chick with a little height on her. Standing about 5-foot-7, she had really pretty hair. She wore glasses and had a large tattoo on her arm. She seemed a little standoffish but also very direct with an East Coast vibe about her, for sure. That DC accent was heavy, too. With more exposure, I became great at detecting where people were from based on their accents. After class, I returned to our room and found Devita talking to a guy who happened to be sitting on my bed. My eyes widened in amazement, and I was speechless for two reasons: First, he was sitting on my bed, and second, she boldly had invited a guy to our room, and she and I hadn't even gotten acquainted. The first thing I said when I saw him was, "You know it's a $150 fine if he's caught up here."

She calmly replied, "Yeah, I know," and they kept right on talking. I walked over to my bed and started straightening up my sheets. He must've gotten the hint because he got up and moved. I looked at him. "You must be from DC, too, because y'all sound the same."

"Yeah."

"I'm Dee," I offered. "Did y'all need anything from Walmart?" They both answered no, so I left. "She's rude as hell," I murmured, shaking my head.

As I approached, I felt the bass from the gymnasium bouncing off the buildings around me. Lil' Jon & The East Side Boyz blasted, and the pajama party was rocking! The small house parties I was accustomed to paled in comparison to my first college party. The energy was electric! Beautiful, eclectic black people filled the space, swaying their hips, enjoying good company, laughing, and dancing their cares away. Stepping through the crowd in my white Air Forces, TSU shorts and custom wife beater, I, too, was ready to partake!

I noticed the fellas were cliqued up either by sports team or hometown. Dressed in tall white tees, Reeboks, and Girbaud jeans, the New Orleans guys dressed just like New Orleans rappers at that time. Lots of them wore dreadlocks as well. While displaying their own style, N.O. guys reminded me of guys from Florida, except that Florida fellas wore Polo jeans instead of Girbauds. They were also a bit more thuggish and mannish, in my opinion. Floridians certainly gave me Trick Daddy vibes.

Remember, I was at an HBCU. Now, I will say that the New Orleans guys could dance for sure! Even the most gangsta and tough-looking guys had no problem on the dance floor. They foot worked, bounced, and two-stepped.

I loved watching their style of dance and listening to their native "bounce music."

Walking a little further, I observed the guys from Dallas. They looked similar to Houston guys but were a bit more soulful. Dallas dudes wore gold teeth, leather shorts, and these funny haircuts they referred to as the "booty or south-side Dallas" fade. They danced, too, but not like the guys from New Orleans. Men from Dallas danced like strippers with the body rolling and hip thrusting. Then there were East Coast and Midwest guys. The East Coast people were more chilled, but also had an arrogant cockiness about them. They were few, but they did remind me of Chicago dudes. We had a big Memphis, California, and overall West Coast population there as well. The West Coast people, specifically those from the Bay Area, certainly had a unique style and music. Hyphy music is what they called it, and the dancing was called "going dumb."

What I enjoyed so far about college was the exposure. I had so much to learn and see through the eyes of my peers. College felt more about becoming well-rounded socially vs. academically. I enjoyed the party and meeting new people.

The New Orleans guys stole the show as the night progressed, but the Bruce Hall girls made the party. Girls from our dorm took the stage to twerk and then they started flashing their boobs. The crowd went wild! I felt as if I'd wandered into the middle of a college *Girls Gone Wild* taping.

I ran into the football player from Florida who I'd exchanged numbers with. He grabbed my arm and said hello. I observed his teammates, checking them out but playing it cool. There was one, in particular, I hadn't seen before. He stared intently, refusing to look away. "Hmm, he's cute," I thought. From the way he was dressed, I knew he was from New Orleans. I boldly met his eyes, smiled, gave my Florida friend a hug and kept it moving. I'd been trying to keep things as neutral as possible with the Florida guy. Despite the attraction, I planned to abstain as long as I could that freshman year. I didn't want any drama or trouble, and men were certainly trouble for me.

Besides, he was the "preying senior" type. You know, the ones who snuff out freshmen girls to sleep with. They play the interested role, woo you with their seniority and/or popularity to get what they want and then they're out. I learned that the hard way. In time he slowly wore me down, destroying all my plans. He was persistent and attractive, and I really believed he liked me. We hung out after class and talked on the phone daily, and admittedly, it was kind of cool to be seen with a popular senior on the football team. At least those were my impressionable thoughts before we slept together.

Afterward, I learned that he was seeing a few girls from Bruce Hall, which explained why he had stopped calling, and practically ghosted me. My pride and feelings were hurt, but I took the L gracefully.

Preying seniors are on every campus, and other areas of life as well, any situation where newbies mix with veterans. So, if you happen to be a freshman or a vulnerable young lady reading this, please be smarter than I was.

My first Labor Day Classic was by far my best college memory at TSU. A group of us all went together: Ophelia, a couple of other girls from Bruce, and me. I felt feminine and beautiful wearing my jean catsuit, some sandals, and a big Jennifer Lopez style hat. It was hard not to switch up my style being surrounded by gorgeous girls. Ophelia certainly gave off lip-gloss girl vibes. I couldn't be looking rough or like her stud girlfriend, so I stepped up my game.

The marching band—ah, that band…poetic, vibrant, well-organized, and soulfully hitting every note. Flag girls, drum majors and majorettes danced, paraded, and captivated the crowds. I felt exhilarated with energy, watching them march in synchrony. Sounds from the cymbals, trumpets, and drums reminded me that TSU was my HBCU.

Immersed in Tiger pride, I felt alive and at home. I knew I made the right decision choosing Texas Southern University. I was beautiful, felt beautiful, and was surrounded by beautiful people.

At the Labor Day Classic, we tailgated, cheered, clapped, and screamed our voices out. We played our rivals, the Prairie View Panthers, which happened to be my cousin Keith's school. I hadn't seen him since my flight in. We connected for a few during halftime and teased each other about the score. The game was a massacre; we blew the Panthers out with a final score of 44-14.

There were so many afterparties to choose from, but we decided on the Kappa party that night because that's where the football team was going. Ophelia and I sat back drooling over the frat guys as they shimmied, body rolled, and twirled their canes. We both left the party with a couple of numbers and incredible memories. I made it back to my empty room with feelings of guilt. I was having so much fun, but now my thoughts went to my siblings.

The ringing phone interrupted my concentration. It was him, the Florida football guy asking to come over so I could look at his knee injury. I said, "Boy, please. How are you planning to get up here?"

He said he knew how to get up to the room, and all I needed to do was tell him my room number. It never dawned on me that he'd been to Bruce many times before. Breaking an awkward silence that followed his arrival, I said, "Let's see that knee." I went to grab peroxide and bandages from the bathroom to patch him up. While cleaning his wound, I talked about my classes, the party, and the game. But he soon made it clear that he wasn't interested in any of that.

"Yo, I need a massage; climb up here and rub my shoulders," he said, interrupting my chatter and flipping over on his back.

I thought, *He's pushy, but OK, very well, then*. I didn't feel afraid or anything, but I was a little uncomfortable with his aggressiveness and being placed on the spot. He was fine, but just because I found him attractive didn't mean I was willing to sleep with him. I shouldn't have agreed to let him come over, but hey, I was bored, had always struggled with people-pleasing, and didn't know a thing about the importance of boundaries, so there we were.

He started to kiss my hands, setting off shooting thoughts in my head. *Is this really about to happen? Get it together, girl. Don't come off too difficult or immature.* I had a flashback to Angel's advice. "You're in college and grown. No one cares what you do." *He'd probably lie about it anyway and say we did even if we didn't.* I never understood why guys lied about who they slept with.

I knew too many guys who boosted the number of partners they'd had, as if it solidified manhood. Totally, a telltale sign of toxic masculinity. Toxic masculinity teaches domination, control, projecting, and pretending. Most of the guys I knew were raised under that tutelage and lacked emotional availability, wholeness, vulnerability, and a healthy respect for women. It was all about smashing, bragging, and passing that provided self-worth.

Admittedly, I wrestled with the power dynamics of being "smashed" and subjected to a male's prerogative. I hated the double standard and celebratory tolerance of guys sowing their wild oats while females got a bad rep. So, I wanted to exercise my own power but got lost in an equally toxic perspective of feminism.

I watched his chiseled bare back while putting on his shirt, while reminded of Tina. Her infamous phrase, "You betta be careful 'fore you get somethin' bleach can't take off," made me belatedly realize we hadn't used protection. He didn't say a thing, and I gave no thought to it, either. Protection wasn't really talked about in high school or among my peers. I knew a little about STDs from occasional PSAs and health books, but it wasn't a reality for me. I believed that only nasty or really promiscuous people got diseases. I didn't realize that it could only take one episode of unprotected sex, or that STDs could be transmitted without actual penetration.

The freedom associated with college both tempted and challenged me. The lack of boundaries and adult supervision required massive levels of self-discipline that I didn't realize I lacked. I felt like a kid in a candy store. The freedom to explore and do whatever I pleased in college without consequence blew my mind. At least, I didn't *consider* the consequences. I was sadly mistaken, learning the hard way that there are always consequences. And for every action (negative or positive), there is a reaction. Therefore, having a solid moral foundation, self-respect, and boundaries *before* college is important.

For many of us, college is—or was—that wonder-year period where we aimed to find and define ourselves. Sadly, some wander too far away, never returning to who they were created to be.

Attention, younger ladies reading this: please know your worth and how valuable you are. Avoid the seniors on campus, or at least check their references, do homework on them. Every guy doesn't truly want or deserve you. For some, it's just a game of bragging rights and self-gratification. Furthermore, you don't owe a man anything, especially not your body. And sex will not make anyone truly like you.

You can find someone attractive, spend time with and even kiss them, but that doesn't mean you are obligated to go all the way with them. Even if the time and opportunity present itself, that still doesn't mean anything; it's not a sign. If any guy gets upset over your decision to say no or even not yet, then he doesn't respect or truly care about you. Time is always a really great revealer; time tells on everyone, revealing their true intentions. Just watch. Just wait.

For me, I had to force myself to pretend he didn't exist. I hated the feeling of having been hunted, preyed, and played. I needed to refocus and avoid melting down. After all, he wasn't my boyfriend, nor did we really get to know each other. I interpreted surface conversation, flirtation, and his expressing interest as a sign, assuming he liked me. Sometimes you have to ask people's intentions upfront. Sure they can lie, but you might be surprised by asking anyway, especially with sex being as casual these days.

Certainly, I didn't like the strings that entangled my emotions when it came to the guys. Learning to be physical yet feel no emotion is how I survived high school; it was my defense mechanism. However, that strategy was corrupted and illogical, breeding no reward. Surely, I didn't want to revert back to that, but the notion still lay dormant. College was my opportunity to grow and even possibly find love.

I got over the football guy, and as time passed and I became focused, the temptation to deviate from my plan presented itself in the package of someone else. Space and opportunity conveniently presented my dark-skinned track crush right before me. He was sitting in the café, eating alone. We made eye contact as soon as I walked in. *Forget this*, I told myself while making a beeline straight for his table. "Hi, I'm Dee."

"What's up, Dee?" he responded. "I be seein' you starin' at me and stuff."

Hmm, he's charming. I laughed before using an old *Fresh Prince of Bel Air* line on him. "You wouldn't have known I was looking at you if you wasn't looking at me."

He laughed. "I'm Zaire."

"I love that name. Where are you from?"

That was how it began. We progressed to daily phone calls, study sessions, and lots of time together arranged around his track schedule from that initial conversation. Zaire wasn't into the party scene, which explained why I never saw him out. My first impression was that he was the good guy type, someone I could truly settle down with. Zaire was chill, laid back, intelligent, respectful and, like me, very witty.

We grew steadily closer and dated unofficially. I adored everything about him, and the feeling seemed to be mutual. However, the more time we spent together, the more timid I became. I grappled with the notion that he was too great of a guy for me. Those private memories of seeing myself as broken had never left. I struggled with imposter syndrome and was afraid he'd find me out. Like a slow leak in a punctured tire, my own insecurities started to flatten our growing friendship.

As bad as I liked Zaire and wanted to move forward, I didn't think I deserved him. He preferred to spend leisure time playing video games, chilling, or studying. He didn't drink or use profanity and came from a two-parent home. Clearly, I saw being opposites as a negative, which persuaded me to put him on a pedestal. Zaire was a solid, wholesome guy.

On the other hand, I preferred to be at every party, meeting new people, smoking, drinking, exploring, and maximizing my new freedom. Still looking for worth and to fill my voids, I wanted the full college experience. I didn't think those wishes were too, too bad, but I also wasn't comfortable with our differences.

I wanted to be a "good, wholesome" girl. However, I didn't see myself as one. As a matter of fact, my definition of "good" was flawed. I created this imaginary high standard of what "good" meant. Most of my ideas stemmed from the perfectionist in me. Those unattainable standards and expectations became ingrained long before college. There was no room for self-forgiveness, grace, humanity, or growth. I consistently compared myself to my made-up standards and other people's lives; primarily contrasting what I wish I had and was to what I didn't and wasn't.

My consuming self-sabotaging cycle was most prevalent and triggered by interactions with men. That chip on my shoulder kept growing. Zaire didn't have a problem with me or our differences; I did. Unaware of this revelation at the time, it was easier to reconcile that he deserved someone better. That would be my go-to conclusion. Hardly giving myself a real chance, subconsciously, I pushed him away. I didn't know how to separate who I thought I was from what I been through.

We took our relationship to another level, the night he insisted on studying together upstairs. We usually met in the library, but I let him come up. I felt comfortable since we had been talking for nearly two months already. We hung out all the time, so it wasn't a big deal. I had him climb the tree outside the laundry room up to my floor. Prior to his starting the climb, I cracked the window and left my room unlocked. His track abilities did the rest, getting him there ninja fast.

He was the second guy to visit my room. Devita, my roomie, was hardly ever around anyway, making it easier. I sat in admiration that night, watching Zaire as he worked on Ophelia's laptop. I didn't have a laptop, so she let me borrow hers to avoid making the hike to the library. Zaire sat there, staring at the screen and barely blinking those curly lashes of his. I couldn't help but stare at him, thinking how smart and perfect he was. I lay with my legs sprawled across his as he sat up typing, determined to properly revise my paper. It was comforting to have him around, and that night I showed him just how much.

After we finished my paper, we passed the rest of the time with each other. Thinking about my first college experience, I asked if he had protection. He told me "No, but don't worry, I done it before without one; I'm safe." My easy acceptance of that response was just as distressing as it sounds. But, at eighteen years old, that was enough for me to trust and move forward.

After sleeping together once, we decided to continue getting to know each other. I loved the fact that our relationship wasn't built on sex. Zaire seemingly liked me for me, and I was fine with that until I wasn't.

I met this other guy named Dallas at one of the campus mixers who I started seeing as well. He was fun, outgoing, and flawed, like me. He wasn't a rule follower like Zaire, and he was just more exciting. Honestly, I liked them both. However, I didn't want Zaire to think I was trying to play him if he found out.

Casually hanging was nothing for me, but crossing the line sexually was different, and Dallas and I slept together almost immediately. Being entangled with both of them provided my first lesson in staying out the gray when entertaining guys. I discovered how problematic ambiguity in relationships can be. Without clarity, intention, and a destination, it's like driving around wasting premium gas and time. I also became sloppy when it was my turn to sneak over to Dallas' dorm. After all, he and Zaire lived on the same floor, just doors apart. It was dangerous, borderline savage, I know, but I was addicted to Dallas. I didn't know how to stop seeing him. He was my destructive drug, and I justified my behavior as being single, "not having titles."

Everything came crashing down the night I snuck over there, thinking the track team was away. My attire of oversized gym shorts, tennis shoes, and a hoodie usually provided a halfway decent disguise in case I got caught. Keeping my head down and sagging my shorts, I made it past Zaire's room before dropping my keys and accidentally kicking them forward. They slid forward, stopping at someone's feet. That someone bent and picked them up. "Aye, here go yo' keys." I had no choice but to look up. Slowing, lifting my head, I looked directly in the face of Zaire's roommate.

"Hey, Dee," he said, confusion on his face. "Zaire is out of town." I swallowed hard, and before I could thank him, Dallas opened his door.

"Girl, get yo' fine a** in here," he playfully ordered. With a mumbled "Thank you," I quickly grabbed my keys and rushed past Zaire's roommate into Dallas's room. My face was hot, and all I could think about was how I'd messed up big time. I knew Zaire would hear about this. I couldn't stop thinking about Zaire, and although we were not official, we kind of had an understanding. Ladies, that's the problem with ambiguity.

Later that night, I went straight to my girl Ophelia's and told her Dallas' condom popped, and we finished unprotected. She and I had become best friends. Crying, I told her how silly and ashamed I felt for having had unprotected sex with three guys. She calmed me down and advised, "Just wait two weeks, then get tested." The mere thought of getting tested terrified me. I had never even made a doctor's appointment myself. Tina took care of those types of things. I planned to take her advice and get tested.

Those were the longest two weeks of my life. I sat in the waiting room of this little clinic we found in southwest Houston, thinking horrible thoughts. *I'm going to have to drop out of college, buy diapers, and take care of a child, and everyone is going to be so disappointed.* Hearing my name called interrupted my dismal prediction. "You're not pregnant, but there are additional white blood cells in your urine," the nurse informed me after my test. I was thrilled not to be pregnant. I wouldn't be forced to drop out of college after all. But... "What are additional blood cells?" I asked. She looked up. "Sweetie, you have a sexually transmitted disease."

The moment those words left her lips, I felt as if someone had run up and stabbed me, leaving me to bleed to death. My face got hot, and I began to sob right there in the office. "Can you hear me?" the nurse asked as she gently touched my shoulder, instructing me to breathe. She then calmly informed me that it was only a bacteria-induced STD called chlamydia and that I would be cured in a week. That didn't matter to me; I felt like the scum of the earth.

"Here," the nurse said, handing me a tissue and a bottle, "drink this pink elixir and refrain from sex for two weeks. You'll need to use condoms; we can give you some. And contact the people you've slept with. Have them come get tested as well," she calmly instructed. Snapping back into reality, I realized she said it would clear up in a week, but still, I was devastated. During the bus ride back to school, I rehearsed how to deliver news of my chlamydia to my partners. I knew I had been tested and was negative before leaving for college, which meant I contracted it from one of the three people I'd been with. But because they were all unprotected, I had no clue which one gave it to me. I felt terrible, stupid, and disgusting. I suspected Dallas had given it to me since we slept together so frequently. I only messed with the football guy and Zaire once. I not only felt overwhelmed but frightened at having to share the news of my diagnosis with others.

I disappeared for a week, trying to gather myself. I didn't take any calls and laid low. Dallas finally came over, demanding to know if I was OK after avoiding his calls. We sat on the steps outside Bruce Hall, talking. I told him I wasn't pregnant but did test positive for chlamydia and that it had cleared up. I told him I wasn't even mad at him because it was my fault for having unprotected sex with him. He said, "Wait, don't put this on me. How do you know I gave that to you?"

Our exchange grew louder, and our conversation was no longer private. People gathered around listening to our feud and chatting among themselves. Furious, I stormed off to my room. I needed someone else to talk to. I wasn't getting anywhere with Dallas.

Guess who decided to show up? That's right, the devil on the left, making the situation far worse. I anticipated the rumor mill to fire up. Once again, I'd be a laughingstock, just like in elementary and high school. I sank into a rapid slump, driven into depression because of the STD diagnosis.

Dodging Zaire for a couple of weeks was fairly easy, but I knew we needed to talk soon. Locking myself in my room felt just as miserable as breaking the news. I didn't want to go anywhere, not to class, not to the café, but I understood that life would go on with or without me. I hoped my help would visit with uplifting words, but I actually didn't hear from him the rest of the year.

Experiencing that STD debacle in my first semester of freshman year was a valuable turning point for me and my college experience. From that moment forward, guys became dead to me. If I wasn't in a relationship, I planned to be abstinent. Turning my attention to my studies, academics became my supreme motivation.

I saw a flyer for dance team tryouts and figured that would be a great outlet. Snatching the flyer off the wall, I lit up with excitement.

But before tryouts, I needed to take care of something. I finally called Zaire and asked him to meet up with me. I picked up on a streak of eagerness in his voice, but he was also still upset. It was approaching a month since we'd last spoken, and I had the hard task of first apologizing to him, followed by advising him to get tested.

Sweat beads formed on my forehead as I stood against the brick wall on the side of the law building. Man, I'd missed him. Taking a deep breath, I began by sharing how much I cared for him. I told him at times I truly felt as if I loved him. "You're an awesome guy, who I didn't think I deserved. I apologized for hurting you and for the way you found out about Dallas," I confessed. He stood there, arms folded, emotionless, staring me directly in the eye, not saying a word. The longer he stared at me, the harder it became to talk. My throat tightened up, and it was hard to swallow. "I'm sorry for misleading you, but I did want to be with you. Please forgive me." I ended by telling him that I recently tested positive for chlamydia, had it treated, and suggested he get tested.

His brows slightly raised, showing only a hint of emotion. Then he asked, "Are you finished?"

I couldn't hold my tears back any longer. "Yes."

"Thank you. I'll have to think about this hard."

He walked off, and I took a few minutes to regain my composure before walking to Ophelia's room. She always knew what to say to encourage me. Supportive but carefree, her perspective was always more liberal than mine. I appreciated that about her. I was super hard on myself, tripping over everything. She kept my neurotic tendencies balanced freshman year. "Girl, stop crying," she urged. "I know girls that have had twenty partners and multiple abortions by our age. You're tripping off three people."

It's funny how in comparison to others, what we have going on can either amplify or elevate our feelings. Personally, I was more upset by the consequences than the behavior that garnered those consequences. If I can be honest, that is typically the real problem for many people—disregarding the behaviors that jam us up in the first place. It would take years for me to unlearn that way of thinking.

Devita finally started staying the night in our room, which provided us an opportunity to get closer. Speaking in passing turned to talking for hours. Despite her not being around much, she knew something was up with me. I went from Ms. Social Butterfly to staying in our room for days at a time. In a plan to get me out of my funk, she insisted that we get out and invited Ophelia to come with us.

Devita had ties to an up-and-coming DJ who picked us up on weekends. Climbing over all this equipment, we got into his truck. Riding with the DJ got us free entry and drinks. Because we were under twenty-one, none of us were big drinkers, so we only stuck to apple martinis. Riding with the DJ became our thing. We blossomed into quite the party animals.

Our weekly lineup was Club 713 Tuesdays, Red Rooster Wednesdays, T-town on Thursdays, and 8 Mile Fridays. Saturday nights were reserved for campus and frat parties. I thought I missed out on partying in high school, but those had nothing on college partying.

The dance tryouts were disastrous! I was determined to make the team and excited about dancing again. I practiced feverishly to the fast-paced routine to Sir Mix-a-Lot's "Baby Got Back." The dance was difficult, but I learned it. The day of tryouts, I was ready and pumped...until I learned they were open to the public. Boy, did that make me nervous. The football team, frat guys, SGA, sororities, and everybody and their mama was there. They paired us in groups of two. I hoped to be paired with a cute and agile partner. Instead, they teamed me with an uncoordinated, awkwardly built

Hunchback of Notre-Dame type chick. Sis was downright scary.

She wasn't a bit friendly and refused to rehearse with me before our turn to worsen matters. She even had the audacity to tell me, "Every man for himself." I thought, "OK, bring it, I'm about to shut her down out there." They called our number, and we took center stage. The sound system boomed with the song's opening.

The beat dropped and I started dancing, hitting all my kicks and turns on target, but I started to hear booing. *This is one tough crowd.* Then I made the epic mistake of looking at my partner and saw it was she who the crowd was booing, and no wonder. She was completely trolling, doing her own routine. She did none of the things we'd done in our weeks of practice. Looking at her completely threw me off beat, and before I could get back into the rhythm, she bumped me out of the way with her massive hips to steal the show.

People were laughing hysterically at her jiggling meat that bounced all over the place. My small, 120-pound frame couldn't stand up to her. Her hip check threw me flat on the floor. All I could hear were the frat guys chanting, "It don't take long to judge that sh*t." The laughing kept going until they stopped the music, and the host thanked us. I didn't know whether to pick my face up off the floor first, or my pride. That was the moment I stopped dancing forever.

The rest of the semester was eventful, to say the least, for several reasons. A couple of us got into a car accident on the way to our first strip club, we got more tattoos, attended more parties, the B3 crew split up, and I got into a few verbal altercations…and then I met another guy who changed my life over the next three years.

His name was Virgil Scott, an unusual first name very fitting to his style and unique look. I saw him around Bruce a few times. He was the same guy who'd stared at me at that first college pajama party. We never spoke, but I knew exactly who he was and a lot about him, courtesy of one of my suitemates who had a crush on him and talked about him 24/7.

He was from New Orleans, and they had attended the same high school. He played football and had an air of mystery about him. He wasn't interested in her and made that clear in my fruitless attempts to hook them up. Virgil was actually planning to make a move on me.

Minding my business, and wolfing down lunch between classes, I was in deep thought about Zaire, Dallas, and the dance team. Days prior, Dallas told me he had tested negative for chlamydia. I thought that was strange but didn't think he would lie. I had no clue of Zaire's status, because he still refused to talk to me.

My thoughts were interrupted when a funny-looking guy came over to where I sat.

"Hey, my guy wants to talk to you," he told me.

"Who?" I asked defensively, looking in the direction he had come from. My eyes settled on Virgil, and our gazes locked. Virgil stood about 6 feet and weighed about 200 pounds. He had a solid muscular build with a gorgeous caramel complexion, light brown eyes, and wavy hair visible through the stocking cap that held his braids in place. I'd never really given Virgil any thought at all. I'd been doing great with my focused, anti-guy strike. I gave him an uncomfortable smile and waved. I looked up at the frail guy before me and retorted, "Ask him why he can't speak for himself." I knew this was my suitemate's crush, so I figured I would exchange numbers with him in another attempt at hooking them up.

The guy said, "OK," and walked off. Then Virgil slowly approached me with a smirk on his face. This man had the coolest walk ever and looked like the smooth operator type...

trouble. "Hey, here's my number. What's yours?" he asked. He had that very deep New Orleans accent going on. I'd seen him watching me for a while but never gave it any attention until then.

"'Hey, what's my number'? Rude. My name is Dee," I pointedly responded before taking the paper with his number. I looked at it and chuckled. "I'll call you later. Bye Virgil." I decided to wait on calling him but definitely planned to...only for the sake of my suitemate.

Ophelia got a kick out of the fact that my suitemate's crush was crushing on me. She advised me to at least see what he had to say. The fact that Virgil played football was enough. After that one guy, I felt my name had circulated enough with the team. For that reason, I didn't rush to call. We finally had a conversation a week later. I asked him what the deal was with him and my suitemate.

"She's delusional. I wasn't checking for her in high school, and I'm definitely not now," he replied. She and I were cordial but not friends. So, after sliding her name in as many conversations as I could, I realized he wouldn't budge and just wasn't into her. Virgil was pretty quiet and chill on the surface, but he was very persistent in his pursuit.

We started to talk more often, and he started to grow on me. He gave me a bit of escapism and a mental reprieve from Zaire, whom I thought about every day. Virgil was a great listener and had no problem letting me vent about Zaire, either. Virgil was the first to ask me out on a real date, since he had a car. I thought he was sweet. He said he wanted to get me out and cheer me up. His compassion and tolerance of me lamenting over another guy earned him lots of points.

Our first date was dinner at Popeye's followed by a movie. Oh, stop laughing...that was big for broke college students. Virgil was quite the gentleman. We started talking a couple of times a week and some weeks, we talked every day. I stayed mindful of taking things slowly and getting to know him. I was serious about that but enjoyed him in the interim. The more we hung out, the more my walls came down. We had a weekly study session in our favorite spot in the library on the second floor. During one session, his mother called his cellphone, and he told me he wanted me to meet her. That was by far the sweetest thing I had experienced with a guy. His conversations were always intriguing, and I found him remarkably interesting, too. What I liked most about him was his low-key and private nature. For example, he never let being an athlete go to his head. He was talented but humble.

The more time we spent together, the more I gave up hope with Zaire. I still emailed Zaire occasionally, but he never responded. Virgil helped me pass the time wonderfully until the semester ended.

Everyone had to move out of the dorms at semester's end. Finishing the semester with honors, I was proud to have survived the first half of my freshman year. I looked forward to a break from college and was eager to see my siblings.

As it turned out, my trip home was uncomfortable. Pee Wee was still staying with our aunt and barely passing senior year. Taylor was running the streets and planning to drop out of school. I knew he didn't have the necessary support, stability, or encouragement he needed to be successful after I left. Taylor told me about Tina's new alcoholic boyfriend and how she'd started back drinking, even more than before. He painfully added, "That's all they do. I hate it here."

I hated that Taylor was essentially on his own, and I hated worrying so much about them knowing I couldn't do much. It seemed like they were always on my mind. The conflict of enjoying my life vs. knowing my siblings' living conditions weighed heavy on me.

I kept up with Virgil and Ophelia during the break; they were both doing well. In what would be my last attempt at contacting Zaire, I emailed him to wish him a happy holiday. After a week or so, I was ready to get back to school. I missed hanging with Virgil; every New Orleans song or artist I heard while away reminded me of him. I found myself thinking about him a lot. We had been spending time together for over a month, and I was proud of myself for following through with getting to know him. He had been the only guy I felt comfortable being my full self around. After talking Angel's and Pee Wee's heads off about him, they asked why I didn't date him. At that moment, I figured I needed just to close the door on Zaire.

In some kind of sign that I'd made the right decision, the day before I returned to Houston, Zaire finally broke his silence. He emailed me back, telling me he had been diagnosed with chlamydia as well and that I'd really hurt him. He accepted my apology and said he forgave me. He said he didn't want to be with me anymore but was willing to be friends at least.

CHAPTER EIGHT

US

Campus was a ghost town! It lacked the vigor and excitement generated at the start of a new school year. Just as Angel predicted, people dropped out, fell out, or simply didn't return. Many of the girls from Bruce didn't return for the next semester, either. Needless to say, B3 was a wrap.

Devita and I remained roomies that semester, and our friendship grew stronger. Anticipating the start of a new year, I knew the semester ahead would be different from the first one. I could feel the possibilities.

Heading to the café my first week back, Virgil would be the first person I ran into. Locking eyes and smiling, it was great seeing him. We shared a warm embrace, and he asked, "How was your trip? When did you get back?" Distracted by the little diapered baby flying over his shoulder with a bow and arrow in hand, I couldn't get my words out. Cupid's arrow hit me in the center of my heart. It wasn't fair—I fell instantly in love with Virgil! *I was supposed to be with him all along,* I happily thought before responding.

We were inseparable from that day forward, and a few days after Valentine's Day, we became official. We did our homework, studied, traveled, worked out, ate lunch, took classes together, and I slept in his high school shirts every night. We met each other's families, and Virgil became my world and I his—second to football, of course. He was protective, assertive, and super crazy about me. Although Virgil was cool with his teammates, he was still pretty private and a loner who kept a low profile. Definitely a mama's boy, he was an only child who loved his entire family. He shared a bond with his family that I could only dream of.

Sweet, compassionate, and fun-loving Creole people, Virgil's family took me in as if I were one of their own. His mother and I developed a close relationship. She became like a second mom to me. We talked often, just like girlfriends. She thought I was beautiful and smart, and she appreciated my commitment to her son and our academics.

She was right, her son and my education consumed me, they were all I had. There was no balance, boundary, self-discovery, or breathers from my relationship and schoolwork. I became so committed to Virgil and my studies that I didn't have much of a life otherwise, but at the time I was comfortable with that.

I failed to allow myself time to transition, learn more about me, and get comfortable and acclimated to being away at college. I hadn't truly reflected on anything, and everything moved so quickly. However, my relationship with Virgil did put a halt to my smoking and partying. I traded in my Jordans for wedges, sandals, and heels. With Virgil I desired to be more feminine. He said he didn't like hood girls who smoked, fought or dressed like dudes, and I aimed to please.

As the semester ended, my friends took notice of my changing personality. My academic obsession and fantasies of success only heightened after Pee Wee announced she was pregnant. It happened at a hotel party that I snuck her into over the holiday break. Tina was upset and blamed my aunt for not keeping a closer eye on Pee Wee (as if *she* watched us closely). It was what it was, so we shifted to excitement at the thought of a new baby. Admittedly, I did feel responsible.

US

I stopped home to see her before heading to Chicago, where I planned to get a summer job. Pee Wee was about five months along by that time. She was glowing and seemed excited about becoming a mother. Living in separate homes the previous year had stifled our relationship quite a bit. We weren't as close as we used to be, and my leaving for college didn't help our connection. We did keep in touch while I was away, but still our sisterly bond had been disrupted.

Two things I knew for certain were that the baby would be loved and Pee Wee was going to make a great mom. We all knew this since she was nine years old and desiring to be a wife and mom. Personally, I knew the baby would motivate her to work harder in life. Only the financial part concerned me, chiefly because her sperm donor disassociated himself as soon as he learned she was pregnant. As for me, I planned to commit the rest of college and my pursuit of success to the unborn child. I wanted to ensure that I was in position to help my family. I couldn't wait to be an aunt!

I made the difficult suggestion that Tina put Taylor in Job Corps to avoid his dropping out of school without a GED or a trade. He failed all his classes, making it impossible to avoid repeating his grade. Still lacking the necessary support, Tina apparently gave up trying to rear Pee Wee and Taylor after I left. She was still seeing her alcoholic boyfriend and had moved into the same apartment complex where he lived. Pee Wee was asked to leave our aunt's home when she got pregnant. She and Taylor confided that Tina was never home, they hardly had any food to eat and, again, that all she and her boyfriend did was drink. That news and the associated stress was challenging to learn.

Arriving in Chicago in early June, I stayed with DeDe and landed employment fairly quickly. I needed to save money for my next move in Houston. I couldn't return to Bruce Hall, as only freshmen were allowed there. Chicago felt different that stay, because I'd evolved tremendously since leaving just a few short years prior. I returned to my old stomping grounds my first week in town and made a surprise visit to the market down the street from where we used to stay. I was hoping to run into Darius but wasn't sure if he still worked there. Entering the store, I headed straight to the back and saw Darius stocking groceries. He looked up, and we smiled at one another before coming together for a tight hug.

"Ayeee, when you get back, G?"

"Man, I'm only visiting for a couple of months," I answered.

He looked me up and down, observing the transformation I had begun. He still looked the same, handsome as ever, and had started to fill out more. He wasn't the only one; I had gained about fifteen pounds freshman year, just like everyone said I would. I was cool with it, though. I had it to spare, and it looked great on me.

Being back on the West Side felt good and being in the area also felt humbling. I went to holler at my cousins and some friends. They were up to the same things they'd been doing when I left years prior. I was the only one doing the college thing, and that soon started to show. My speech was different, as were my priorities. I was focused on opening my first bank account, finding a place to live for sophomore year, and my future career. My friends from the hood were still selling drugs, having babies, going to prison, and not thinking beyond the moment. Making my own money was always rewarding, but it was going toward a down payment on campus housing this time. The fall semester would be here before I knew it, and I had no clue of where I was going to stay. I was a couple of hundred dollars short and putting in overtime in an attempt to pull off a miracle.

US

Over the summer, a new passion for poetry writing emerged. I mean, I was artistically inclined and solid with writing lyrics, but being in love propelled me toward producing poetry. I wrote poems about life, Virgil, being black, and my community.

The semester prior, Virgil and I had taken a political science and black history class that awakened the future activist in me. My interest shifted and putting it all on paper was therapeutic.

Summer's end brought two mammoth moments in my life. First, on August 7, 2003, I welcomed my first nephew into the world. My heart felt full just knowing that he was healthy and Pee Wee was well. My only issue was that I'd have to wait months to see him. The next piece of good news came from a conversation with my dorm mother. She called to offer me an RA position, the timing of which was nothing short of the miracle I'd prayed for! It was a major blessing as time dwindled without my having earned the full housing deposit. Ironically, my help kept instructing me to relax, assuring that everything would work out, but I was so fixated on what I saw vs. trusting God.

As an RA, I would have neither rent nor food expenses. My meal plan and housing were free. I knew the big man upstairs shot me a favor with that blessing. I didn't even apply for the position or interview (and typically, the process is very tedious with several interviews). The dorm mother specifically shared with me, "I noticed how responsible you are and how well you communicate. You would make a great RA." I tearfully accepted the offer. *OK, God, you really do hear me...*

Virgil waited for my arrival just outside the security checkpoint with flowers in hand. Like a scene out of a romantic movie, I ran to him, jumping in his arms and affixing my legs around his waist. We embraced for a long moment before he put me down. I had never been big on PDAs, but I didn't care who saw us. Seeing each other prompted that new love feeling all over again as we closed in on sixth months together and were about to embark on our second year of college.

The year started similar to how it ended, except we both had more on our respective plates. Virgil became a starter on the football team, and I had two jobs on campus. In addition to my RA duties, I took a job at the radio station my cousin had told me about. KTSU, 90.9 FM ("Jazz And All Its Colors") would become a second home and where I developed professionally. I was grateful for the introduction to KTSU, as it truly changed my life's trajectory. I started off answering phones and making copies, then soon progressed to writing scripts.

Working a couple of hours between classes was just the right amount of exposure I needed. KTSU was where I first fell in love with the sounds of jazz. On my very first day at the station, one of the announcers, with his smooth vibe and raspy voice, told me words that changed my life.

Dressed in a dashiki, he reminded me of one of those revolutionary cats from the seventies. He said, "Hey kid, what's your name?"

"Dee," I replied.

"Good to have you with us, Dee. Stick around here long enough, and not only will this music change your life, but your grades will increase," he advised.

I soaked up everything I could while there. Learning quickly, I was able to identify different artists' signature sounds and fell deeper in love with the trumpet. I have always had an affinity for the sax and trumpet since attending Pastor Sumrall's church as a kid. We had a saxophonist whose notes accompanied worship. I admired him, and the sounds of the trumpet had always done something to me. Music placed me in a happy and safe space.

US

Being around jazz music made me feel more hopeful and a lot less mentally scattered. I did, in fact, study better to that type of music. Herbie Hancock, Duke Ellington, Louis Armstrong, Miles Davis, Dizzy Gillespie, Thelonious Monk, and even modern musicians like Christian Scott kept my spirits up. I learned about the Harlem Renaissance and soaked up every learning opportunity like a sponge. Absorbing all the knowledge I could, my vocabulary started to expand while in that environment. I started to transform; my rap intake decreased and so did my potty mouth. I went to sleep listening to jazz and awakened to the sound of it as well.

Music wasn't the only abundant learning opportunity. The radio station also taught me about production, different departments and their functions, station operations, underwriting, switchers, editing, and fundraising. Our station's GM (general manager) became a father figure to me, a well-connected big shot, get-things-done type of guy with plenty of heart.

He played the trumpet, too, and promised my cousin that he would look out for me while I was working there. He kept his word all the way to graduation. I stuck around the station for hours on end while Virgil was at football practice. Mama D from the partnership department became a mother figure to me, having daughters only a few years my senior. Very street smart and candid, Mama D kept it real all the time. She didn't sugar coat or cut corners with any of the students. I liked her style, and I needed her presence in my life during that time. We talked about life, family, Virgil, and everything else.

No subject was off-limits, and she became my biggest advocate. She often reminded me, "Take care of you first, and the guys will always be there as long as you have a vagina." She liked Virgil but cautioned me not to get lost in him. She saw something that I didn't see.

Friday mornings we played old school music and dusties at the station. The music was reminiscent of my childhood. Tina always had some Al Green, Otis Redding, or Ray Charles on deck during Saturday morning cleanings. We hated getting up early to clean and loathed washing the walls. I recalled those memories as I made a beeline through the station to grab donuts on my way to class. "Good morning, Mama D. Is that my boy Ray Charles?" I teased, picking up my donuts before exiting through the back door. The Friday morning host also happened to be one of the sports announcers.

I loved those guys! They were hilarious, passionate, and so knowledgeable about sports. The play-by-play announcer loved to tell the story of getting me off the phones and onto the field.

"You know, I saw all that potential jus' goin' ta waste," he claimed. "She sat there, answerin' them phones: 'Hello, thanks for calling KTSU,'" he said, mimicking my voice. "I looked at her and said, 'You need to be back here in the studios and on the field interviewing these athletes. Get off those phones, girl.'" Hearing him tell that story cracked me up every time. He ain't lying when he tells it.

He knew that I had an interest in sports and was studying broadcast media, so they took a chance on me. But first, I had to shadow the current sideline sports reporter. Her name was Kelly, and she was a year older, belonged to a sorority, was a member of the track team, and also hailed from Zaire's hometown.

Kelly initially came across as standoffish, stuck up, and not welcoming of me shadowing her. She pranced around the station barely speaking to anyone but carrying a Bible with her eighty percent of the time. That amused me. *How she walkin' around with a Bible but not speaking?* What really ground my gears about her were her post 10:30 PM calls to Virgil for game stats. Answering his phone, I asked who was calling, knowing it was her, before handing the phone to him. *She's the reporter; she needs to do her own homework,* I thought.

Virgil was just as protective of me, if not more. I only gave Kelly a hard time because she gave me one. Virgil, on the other hand, intimidated everyone and even ran guys off for looking at me. Front and center, I supported my man, wearing the number 26 painted on my cheek. After each game, Virgil came up to the stands and leaned over the rail to plant a kiss on my cheek before hitting the locker room. Those moments and public display of affection meant everything to me. Other athletes I knew hid their girlfriends, but Virgil's kisses said he wasn't ashamed and wanted the world to know that I belonged to him.

His moving off campus allowed us to play house the majority of the year. Having him to take care of provided a sense of purpose for me that made me feel empowered. Virgil became my baby, and I didn't even realize it. I started prioritizing his needs over my own. My lack of self-worth and self-love blinded me from seeing the problem with my behavior. I had needs, too, but I was only concerned with taking care of *his* needs. There wasn't a thing I wouldn't have done for him, either. I cooked, cleaned, catered, nurtured, and assisted him academically, physically, and emotionally.

From the back seat, my friends strongly suggested that I slow down a bit, but I wasn't trying to hear any of that. I'd placed them in the back seat for a reason. I had finally found true love and was content with being a bookworm, unofficial wife, and campus worker.

It would be several years before I saw how problematic and unhealthy our relationship was. Our differences in values and between our still-evolving personalities slowly became more prevalent the more time we spent together and apart. For example, my love for activism increased through my "woke" and pro-black community contacts. Which was to be expected from attending an HBCU.

I had professors dressed in Afrocentric fashion while lecturing and engaging me in conversations on revolution, systematic racism, Juneteenth, and culture changes. My healthy curiosity appreciated that type of talk and birthed a deeper desire to educate myself while engaging in social change. The more I learned about disparities in the black community relating to government, the more passionate I became about implementing racial equality and change. Activism-related content started to fill my poetry book and notepads. My coursework became devoted to social justice. I wrote and produced short projects and films related to it. I wanted to volunteer and support the underserved. But trying to engage Virgil in my newly growing passion was an uphill battle. Not only didn't he share the same passion, but he laughed, saying it was stupid of me to be interested in social activism.

Luckily, I had Ophelia with whom to share thought-provoking conversations. She was my outlet and attending TSU with aspirations of becoming a judge. She was a political science major, and her liberal perspective and deep connections to social revolution were rooted in growing up in the Bay Area. Her passion for our culture was infectious! Being on the same wavelength with her fulfilled that need for thought-provoking conversations.

Homecoming was days away, and I wanted to do something nice for Pee Wee. So, I sent for her to come down and get a taste of college life. I knew as a new mom, she likely needed a break as well. Surprisingly, she didn't object, although my nephew was only two months old. I had a full weekend planned and was excited to show her a portion of my world and also for her to meet Virgil.

US

Pee Wee and I went to the step show, to dinner, and a couple of afterparties. I showed her the radio station, the yard, and she thoroughly enjoyed the game. During a heart-to-heart talk, she shared the difficulties of being a young mom taking college classes and how tiring and difficult it was.

We talked about Tina and Taylor. "Taylor be in the streets doing what he wants while Tina acts like she doesn't care," she shared. She revealed that Tina had gotten evicted again shortly after my visit and moved in with her boyfriend. She said that she and the baby had been staying at a friend's and Mel's. My chest burned with fury because I had recently spoken with Tina and she didn't mention a thing about having been evicted. This news came as a shock, and it distressed me to hear that Pee Wee and my nephew were living in such unstable circumstances.

Fortunately, Pee Wee was a fighter. I knew she'd make a way for the baby and would continue to be a great mom. I reassured her that I'd be there for whatever she needed and didn't plan to leave them.

The rest of the semester flew by quickly. I went home with Virgil for the Thanksgiving holiday before heading home. I enjoyed a true New Orleans holiday feast. Tasting deer meat, gumbo, boudin, and other Cajun dishes, the food was delish! I loved the city; his family was beautiful and I finally got a chance to put a face to stories heard. New Orleans, a jazzy, warm, and welcoming city, captured my heart.

My nephew was all I'd thought about since Pee Wee's visit. During the short fight home, I imagined how he looked and how he smelled. Seeing him in person brought tears to my eyes, he was absolutely the most vibrant, alert, beautiful, happy, brown-eyed baby I had ever seen. Just a giggling bundle, he smiled and laughed at everything. It felt as if he was excited to meet me, too.

When I extended my arms to hold him, he raised his arms toward me. My sense of wonder at this perfect little person was overshadowed by a sense of hope for his future. Holding my nephew felt as if I were holding my own child. I wanted to protect him, teach, and to comfort him. I vowed to give him the world.

Pee Wee had, in fact, stayed in the back of Mel's home. She and Tina had fallen out after the eviction and Tina's move with her boyfriend. The home where Pee Wee stayed wasn't anything like the home I had left. Dilapidated and desolate, there was no heat, food, or even a door to the bathroom. Pee Wee and the baby slept on the remains of a torn bunk bed with a filthy mattress. She kept him clean, and they rotated between staying with different friends, including her new boyfriend.

Pee Wee was secretly dating the brother of my ex, Devin. She kept this little detail secret from me because she didn't think I'd approve. It didn't bother me, though, because he did a fantastic job caring for them both. He bought them food, diapers, and whatever else they needed. My admiration for Pee Wee's diligence grew.

Taylor, on the other hand, was crashing with Tina and her boyfriend from time to time. But he also stayed at Mel's, and so did Tina when she and her boyfriend fought. Now sixteen, Taylor worked a part-time job to provide for himself and as an outlet. Emotionally, he was frustrated with life and, most importantly, with our mother. The displeasure in his eyes was obvious, and he had nothing but harsh words about her drinking. Seriously, our mother needed help, but it was her life to live. Collectively, we didn't take issue with her per se, but the drinking made her a different person. Drinking turned her into someone we didn't like.

Tina carried such an easily offended spirit that she lacked accountability and acceptance of her own behaviors and reality. She still struggles today, and continues to neither admit nor identify problems. But I guess if you don't see something as a problem, then you can't admit there is one.

She lived in denial that holiday season, with conflicting perspectives of Pee Wee and Taylor. To let her tell it, everything was great, and she was gearing up for a wonderful Christmas dinner. It always presented a challenge to me to call her out on her crap. Not only was she my mother and I felt sorry for her, but I had grown accustomed to aiming to please her and gain her approval.

Therefore, I forbid myself to speak truth. I remained quiet, pretending to be excited about being there and supportive of her out of respect, but inside, I burned with anger because not only did we not celebrate Christmas, but Pee Wee, the baby, and Taylor were left stranded, fending for themselves.

My silence and pretense consistently enabled her, and it hurt me deeply to see my family's living conditions. I wanted to be as angry with Tina as my siblings were, but instead, I just felt sorry for them all. I was only nineteen and still learning about life myself, transitioning and growing. I didn't have the skills to defuse the situation, and I wish I had more to give that visit. But I had nothing to offer besides my presence. And now, at thirty-seven, I realize that just my presence was enough.

Christmas dinner was a disaster, as Tina got into a drunken altercation with Pee Wee. I sat watching it escalate into verbal abuse and extreme profanity toward each other. Pee Wee didn't hold her tongue like I did. She called Tina out and held her accountable. Tina never appreciated that.

The baby cried as they yelled. Taylor was over it, Tina's boyfriend was silent, and I was torn about who to side with. Never before had I heard Pee Wee curse at Tina, and her disrespect toward our mother angered me. The argument was so bad that it ended with Pee Wee declaring, "B*tch, you'll never see your grandson again," as she stormed out into twenty-five-degree weather with Jamari, the baby. Crying uncontrollably, I grabbed the car seat and begged Pee Wee to at least bring the child inside until her ride came, but she refused. They sat outside in the cold until her friend arrived. Taylor and I also left with Pee Wee.

Our eyes were swollen and damp from crying, but the three of us stayed up talking for hours. That night I contemplated if I had made the right decision in leaving them. My heart felt heavy on the flight back to Houston. I hadn't wanted to return, and I chose not to speak with Tina before I left. At the same time, I felt motivated to work harder. That semester, I advanced in my major coursework, doing more media-related projects. I made the dean's list for a third semester straight and learned to celebrate my own successes.

Virgil was there, but he tended to downplay my achievements. My other girls, Devita and Ophelia, had transferred from TSU a couple of semesters prior, but we still talked all the time. And ironically enough, Kelly and I became the closest of friends. I was grateful to have them. I was also grateful to have Angel's presence in the same city, although we didn't see each other or spend much time together. She had enrolled in a graduate to a PhD program in Houston.

She celebrated and encouraged me. The Angel I had known and grown up with had transformed the last few years. She was now calmer and spiritually aware. Miraculously, she had converted from atheism to Christianity but wasn't overbearing about it. Actually, I found her transformation inspiring, and it encouraged me to revive my own relationship with faith. I still prayed every now and then, but primarily when I needed something or out of habit, such as my nightly prayers. I had no clue how prayer truly worked or that current prayers planted seeds that would bloom later.

Today, my life is largely a result of answered prayers from long ago, and I'm sure it's the same for you, but you might not realize it.

That spring produced not only flowers, transitions, and reconnections, but more baby news from Pee Wee. She called my dorm room excited to announce that she was having another baby! Initially, I was surprised and more than a little disappointed, being concerned for her future as a young single mom of two. However, she and her boyfriend, Devin's older brother, were happy and doing well. That gave me comfort, especially knowing the family. I had always respected Devin's older brother. I chuckled, thinking, *now my ex is going to be my sister's brother-in-law*.

Daniel called on my twentieth birthday. It had been years since we talked. His voice greatly comforted me, as I'd wrestled with feelings of disconnection, being so far away. I longed for the days of barbequing at Grandma's and laughing with everyone. He said he was doing well, and that was all I needed to hear.

Bruce Hall was being demolished and many of the RAs, including myself, were displaced. They didn't even have the decency to provide a thirty-day notice or to assist in placing us elsewhere.

Advocating for myself against the board and staff was an uphill battle, but like a true Shelton woman, I fought, demanding compensation, writing letters to media outlets, and contacting the president's office.

If I didn't learn anything else from attending an HBCU, I discovered resilience through hardship. I learned to advocate for myself, put things in writing, not to take the first no for an answer, gather names, and document everything, from the financial aid office to advisors and administration. Because of the housing debacle, the activist in me arose, and I became more vocal, confident, and adamant.

Fortunately, I had Virgil's place to crash at but needed cash to find a space of my own. Starting to outgrow our relationship, I became agitated with cooking and cleaning for him and his roommate. I ensured his homework as well as mine was good. And as a star athlete, Virgil had it easy. He didn't have to work; administrators made sure he had housing, teachers curved his grades...heck, at times he didn't even have to attend class.

Paying for our outings and taking care of everything had gotten old. At first, it was fun—kind of like playing house—but I wasn't the same person I'd been two years prior. The relationship didn't feel reciprocal. All he cared about was football and going pro while I supported him and his dream. I couldn't compete with his passion and living together revealed our brutal truth. He didn't see an issue because I was the benefactor. I started to feel stagnant, and I wanted so much more out of life. I longed to grow, explore, transform, and evolve. Life held something huge for me, of that I was sure. I *felt* it and was eager to find it, whatever it was.

My advice to you is to avoid wearing out your welcome. If you've identified that you've outgrown a partnership, relationship, job, or whatever, please...just go! Move forward because you can't recoup the precious time lost in waiting and hoping the situation will improve. Vibes don't lie, so trust your gut...your own help is leading you!

Working my first-ever fast-food job, I saved enough to move into an apartment with another former RA by late summer. I finally had my first place and immediately set my next goal: purchasing a car. I started driving lessons with Angel on the weekends. Lord knows, she was so patient and a better teacher than I could ever be. Mama D took me driving around the station and campus as well. She and the GM were also fundamental in helping me garner scholarships. I was awarded a partial scholarship and transitioned into Kelly's former role as lead sports reporter. Both opportunities came right on time for me, as things so often did.

Junior year was all about growth, preparation, and realization. I had an idea of what I wanted to do, but had quite a few passions. Sports reporting, producing, filmmaking, and activism were all on my radar. If I decided to stick with sport or film, my goal was to produce more progressive images of Blacks in the media.

Living off campus, budgeting, paying rent, car insurance, and other bills, developed a deeper sense of independence and responsibility in me. However, I gained a new friend in Visa and Mastercard; the credit card industry aggressively pursued college students looking to establish credit. But it wasn't a real friendship; it was more of a temptation that I couldn't always resist. In hindsight, I sincerely wish I had someone to educate me on credit and finances in advance... but, nope! The only philosophy I knew was from Tina's flawed money ideologies.

Growing up, I watched her borrow money, make partial bill payments, pawn things and often get hit with high payday loan interest. I knew I never wanted to live like that, and therefore, I paid all bills early and the full amounts. However, I didn't know the danger of credit cards and the sneaky 0% APR bait. So, I gave in to temptation, spending money on flights, dates, gifts for Virgil and me, whatever he wanted and we "needed." There was no reciprocity.

Shortly after my twenty-first birthday, I met a young lady who imprinted my life instantly. We shared mutual friends and the same college major. Her name was Stella, and she had a quiet confidence about her that I liked. She was warm, soft-spoken, and super sweet. Our first interaction gave me lip-gloss girl vibes because she was so polished. She dressed fashionably, and every hair was in place. She came into my life at the perfect time. I needed outlets outside of Virgil. We ate, laughed, and cried together, sharing personal stories and developing a sisterhood. She became one of my closest friends next to Ophelia, Angel, and Kelly.

I shot, produced, and edited my very first thirty-second commercial, which aired on local television. My KTSU family sponsored, supported, and trusted me with one of their clients, and I ran with it. Eager for the opportunity, I invested in my first camcorder, computer, and editing software. My goal was to finish the commercial before attending my first National Association of Black Journalists Conference.

The GM and Mama D had to have been tired of me asking for business cards. Their budget didn't include the miscellaneous needs of student workers, but I persisted until they not only funded my cards, but also sponsored my travel: flight, hotel, and admission to the conference. My KTSU family were my guardian angels. I wouldn't have had half the exposure and experience or be who I am today without them. God placed them in my path, and I knew it.

Virgil displayed little to no excitement about either my first conference or all the buzz I started generating on campus. What I wanted from Virgil, he didn't have the capacity or desire to give. Encouragement, support, and validation were what I sought for our relationship to be reciprocal. I remember begging him to attend my scholarship gala. He refused and accused me of trying to change him into something he wasn't. My evolution wasn't ours. So, as he dedicated himself to his craft, I became fixated on editing, creating, reading, and plotting. Our relationship grew so distant that I began missing him while in the same room, but we weren't freshman kids anymore.

Like a ton of bricks, it hit me, and this time I accepted the truth. *I* was the only one showing up in our relationship: giving, serving, and loving. He wasn't on my level academically, emotionally, intellectually, or socially…and staying

US

with him only stifled my bloom. Because I loved him, I turned a blind eye, wrote things off as me being silly or over the top…petty, even. I used the standard, "If that were me, I would have…" as an excuse. I didn't love myself enough to see this as an issue. I questioned my own desires and motives for being with him. When he downplayed and disregarded my accomplishments, I did, too. I missed out on so much because he didn't think things I wanted to do were a good idea, or he thought that things I was interested in were stupid.

Don't get me wrong — this is the thirty-seven-year-old me writing this. But at twenty, I couldn't articulate what was happening but knew something wasn't right. My desire now is to inspire young women out there to reflect on their own relationships. Toxicity like this occurs all the time, so it's not limited to collegiate or puppy love. You probably know people in relationships now who give without reciprocity. You probably know people with jealous and insecure partners who criticize their growth and progression. Shoot, I currently know people dealing with similar and even worse situations. If any of these shoes fit your feet, please choose you and the future you deserve.

The rain, the flood, the floating bodies, and the overall tragedy of Hurricane Katrina incited our split. The night before August 24, 2005, we had stayed up late, watching the news. There were numerous weather warnings and reports of flooding coming our way. Typically cool, calm, and collected, Virgil paced, watching his hometown under a severe weather warning. His concern tugged at my heart, as anything concerning him did. I had been with him through surgeries, injuries, finals, and everything else major in college; this was no different. Massaging his broad shoulders, I promised it would be fine.

We prayed, and the following day, horrific and heart-wrenching images plastered the news. The city that we knew and loved had been devastated. Virgil couldn't reach any of his family members for weeks. Hurricane Katrina was one of the most costly and deadliest hurricanes ever to hit the United States. People were lost, hungry, stranded, dying, and dead. Every image of the aftermath brought tears to my eyes…and the government's lack of response and urgency to assist those trapped in the city had me furious! After much searching and weeks later, Virgil managed to locate his entire family. Everyone made it out safely but lost everything.

The emotional ramifications of the storm lasted for months. Hurricane Katrina touched Virgil and me in two different ways. He became more focused on making it to the NFL so he could help his family. Angered by the racial disparities exposed by both the media coverage and the government response, I became more focused on making a difference nationally. I purchased items with my own funds for care packages filled with toiletries, socks, undergarments, and random snacks, neatly packed them, and sent them to his family and other victims. I partnered with the Red Cross on a volunteer basis to serve those relocated to Houston. Hurricane Katrina ignited and defined a part of my purpose.

On a whim, one night, I went out with some friends to a spot called Shadow Bar. It was reggae night, and my friends knew how much I loved to wind my hips. Surprisingly, Virgil had no objections to my getting out. That night I sweated out all my fears, problems, and cares on the dance floor to the sounds of Buju Banton. While dancing, I caught the attention of a tall, light brown, handsome fella wearing locs and a matching gorgeous smile. Noticing the level of attention he gave me, I put on a show, climbing on the stage in my Steve Madden heels and dancing more intently. He made his way over to me and, in the sexiest island accent I'd ever heard, asked if I wanted another drink. I declined but complemented his hair. He told me he loved my moves and that I was beautiful. It had been forever since I heard a man compliment me. Virgil stopped ages ago and even discouraged my attempts at dressing up.

There's something about being called "beautiful" that resonates deeper for me. "Beautiful" is a super adjective that, in my opinion, is all encompassing and refers not just to the physical. I felt flattered that this strange man had recognized my spirit and compassionate heart and called it out almost immediately. Batting my lashes and smiling, I thanked him. He introduced himself as Jay and told me he was Bahamian.

He was on a track scholarship at the university across from mine. I knew he'd ask for my number, but I didn't know how I would turn him down. As the night ended, he asked if he could call me sometime. Heartbroken, I had to tell him no, that I was in a relationship. Jay politely said that he understood and stated my boyfriend was a lucky man. "I hope he knows it," he added before kissing my cheek. "Goodnight, beautiful."

I thought about Jay for weeks. More than that, I found myself daydreaming about a charming man who'd appreciate me and tell me I was beautiful. My "perfect" man supported my dreams and goals and would kiss away the scars from my past. He also loved me unconditionally and gave me the attention I craved. The man I daydreamed about catered to me and loved on me, matching the love I gave him. That man was not Virgil.

CHAPTER NINE

Starting Fresh

By the grace of God, I was in my second year as lead reporter, had a commercial on TV, scholarships, and my voice rotated on the campus radio station. Virgil and I broke up after celebrating our third anniversary. That night, over dinner, I expressed my dissatisfaction about our relationship. Acknowledging some of my frustrations, he claimed to have held back because he had trust issues. He actually used a football analogy to explain, telling me that when you're injured in a game, you can't show it, or you'll be targeted. While I appreciated his acknowledging how I felt, my heart sank when it became apparent that he had no intention to do anything about it. "I'll never be that soft dude you're looking for," he proclaimed.

"Well, we're not on a football field and I'm not your opponent. Furthermore, I don't want a soft dude; I just want to be supported and to have you go all out for me as I do for you. And I can't do this anymore," I declared.

Nothing could have prepared me for his reply. "Look, man, my money comes; first, my family comes second, and you can follow if you like. Furthermore, I need space." I felt completely blindsided by his rapid reversal. I suppose his pride wouldn't let me break it off first. But at least his words confirmed what I already knew. I had been wasting my time,

"I can follow if I like?" I repeated. "Really, Virgil? After all I've been through with you?"

We didn't talk to each other for weeks after that, and during that time, I stayed at my computer, editing videos, creating scripts, working out, and finding other ways to keep him off my mind. The breakup was tough; he'd been my best friend and a large part of my identity.

My girls were tired of seeing me mope around. Heck, I was tired of it myself. I was pitifully struggling until the night I decided to get out and have some fun. It was time to make my moping a distant memory. My dentist's assistant randomly texted me one day, asking if I wanted to go out. We were cool and coincidentally, she asked the night of the pre-draft NFL parties for top 2006 candidates. That sounded like a perfect opportunity to network, so I was happy to oblige, and I needed to get out anyway.

We went to the Shadow Bar, the same spot where I had met Jay a few months earlier. My roommate assisted on finding my attire that evening. Settling on a pair of rusted green denim pants and a light green army vest, I pulled out my special occasion, rust-colored Steve Madden pumps, and gold bangles. Slicking my hair back into a ponytail, I threw on a pair of hoops. I hardly ever wore my hair pulled back, but I needed to step out of my norm. I had gotten my brows freshly waxed and my lashes and nails done earlier that day. Pulling myself together, I applied a coat of lip gloss and grabbed a handful of business cards before heading out.

The assistant and I had spoken in passing while getting my teeth cleaned, but nothing more than that. I didn't really know her, but she had always been sweet. She was older and certainly on the social scene. She had that "Bad B," video-vixen, groupie type of thing going on. Today, we'd call it Instagram modelish. Drop-dead gorgeous, she had a body full of curves. I was surprised that she wanted to hang with little ol' me. I didn't care; she was right on time with her request. I must say, I felt nervous and intimidated but eager for a night out.

She had a couple of friends in the car with her who were bubbly, very feisty, and fun. Over the last few years, I had become super serious, focused, and rigid. I needed to lighten up and wanted to project and match their energy, too. One of the girls handed me a cup of vodka and loudly said, "Drink up, we're catching us one tonight!"

I accepted the cup. *Lord, please don't let us get pulled over.* I had to tell myself to relax several times because I was all over the place and emotional.

We made a beeline for the bathroom to adjust our hair, makeup, and cleavage when we arrived. I ordered another vodka just to loosen up a bit before following the girls over to the VIP section. As we approached, I spotted a couple of first-round draft picks and current players. I had a keen sports knowledge, being a fan...but not the same type of fan as my companions. They were trying to get chosen while I was thinking about life after graduation.

The place was rocking. People were showboating and making it rain—throwing money in the air. Following behind the girls and trying not to get lost in the crowd, we positioned ourselves directly in front of the velvet ropes. It didn't take long before we were invited in and they split, all of them selecting an athlete to dance with. I stood there, awkward and solo, looking through my phone for people to text. I texted Ophelia and told her how much fun I was having. Of course, I wasn't.

Instead, I stood there wondering what Virgil was doing and if he missed me. Occasionally I looked up and kept making eye contact with this one guy. I noticed he wasn't drinking alcohol; instead, he had a bottled water in his hand. Our eyes met a few times, and each time I got nervous and looked away, but we kept locking eyes. Even in the dim lighting, I could see he had beautiful eyes. He had the most amazing curly lashes that I could never achieve naturally.

My eyes wandered, thoroughly checking him out. He had a most attractive build…nice broad shoulders and a wide back. He looked very fit and was a good height, too. My friend came over to check on me and noticed him as well. "Dang, he fine," she observed. "You better holla at him before I do."

I chuckled. "Who? Him? Oh yeah, I see him." Her comment propelled me into competitive mode. I began to stare at him without looking away. I hoped that would lure him over because I was rusty when it came to approaching guys. My strategy was to make eye contact long enough for him to notice. I flashed a forced smile. *Oh my God, I probably look stupid.* However, my plan worked with assistance from a flying twenty-dollar bill that rained and landed near my foot. There he was, right in front of me, presumably to be chivalrous and pick up the money for me. Instead, he picked up that twenty plus another one nearby and stuffed them into his pocket. I chuckled. *Dang. The only thing separating us is a measly velvet rope and an outgrown tie to my ex.*

Suddenly, another guy showed up, delaying our pending conversation. I heard this new guy's raspy voice clearly over the music. "What up, Charles? What you doing here, bro? You gettin' ready?"

Charles and I exchanged glances before he responded. Looking at the guys behind me, he answered, "Bro, I'm out here training and trying to get ready." I stood there, awkwardly listening to the conversation. The content of the conversation plus his broad shoulders and thick neck told me he played football. He just didn't look familiar to me. Making light of the moment, I asked, "Are you trying to get closer to me, or what?"

"Nah," he replied with a laugh. "But where you from? Who you here with?"

I pointed in the direction behind me, noticing the girls were now sitting on the athletes' laps. Quickly, I looked away. *Oh no, he's going to think I'm a groupie.* We both chuckled, and I asked him the same. He replied that he was visiting from college on business, but Houston was his hometown. *Hmm,* I thought, *he's humble and drinking water, how nice.* We chatted briefly before he asked for my number. I paused a second, reflecting on Virgil's last words before boldly telling Charles, "Well, I have a little situation."

He smirked. "Yeah, I have a situation, too. How serious is your situation?"

"A three-year situation," I replied, but nevertheless handed him my business card. "What you doin' with business cards?" He sounded amused. I smiled, knowing the cards distinguished me from the other women. I wanted to establish my growing professionalism. "Boy, just lock my number in," I answered. Just then, my companions tapped me on the shoulder for a restroom break (ladies, you know how we do, hitting the bathroom together). I told him I'd be right back and walked off.

When we returned, all the football players were gone. The whole section had cleared out. The ladies were ready to go, so I texted Charles, asking if he'd left. He texted back that he was outside and asked me to meet him out front.

The girls planned to hit a strip club next, and I had never been to one. I was a bit uneasy about going, but planned to stick with wherever the night took me. I walked outside to connect with Charles for a few. The girls followed me out, lagging behind a few feet as I approached him. "You need to get on that ASAP!" they whispered. Charles stood in front of a fancy car with rims. I thought, Dang, he's fine. The dim lights of the club did him no justice. My heart pounded, and my thoughts blended as I inched closer to him. *That car is so fancy. You probably look stupid. Ah I feel uncomfortable standing near that car.* I turned around to the girls and announced, "I'll be right back." I didn't want them following me, they might say or do something I'd find embarrassing.

He greeted me with a tight hug. Charles was every bit of six feet, maybe two-twenty-five pounds of what felt like solid muscle. He had a dark, sun-kissed, toffee-brown complexion. He was much bigger than Virgil, and he smelled good. His arms felt so strong wrapped around me. "What y'all 'bout to get into?" he asked.

"Hmm, depends," I teased. "We're going to Onyx, the strip club."

"I know what Onyx is. Cool. I'll meet you up there so we can talk." Deep down, I was afraid of anyone I knew seeing me at Onyx. I also worried, *What if one of Virgil's friends sees me talking to a guy?* You know how breakups go; you can't be seen right away with someone else. I decided to take my chances.

One of the girls knew the owners and got us in for free. As I walked through the dressing room, I felt like I was moving in slow motion, it was so surreal. I saw nude breasts and exposed vaginas poking out of skimpy costumes. I felt bad seeing these girls, who looked about my age.

On the way to the bar, I spotted one of my old friends from Bruce Hall. She saw me, too. We looked at each other for a sec. I wanted to hug her, but she was serving…topless. It was an awkward exchange for both of us. I asked how she'd been, remembering that she'd gotten pregnant our freshman year and didn't return. She said she'd been doing great and was working there to support her daughter. I told her it was great seeing her and to take care before walking to meet Charles.

We found a cozy space in the back corner, and he sat facing me with his back to the stage, an action I thought was very considerate. He gave me his undivided attention, and we talked about everything…or at least I did. Putting my foot in my mouth, I vented about Virgil the entire time. He listened patiently and was very sweet, attentive, and compassionate. I asked about his situation, and he kept it very simple, saying that they were off and on. He said he'd be returning to school in a couple of days and asked if he could see me before he left. I said yes, thinking, *What the heck; why not?*

"Great. I'll call you tomorrow," he replied. "Let me know when you get home safe." We hugged again, and then he was gone. We left, too, and I thanked the girls for getting me out of the house. As I turned the key to my dark and lonely apartment, I received a text from Charles: *It was a pleasure meeting you. I look forward to seeing you – goodnight, beautiful.*

I smiled at the text, and tears formed in my eyes. It had been so long since I'd gotten that type of attention. I wished I had a "fix it" button with Virgil. I missed him, but instead of calling him, I cried myself to sleep.

The following day, my roommate took me to breakfast to cheer me up. While there, Charles sent a text wishing me good morning. Then he asked if he could stop by later and if I would accompany him to a relative's birthday party. I was down, and when he came over, I showed him my sports projects, software, and cameras. He seemed impressed and genuinely interested, asking questions about my work. "You're very talented, Dee. Your projects are dope. You seem very ambitious, and I'm confident you'll do well," he remarked. His feedback blew me away. From that moment on he had my undivided attention. Subconsciously, I kept comparing him to Virgil, but still managed to enjoy the time. We hung out the rest of the day and that night as well.

Charles seemed far more mature than Virgil, although we were all the same age. When he brought me home, he invited me to church the next morning. *Wow...where did he come from?* At that point, I was convinced he'd fallen out of the sky. I answered, "Yes, of course. I would love to go to church with you." I thanked him for the lovely time I had and leaned in to give him a peck on the cheek before he got out to open my door. "Thank you again," I whispered. Everything about Charles impressed me. He showed more consideration and interest in me in less than forty-eight hours than I had received from Virgil over the last couple of years.

Church service went well, and we did brunch afterward. While enjoying our meal, his phone rang consistently. I assured him it was OK to answer, and he did. My jaw dropped when I heard him lie to whoever was on the other end of the line about what he was doing and who he was with. I lifted my head to stare at him in amazement, then quickly looked away, deciding to pretend that I hadn't heard anything. As he ended his conversation, my phone rang, and I almost leaped out of my skin when I saw Virgil's name in the caller ID window. Although I let the call go to voicemail, I was curious about what he had to say. It had been nearly two weeks since we talked.

This was the last day of spring break; classes would resume the following day. I knew I wouldn't be able to avoid Virgil, anyway. I thanked Charles for a great weekend, and was convinced that meeting him was designed to open my eyes. I needed to know that better quality men did exist. Meeting Charles helped me bury Virgil...at least for a little while.

I spoke with Virgil and learned he wanted me to attend his combine. He had an NFL scout scheduled to see him and asked for my support. Despite everything that had happened between us, I knew how much this meant to him. After all, next to his mom, I was his biggest cheerleader and supporter; I wouldn't have missed being there for him. Kelly knew how important this was for me, and she said she'd be right by my side. I really needed her support. As she was dating an athlete herself, she understood.

"Going to this combine is the closure I need. Girl, if I don't feel anything during his tryout, then it's meant for me to move on. But if I do feel something in my heart, I may consider working things out," I told her.

We stepped on the field wearing matching oversized dark shades, with our hair together and lip gloss popping. Sitting in the back of the stands, I noticed a single scout. I knew they had come to see Virgil. He was coming off an incredible season and had lots of public press. He was balling that year, fighting to garner the needed exposure. Athletes attending black colleges didn't attract the same attention as those going to private white institutions. We didn't have all the media coverage and access that bigger schools did, despite our schools—especially the SWAC football division—having monstrous talent.

Virgil took his stance and began to run. As he ran, I felt tears welling up in my eyes; I knew I had to make a huge decision. I didn't want to make it, but had to. I didn't feel much of anything besides my not wanting to "follow" him. I wasn't a follower and refused to start. He walked up to the stands afterward, and we looked each other dead in the eyes and I could tell he knew it was the end as much as I did.

I planned to stay focused, move on, and properly adapt to new single life. I knew it would be hard, but I was up to the challenge. Planning to stay extremely busy, I found a trainer, took up boxing, and started writing a lot. I had a hectic semester ahead, anyway, so I knew that would help. A friend and one of my professors both recommended that I enter the HBCU student Film Fest. They knew how hard I had worked on my latest project. I thought, "Maybe I will." It was a big step for me. Still, I underestimated my own talents and struggled with imposter syndrome.

My inner negative voice and the devil on my left often tripped me up. There were times when I felt I needed permission or a cosigner to unleash my skills and authentic self. I didn't know that I didn't, that my creator was my cosigner. After all, he made me and equipped me with skills and creativity. Stepping out of my comfort zone with encouragement from my help, I talked myself into entering the contest and was glad I did. I beat out a number of other talented classmates to pull off a win in the Best PSA category.

My project addressed HIV in the black community among women. I believed the film was good and the content solid. It was insightful, and Lord knew I worked endlessly on the filming, script, and editing. I can't tell you why, it never occurred to me to submit my work in a competition or that I would win. I lacked confidence and was fearful of rejection. But winning was such a proud moment, and just think… had I never gone for it, it never would have happened.

The more I succeeded, the more I believed in myself. The problem was my default setting, which was to question and discount myself. Although my prize was only a small, framed certificate, I left with an elevated awareness and sense of hope, which turned out to be the catalyst for future risks that I would take that year.

Now relentlessly determined, I decided to apply for the highly competitive and coveted Tavis Smiley internship. The internship would send four top media students to Los Angeles, sponsor housing and transportation and provide a $2,500 stipend. The winning students would work on both Tavis's television and radio shows. There was so much going on, and a wealth of opportunities had presented themselves before me, but only after I made myself available to receive them. Most importantly, I was prepared!

A wise woman named Oprah Winfrey once said, "Luck is preparation meeting opportunity." I couldn't agree more, besides my view on luck being synonymous with God's favor. Remember, the key for me was to also make myself available to the opportunities, i.e., looking for them and going for it. Seriously, you can't expect to be successful at anything if you're not prepared and available. For me, availability meant being single, focused, seeking, and stepping out of my comfort zone.

Currently, my husband jokes, "God can't steer a parked car!" I find this to be true. It's extremely important to get moving, whether you believe in God or not. Opportunities are ready and available to those who go searching for them. Sure, you can pray, meditate, or even ask the Creator of the Universe for clarity, but we also have to give Him something to work with. So, get going!

On Thursday, April 6, 2006, months away from starting senior year, I nostalgically entered the doors of the Sawyer Auditorium. These were the same doors I entered with my girls from Bruce Hall during freshman year orientation. The occasion this time was Honors Day, which celebrated students' academic success. I'd worked exceptionally hard, doing extra credit, studying, reading, and fostering relationships with professors, and I managed a 3.7 GPA and hoped to do so through graduation. I had never truly been naturally smart but always determined to achieve academically.

I quickly took a seat in the rear balcony, mesmerized by our guest speaker. Speakers came and went, all selling the same or similar motivational lectures. But this speaker was different, I could tell before she even opened her mouth. She was beautiful, graceful, young, and black, a professional who happened to be the SVP (senior vice president) of HR (human resources) at New Line Cinema. The intense bling and sparkle produced by her mammoth wedding ring really captured my attention. She used the word "goal" as an acronym. She stated, "G, you must go. O, where the opportunities are. A, always work hard, and L, love yourself."

I nearly jumped out of my seat. *Oh, my God! She's talking about me!* Her words resonated deeply, confirming exactly where I was in life. She was a reflection of who I wanted to be in the future. She came across as a boss...fierce, composed, intelligent, and a well-put-together beautiful black woman.

My lips moved as I silently repeated her words. "I must go where the opportunities are, always work hard and love myself. That's it, that's it!" Her speech ended with a standing ovation. I quickly left my seat, raced down the stairs and through the crowds, eager to meet her. She was surrounded by dozens of people, taking photos and chatting, but I kept inching closer. I saw her hug the radio station's general manager, so I promptly tugged his jacket. He immediately introduced me. "Lita, I want you to meet Danielle Shelton. She's our top scholarship recipient and reporter."

I firmly shook her soft hand, nearly blinded by the whiteness of her perfect teeth. *Calm down, girl. Be cool.* I managed to blurt out, "Your speech really spoke to me. I appreciate your work and desires to give back to students like us. It means a lot!" Very personable, she smiled and thanked me, so I stuck around the GM and followed them outside.

I overheard her mention to him that she'd be back on campus later for a private workshop. I quickly interjected, "I would be honored to attend and would love to share my work with you."

"That shouldn't be a problem. I hear great things about you. I would love to see your work! You have a very bright future, and I'm looking forward to your progress. I'm happy to help you," she said with that brilliant smile. With those encouraging words, we parted ways.

I ran home to grab resume copies and a few of my DVDs. I had picked up a few networking hacks from working at the station, but I didn't know how to pitch myself properly and establish my value. No one wants to be pulled into a what-can-you-do-for-me type of relationship. However, I was only twenty-one at the time and still learning. I've learned that networking is all about adding value, supporting others, and nurturing existing relationships in my adult life.

Charles flew into town and took me out to celebrate my accomplishments. We had been talking casually but consistently for a few months. He was very charming and well put together but also deceptive. I learned that he and his "situation" actually lived together at one point, but he consistently masked it with vague and misleading responses. *We're just having fun,* I told myself. *And he's the rebound. No one falls for the rebound.* This rationalization pacified my feelings, but I felt conflicted about being with him, as he consistently lied to his other woman. I was becoming that chick I despised.

I tried to enjoy things for what they were with him. Charles offered companionship, chivalry, and he truly cared about what I was doing...at least he did a great job pretending to be. Besides, we had a blast together. Soon we became intimate, only further complicating matters, as sex usually does.

Reflecting on Charles' entry to my life now, fifteen years later, I still believe meeting him was purposeful. However, I never considered the long-term ramifications of casual sex or the power that accompanies the creation of soul ties it produces. I never considered how a possible future husband would feel about my past. Like most of us when meeting new people, we only consider how we feel in that moment, thinking *Dang, she bad,* or *He's fine as heck.* I figured when you're dating and vibing with someone, sex is just what you do.

I didn't have, nor did I see, an issue with casual sex. My perspective was flawed, thinking, *It's my body, I'm grown and I'm not hurting anyone.* I couldn't have been more wrong. Not only was I hurting myself by accumulating more partners, but most importantly, being intimate with Charles twisted my ability to see him for what he was. And now, fifteen years later, more seasoned and more mature, I see sex differently. Sex is an exchange of energy, and it's spiritual more than anything.

Now as a Christian, I don't believe my body even belongs to me. My body is a house for the Lord's spirit that dwells within my body. I believe this is the same for you. Think of it like this: Our bodies are similar to avatars or vehicles, chauffeuring and transporting our spirit throughout life.

Because our spirits are sacred, our bodies and the energy they give, and exchange are to be protected. Regarding sex specifically, we're created for our soulmates (husbands and wives), not to be entangled with random people whose names we sometimes can't even remember, just because they were fine or gave us a little attention. Believe that or not; I'm not trying to convert you. I'm simply sharing my beliefs, my story, and what I wish I'd known then. My goal is to also tell you there will always be a consequence to whatever we do, whether good or bad, even if you don't see it immediately… even if you see it fifteen years later.

Intimacy with Charles only confused my conflicting emotions. He wasn't honest about his personal life, and because he satisfied certain desires I had, I chose to overlook his deception. "Never fall for the rebound" might have been the standard rule, but trust me, it happens…especially if you're emotionally unstable. I missed Virgil and wished he offered what Charles did, and I only missed Virgil because he no longer filled that void in my life. His absences forced me to sit with myself, and it was uncomfortable. Still, I attempted to fill his void and other voids, masking my personal hurt with men and achievements.

I was all over the place emotionally, and each day brought new feelings. At times, I thought I loved Charles and wanted him for myself. Other times, I missed Virgil and felt pleased to know he still loved me. At times, I hated myself for letting Virgil into my life at all. I felt stupid and upset because things weren't working. I was even upset at myself for being unable to settle my feelings one way or the other. Privately, my life was a wreck.

One day, my help whispered, "This is not real love, Dee." Sobbing, I silently asked, "Well, what is?" I heard, "I am love. Follow me." At the time, I had no energy to decipher what that cryptic message meant, I didn't even know what this help truly was until years later.

In the meantime, I continued to stay busy and picked up new hobbies. I started volunteering with kids a couple of times a week and loved it! I was also selected to interview for the Los Angeles internship around the same time Virgil found out about Charles. He had always been insecure and overly protective. I should have known he was watching me. One night, he saw Charles's car parked in front of my place and blew up my phone with calls and derogatory text messages. I didn't realize the relatively small size of the football circuit, but Charles and one of Virgil's close friends shared the same agent. Virgil knew all about Charles and that I had filmed Charles' draft party. The two of them had attended the same events plenty of times as well. Stepping away from a sleeping Charles, I took Virgil's call.

We initially argued back and forth before he broke down, apologizing, insisting that he loved and cared for me. He apologized for hurting me and not being the man I needed.

He told me he'd never loved anyone like he loved me, explaining, "I don't trust women because of things I saw my own family do. I saw women I love cheat on their husbands. That's why I don't trust." His words truly touched me, but I knew I couldn't go back to him. Our conversation provided some closure, but it wasn't enough. It did help me to stop thinking I did something wrong or that me and my best efforts weren't enough. Nonetheless, my issues ran deeper than those related to him. We agreed to make an attempt at being "friends."

That was it for Virgil and me…and after filming Charles's draft party and meeting his girlfriend, I knew for certain that she was a big part of his life, no matter how he tried to downplay her. I also knew what I needed to do about him as well.

My twenty-second birthday was filled with a few surprises. That morning, I did something I hadn't done in a while. I actually prayed and reflected on everything in my life: how much I had grown as a woman, areas of stagnation, the obstacles I overcame, my family, and the direction my professional life was taking. I didn't have it together personally, and I worked hard not to beat myself up about that.

Remembering the Honors Day speaker's advice, I decided I would leave Houston after graduation. I wasn't sure just where I would go, but I was ready and willing to G.O.A.L! About twenty-one credits from graduating, I contemplated if I wanted to graduate in the fall or wait until the following spring. Later that evening, during my birthday dinner, my decision was made for me. Dolled up with red patent leather pumps on my feet, I looked and felt fabulous. My friends and I had dinner at my favorite restaurant, Pappadeaux, off Interstate 610. Midway through dinner, my college counselor showed up with a wonderful surprise. After wishing me a happy birthday, she handed me an envelope and insisted I open it. I unfolded the letter and gasped as I read:

Congratulations, you have been selected for the Tavis Smiley internship in LA. I screamed with tears of joy as I knew that opportunity would change my entire life.

I spent a few days visiting home right before leaving for LA. By then, Pee Wee had been married to Devin's brother nearly two months after a quaint courthouse ceremony. Pregnant with her third child, they were preparing to become a family of five and were doing very well. As for Taylor, 'his transformation started around this time. He looked just like his environment and nothing like a college student (which he had been) or soon-to-be father (which he was). At my last visit, I'd begged him to move to Houston with me, but he didn't want to leave because he had a baby on the way. At least he followed my suggestion to enroll in a community college. He started taking classes but decided that school just wasn't for him. The more I grew personally and professionally, the more distant our relationship became. I loved my little brother tremendously, but I was concerned about him being out in the streets.

We lived in two different worlds. When I tried to connect with him and call home, he'd tell Pee Wee to tell me he wasn't there. He sarcastically referred to me as "the college girl who knows everything." In addition to his immaturity, my brother had a complex about where he was in life and projected his personal displeasure onto me. His perception of me was apparent from the way he treated me.

Tina seemed to be holding up, and excited to see me. She was living with her sister at the time and contemplating a move out of state. Thus, Taylor roamed between our aunt's, Pee Wee's, the streets, and Mel's place. His interactions with Tina were rough to observe. Taylor had no respect for her, and neither did Pee Wee. So, I guess they all maintained the status quo.

As for Pee Wee, she made motherhood look easy. She was built for it and was such a great mother and wife. There was so much love in her home. Her family inspired me to the point where I reconsidered not wanting marriage or kids.

I took Tina out for Mother's Day, and we had a chance to catch up. I told her about my work, projects and that I'd been selected for an LA internship. She told me she was very proud of me and excited that I'd be traveling. Moments like those reminded me of my senior year of high school with her. I wondered what went through her own mind and if she was happy with her life. We shared a couple of more glances, laughs, and hugs. In the back of my mind, I still desired to take care of her, and I felt good because LA meant that I was steps closer to being able to do so.

That same spring, I'd been featured in a couple of local and a national publications. One of the local ones highlighted me as a beauty of the month, the other as student of the week. My feature in the national publication was an interview about the internship. I was in a great space and the light at the end of the tunnel was brighter. I saw it...and it wasn't a train.

After landing at LAX, my cohorts and I headed to the rental car pickup. Fortunately, the other classmates were people I knew or had seen around our department. Paired into twos, we spent three weeks each at the radio and TV stations. I felt lucky to have been paired with a friend. We were the closest of the group.

Our living pad was fully furnished and just minutes away from Hollywood. Living with two guys and a girl that I hardly knew certainly felt like being in a reality show. The experience did serve to build character for all of us.

I took the lead that first night, calling a house meeting to strategize our commuting plan and house rules. Privately, I schemed to come up with ways to make myself stand apart from my peers. I worked hard each day, pitching stories and ideas and gathering whatever the team needed. The first few days were easy. By day, we worked and presented ourselves accordingly. By night, we clubbed, partied, drank, smoked and soaked in the Jacuzzi. We had the typical roommate hiccups, like someone being tardy, eating another's food, not cleaning properly or at all, etc. But for the most part, we gelled well.

The tardiness, I couldn't handle, especially since we shared transportation. So every morning, I got dressed early and then woke up everyone. Becoming the mama of the house, I was the most responsible. It was frustrating at times, but I survived. I understood we were a team and all a reflection of Texas Southern University, so I couldn't throw anyone under the bus.

Working with Mr. Smiley and his team was a great experience. I learned so much and gained a plethora of media knowledge. The exposure broadened my perspective on politics, different foods, cultures, audiences, and even more jazz music. His executive producer took me under her wing as a mentee. She reminded me of the Honors Day speaker — a sharp, tough, professional, and beautiful black woman. She was an HBCU alum as well. Watching her affirmed the type of woman I wanted to be. However, she was especially tough on me, and I'm sure it's because she trusted me to get things done.

Because of the damage, Hurricane Katrina did to New Orleans, the Essence Festival, one of the largest black festivals in the South, was moved to Houston that year. Devita, my freshman year roomie, planned to fly in from DC to attend it. It had been a while since we'd last seen each other, so I met her there over the holiday break.

We happily greeted each other. "Hey, girl, hey!" She looked really great and obviously had been doing well. She was still in school, too, but had enrolled at another HBCU in North Carolina. We went to dinner before getting dressed to go out that night. Prancing around my apartment, we sipped Hpnotiq and laughed like the good old days. That night we connected with her DJ friend from freshman year. He had become one of Houston's most premier DJs and had all the hookups that weekend.

The first party we hit was jumping, with a nice grown and sexy crowd. Devita and I took turns buying each other shots of Patrón. As I approached the bar to order our next round, I noticed a familiar face. I squinted my eyes, both shocked and elated at the same time. *Jay, the Bahamian track star I met a year ago at the Shadow Bar?*

He looked up and smiled before making his way over to me. I quickly adjusted my hair and took a deep breath. "Hey, long time," I greeted. "I know, right?" he answered as we hugged. "You still have that boyfriend?"

Smiling, I replied, "No." "So no boyfriend. You should give me your number this time."

"Why, certainly." I grabbed his phone out of his hand and put my number in it. Handing it back to him, I asked, "What're you doing after this?" "Nothing much," he joked. "Spending time with you." That made me smile for sure. Devita and I hung out with some of her friends afterward before I cut out to connect with Jay. I went back to Jay's place, and we stayed up talking until nearly sunrise. We talked about everything, including his track and Olympic aspirations, his family and faith.

Jay was attentive, articulate, ambitious, and all I thought he'd be. He was nothing like the football jock type—he had depth to him. It still felt new, adjusting to being back on the market. I felt like I needed to learn about men all over again. This time, I was grown and not the same freshman girl. As the night progressed, I felt comfortable lying in Jay's arms and grateful for the company. Not once did he press up on me or make a pass. He was a gentleman the entire time, and I appreciated that the most. He kissed my forehead and whispered goodnight. The following day we hugged tightly and vowed not to lose touch. I sent Devita off to the airport and arrived back in LA, refreshed.

As the internship concluded, I was selected to represent the group at an exclusive benefit gala in North Hollywood. CNN's primetime host at the time, Larry King, was the night's emcee. The mayor and other politicians were in attendance.

Nervous and beaming with excitement, I was the only young black college student there. It was a surreal moment. *How did I get here?* The little black, crack baby from Chicago was in Los Angeles on a scholarship in a room with the mayor and other notables. Napkin in lap, and perfect posture, I had my answer ready when asked about my future plans. "To produce more positive depictions of African-Americans in the media." Everyone looked at me intently. Mr. Smiley looked at me with approval. My heart was being molded into one of service, putting me on a path to creating positive social change. That night ended with compliments from both Mr. Smiley and his executive producer, who hugged me and said, "Great job!" I knew I had represented very well.

Entering my senior year that fall was all about legacy and stepping out of my comfort zone. That year's theme was no baggage and no strings attached.

CHAPTER TEN

Dreams Bigger Than Texas

Standing in line on picture day, I adjusted my hair and robe with thoughts of Tina. I wondered if she knew she was responsible for my desire to achieve. I thought about my naysayers, difficult experiences, and all those who doubted me. Despite all I had been through, I realized just how far I had come and how an ordinary person probably wouldn't have made it. *I must be extraordinary.* I wasn't supposed to be here, at least not statistically.

By the start of the year, I had fully infiltrated myself all over campus and the surrounding community. My voice on the radio, my face on campus TV, and my presence while volunteering at the local community center. The girl who'd arrived as a freshman years ago had come a long way.

I knew that time would fly, and I wanted it to be memorable. I could hardly recognize the person I was growing into, a person more confident, ambitious, outspoken, and optimistic. I was eager to take on the world and eager to learn any and everything.

Initially, I felt I didn't deserve any of the good fortune that had come my way. *Maybe God is being nice for all I've been through.* Don't get me wrong—there were still many mountains to climb and areas to work on, specifically in my personal life. Privately, I struggled still with rejection, insecurity, people-pleasing, a feeling of abandonment, and the desire to feel loved, which at times kept me searching in the beds of different men. And the devil on my left still lurked, although he had been dormant.

Sharing the field with Virgil turned out to be easier than I thought it would be. Showing up to the practices and games, I looked unnecessarily fabulous. I got a kick out of his teammate's advances after learning we split. They flirted, and of course, I gave them plenty of attention to make Virgil angry. He had gone too far and said some things that really messed me up recently. He claimed to have cheated on me the entire time we were together...and with girls I considered to be friends. Granted, he could have said these things out of spite, but they did do a number on me emotionally. Naturally, I wanted to get even.

Our senior year meant war. I badgered him with difficult interview questions and incomplete writeups. I avoided eye contact until I needed to speak directly with him. Three long years of being faithful, loyal, and stagnant in my own future plans had left me embittered. Aiming to one up each other, bidding for attention, we went back and forth. And the more my name circulated on campus, the more I felt he knew what he'd lost. One day, Kelly encouraged me to run for the Miss Senior superlative. Miss Senior, the homecoming queen who also represented the senior student body, was a big deal at HBCUs.

"Why don't you run?" Kelly suggested.

My head jerked. *Me? No way.* I wasn't into pageants; those were for lip-gloss girls. "What?" Kelly said, noticing my reaction. "You should go for it. I think you have a great chance at winning. And Virgil will slit his wrists when he sees you win," she added.

We laughed, and the challenge suddenly seemed irresistible. I ran. I enjoyed being in leadership positions but had to admit that Kelly was the ultimate hype woman. Together we were darn good at plotting ways to get a man's attention. We always had some type of scheme going for something or other. We totally could have been private investigators or been certified in post-relationship pettiness if such a thing existed.

I was nominated for Miss Senior and selected to be the Beauty of the Month in our campus publication. The year couldn't have gone any better. Now completely out of my comfort zone, I had no choice but to emit more confidence. My peers already saw it in me, and that year produced the assertiveness needed for life after college. Once on the campaign trail, I dressed up daily, walking the campus, talking, and introducing myself to random people. I had the support of my friends, the athletes, the radio station, and my entire media department.

Homecoming was around the corner, and I felt invigorated. I had a packed schedule and bounced between everything: classes, work, editing gigs, and reporting. The business taught me to manage my time well, and my ability to work under pressure helped me execute. I had been used to working under stress with little or nothing my whole life. Deciding to pursue my interest in sorority pledging, I made time for that as well. *What the heck, let's do it all senior year.* Subconsciously, I felt the need to make up for lost time in my relationship.

Why are you so nervous? You do this all the time. I prayed my sweating armpits weren't visible while giving my speech at the student center. Outlining my plans to implement change as Miss Senior, I laid out the reasons I should win. The speech and support went over nicely, and I won by a landslide just days later. I couldn't believe it! As small as it sounded, I needed all the confidence boosters I could get. Remember, I was the queen of aborting missions before they started. I hardly ever gave myself a chance.

Never in a million years would I have imagined participating in something like Miss Senior in college and actually winning. That familiar lesson I had learned the semester before held up once more: We will certainly miss all the shots we don't take. It's possible to set a goal, stick to it, give it your all, and accomplish it. I was proud of myself and out of my comfort bubble.

I had a few weeks to buy my pageant dress and prepare for homecoming. "Mama, I won! I want you to come down and see me, too!" I exclaimed to Tina over the phone. She already knew about my participation in the pageant, but I wanted her to experience homecoming with me. So, I sent for her with the stipulation that she bring my niece along. The tiny tot stole the show with her cuteness, strutting around my campus like she owned it. She was super smart for her age and just delightful.

Tina cooked, talked smack about my first apartment, and we laid in bed together and watched movies, just like old times. Having her and my niece there with me felt safe and rewarding. Tina beamed with pride as she dressed in her gown for my banquet. We invited our Houston family to attend as well. I had a full week: a fashion show, pageant, parade, and a crowning ceremony to attend. Mama was right by my side throughout it all. I introduced her to my professors and my radio family. Standing there delighted by the compliments I received, I was a proud reflection of her. People thanked her for doing an incredible job with me. There were many moments when I choked on my emotions from her being there. She felt like a real mom in those moments, and her presence meant the world to me. I had always wanted to make her proud.

Slowly swirling my right hand in a princess wave, I greeted little girls in the community from the back of our float. The parade was reminiscent of the Tennessee State

University parades that I'd gone to as a kid. I had always secretly admired the gowns, fancy hair, nails, lashes, and the beauty of homecoming queens. This time *I* was the queen, and all during that ride, I felt as if I mattered, like I was "normal"—someone who wasn't plagued with stains from her past.

I pulled off a Houdini magic trick by game time: I opened kickoff as the lead reporter and had changed into my suit to take to the field before halftime.

While continuously succeeding publicly, my private battles continued. Determined to subdue life's monotony and still searching to fill my God-sized hole, I passed the time entertaining guys and chasing success. I'm here to say over and over again that people or accolades can't fill any sense of void you may feel.

I was a beast, inappropriately justifying my behavior by my "love 'em and leave 'em, no strings attached, I'm-in-power" approach. I spent a great deal of the year behaving as such. In reality, I was truly a broken, hurt, and insecure young woman desperately in need of guidance and a savior.

No one really knew about my struggle, and I didn't want my girls to judge me. They knew I admired a nice man or two every once in a while. However, they didn't know that the roots of my desire to be with them ran deeper. I didn't know, either, but in time, my daddy and abandonment issues were revealed. I wasn't truly happy within, and the more I sought happiness elsewhere, even if only temporary, it blew up in my face.

At times I wondered, *Maybe God is key to me being happy,* but I was intimidated by God and put off by things related to Him. The thought of religion was upsetting for me. The toxicity experienced in the temple messed me up big time. Besides, the temple had led me to believe that I was cut off from God. So, I told myself that I'd try and do right or get saved at fifty, figuring that was a good age to be disciplined. And by fifty, I knew I would be done partying and very serious about life. I also figured God would accept me then. It wasn't until Angel challenged me by asking, "What if you don't make it to fifty? Are you concerned about the now, and where you would go if you died?" At twenty-two, I hadn't truly given heaven or hell serious thought. I'm not sure I really believed in it. My plan was to enjoy my twenties and get serious as I got older. Men were my only "problem" anyway, so I thought.

I attended my final scholarship gala a week before secretly attending Virgil's graduation since he graduated earlier than me. I hid in the top balcony area and out of maybe three thousand people, he spotted me. We made eye contact just before his name was called. His final football season had been by far his best year.

Virgil had a record forty-six solo tackles, sixty-eight assists, five interceptions, and two touchdowns. He was a star in our conference, and I knew he'd be successful. I reflected on the countless hours of studying, writing his papers, cleaning his scars, surgeries, cooking, and our first date. I remembered praying with him the night before Katrina hit New Orleans. I loved Virgil more than I loved myself. As he walked across the stage to have his photo taken with our president, he looked up again, and at that moment, I turned and walked away.

At the scholarship gala, I gave my final words of gratitude. Overwhelmed with emotion, I tried not to cry. The question of the hour, "What's next?" was the catalyst of my anxiety. I had no clue what was next and became mortified by the simultaneous fear of failure and success. I knew I wanted to create change in the media. I knew I loved sports production. But that was about it, and time wasn't on my side. I needed to put a plan in motion, and soon. Staying in

Houston over the holiday break, I got a job to help me save. I began meeting with sorority girls nightly for little tasks and tons of memorizing and learning. My plate was actually too full, but I ate whatever was put before me. I worked two jobs, enrolled in eighteen credit hours, and had my nightly meetings with the ladies while editing projects on the side and volunteering.

Every move was calculated and important to me. Just four months shy of graduation, I challenged myself creatively by filming different projects to build my skills and portfolio. Finally, I had a plan and narrowed down pickings by applying for an ESPN fellowship, a Director's Guild program in LA, and an NPR fellowship in DC. I knew one of those would work out for me.

Alternatively, I thought that if I made it into the sorority community, I could network and partner with them for opportunities. I had a solid interview and knew the majority of the girls. I'd been meeting with a few of them, and everything was in order. In the meantime, I maintained a 4.0 GPA and applied to some local stations. My plan felt failproof and optimistically, I waited.

During the waiting period, something really weird happened one night as one of my male companions left my apartment. I had known him since freshman year, he wasn't anyone special, but someone with whom I had an intimate relationship. As soon as he left my apartment, a heavy feeling that I'd never felt before overwhelmed me. I felt like I'd instantly been convicted for doing something wrong. I couldn't shake, explain, or get rid of it no matter how hard I tried. The dread associated with that feeling was terrible. I must have taken three showers that night. I felt so bad that I started praying. I had to ask God if he was upset with me. After hopping back in the shower, I dropped to my knees and said a prayer of apology in which I promised to try my best to leave the guys alone.

That feeling of dread led to a series of other events that started right after Charles's birthday party. He invited me, and Kelly and I attended. Charles and I only spoke sparingly by that time, but I watched him play any given Sunday or Thursday night. Sitting in the back of the party room, Kelly and I sipped margaritas, talking and laughing. As the night progressed, I received a text from one of the girls who attended the sorority meetings with me:

It's begun.

I looked over at Kelly and exclaimed, "Oh, shoot." I thanked Charles for inviting me, wished him happy birthday, followed by a big hug, and we left. Nervous and eager, I rushed home to check my answering machine because I didn't get a call on my cell. I waited all night, but never received a call, not the next day, either. My chest swelled, reflecting on how much time, dedication, and effort I'd invested in those meetings over the last couple of months. I had a 4.0 GPA, a great interview, strong references, and a passion for serving. I was confused as to why my phone didn't ring.

The rest of the day was spent moping around before it finally occurred to me to check the mail. My box was flooded with letters from ESPN, NPR, the sorority, and the Los Angeles Directors Guild. My eyes widened with a glimmer of optimism as I raced back upstairs to my apartment, carrying the mail. *OK, Dee. You got this. This is your next move*, I told myself as I took deep breaths. I ripped open the sorority letter first, scanning the first sentence that opened with the word, "Unfortunately…" I didn't have to read further. I knew it. *You should've known. Just because you were Miss Senior doesn't mean you fit in with them. You will never fit in.*

Shaking off my negative thoughts, I grabbed the NPR letter next and said aloud, "OK Washington DC, let's go," before the words "unfortunately" and "we wish you the best" jumped out at me.

At that point my chest grew tighter, and I started to tear up as I slowly opened the ESPN letter to read the same thing. By the time I tore open the Directors Guild letter, I felt I would need a paramedic. In less than twenty-four hours, I had gone from hopefulness to hopelessness. A four-time rejection in one day took me out. I had nothing lined up and was graduating soon. My heart pounded as I lay in despair and disbelief. I couldn't bear to be rejected like that all at once. I wanted ESPN and the sorority the most. I also realized that NPR was a no-brainer, my impressive resume over-qualified me. It wasn't a surprise that I didn't get that one. Still, I felt like my hard work was all in vain.

Sobbing loudly, I laid on my living room floor, taking a beating from my negative self-talk, the devil on my left. "You're not talented enough. Remember where you're from. You were a poor crack baby, and you're too damaged. You're trying to fake your way into success, but everyone will see through you. You're nothing." The barrage of thoughts continued...

"Who do you think you are, anyway? Do you really think you can turn your life around? You are a shame, and no one wants you, and you will not succeed."

I lay there, mentally and emotionally tortured for what felt like hours. My eyes had no more tears to shed, and my head throbbed from crying. I called in sick to work the rest of the week and missed class as well. I felt embarrassed to go on campus and had difficulty accepting I had lost at everything. My friends tried to cheer me up as best as possible. After a couple of days, I eventually dusted myself off and did what I did best—kept going with that chip dancing on my shoulder.

While solidifying graduation travel plans with my Aunt DeDe, she inquired what was next for me. Saying I didn't know felt strange to me, because I always had a plan of action or some ideas…but this time, I really had no clue.

"Why don't you move to Chicago?" she suggested.

"Nah. It's too cold for me."

She laughed, "Girl, just put on a coat and come on. You're welcome to stay with me until you get on your feet."

I thought on it a second. Chicago was actually the third largest market in my field, but I never considered living there again. My heart was set on moving to DC or Philly. "Thanks, but I'll just stay in Houston and move in with a friend till I figure something out," I told her.

After the conversation, I laid down and gave the matter deep thought. My mind was racing as I entertained the newly introduced idea of Chicago. *Hmm, Chicago…* And then my help appeared, whispering, "Romans 8:18…Romans 8:18." I sat up and looked around the room. *What does that mean? I don't even go to church or read the Bible anymore. Where did that scripture come from?*

Over the years, my help seemed to have shifted from a good conscience conflicting with my bad conscience, who I refer to as the devil on the left, to more of a positive inner voice and advisor. However, this was a first, as never before had my help placed a scripture on my heart. I tore my apartment from top to bottom, looking for a Bible. I kept repeating, "Romans 8:18, Romans 8:18," aloud so I wouldn't forget the verse. My shoulders slumped in defeat when after looking everywhere I couldn't find a Bible. Lying in the same spot where I'd nearly drowned in tears days before, I asked, "God, what do you want with me?" I propped my feet on the couch, and at that moment, I noticed a green book on the floor under the couch. *Could it be…?* I immediately lowered my feet, rolled over, and reached an arm under the couch to pull out the book.

It *was* a Bible! And I had no clue where it came from or how it happened to end up under my couch. Fortunately, that little green Bible included the New Testament. I flipped to Romans chapter eight, verse eighteen, and read the scripture over and over.

"I consider that our present sufferings are not worth comparing with the glory that will be revealed in us." (New International Version). After reading it a fifth time, it made sense. Not only did the verse echo what I had been going through, but it provided comfort that things would get better.

Although I did feel that I understood it a bit, I still wasn't convinced and thought maybe it was coincidental. I jumped up and called DeDe back and explained that the weirdest thing just happened to me. After sharing my experience, she replied, "That's not weird; it's The Holy Spirit."

"The holy who?" I asked.

DeDe started going off the deep end with her explanation. I wasn't really in the space to hear her, as I'd written off everything associated with the temple, faith, and religion years before. I mean, I still prayed every now and then, in case God was listening. As I mentioned earlier, I planned to circle back at fifty years old. Besides, supernatural and coincidental occurrences were a bit spooky to me.

After I got DeDe to stop her lecture, I called Tina for her take, and she shared the exact same thing. I hung up, got on my knees and prayed. "God, if You know all, are in control, and are listening, please help me get to where I'm supposed to move to next. Amen."

The prayer made me feel hopeful. I stood, feeling strangely calm. *OK, Dee. You can do this. Let's get this life of yours together — something big is out there for you. And maybe God knows what he is doing with these denials and rejections.*

Stella and I planned to meet for drinks to celebrate my rejections. Yes, you read that right, celebrate my rejections.

We called it a rejection party. It was my way of coping and a push for optimism. I needed to shift my perspective to rejection equaling better opportunity.

As I dressed to meet up for my "rejection celebration," my help whispered, "When one door shuts, another opens. Greater opportunities are to come." I chuckled. *Sure; we'll see."* But this time my help's words gave me an incredible feeling of peace. While we laughed over lunch and drinks, my phone rang. I stepped outside to take the call. The female voice on the other end of the line said, "Hello, is this Rahkal Danielle?"

"Yes." *Who is this?*

The woman gave her full name. "I'm with WGN news in Chicago, and I have your resume in my hand. I see you interned with Tavis Smiley. He and I are good friends, and your resume looks pretty impressive. Would you be interested in an internship with us this summer?"

My free hand flew to my heart. "Yes, but I'm in Texas."

"So when can you be here?" she casually replied, as if my being so far away was no big deal. Impulsively, I blurted out, "Two weeks. I can start the end of May."

"Awesome! I'll follow up in writing with the next steps," she informed me. "I'm looking forward to meeting you."

"Bring us another round," I jubilantly informed the waitress. "I'm moving back to Chicago!" The money that I didn't use to join the sorority would cover the cost of my move. Everything was working out perfectly…just the way my help said it would.

I sent off introduction letters and resumes to radio stations, political campaigns, TV stations, and nonprofits. I had other opportunities lined up before my arrival. I wanted to go out with a bang and was prepared to do what I knew best, move around.

"You can't please everyone," were the wise words spoken by my uncle as I battled with my graduation party's dinner menu. Those words were so simple but revolutionary, right when I needed them. They became my exit mantra and the future catalyst for severing my people-pleasing habits.

Just about everyone I wanted to see made it to graduation, with two exceptions: Taylor, who refused to attend, and my cousin Lewis, who randomly became ill and was in the hospital at the time. Something happened to me the night before graduation: I underwent an instant transformation. I was ready to unleash. I was ready to see myself as I was—relentless, intelligent, divinely guided, fierce, valuable…and loved. My help then whispered, "I wouldn't have brought you this far to leave you."

CHAPTER ELEVEN

God, Are You There?

Chicago had treated me well so far, I arrived with a little under twenty-seven hundred dollars months before and started my television internship immediately. I had also secured another job working downtown on Michigan Avenue doing makeup. It was a sweet little job, but my eyes were on something bigger. I was focused on attaining a career in film or the media and chased my dreams tirelessly. I loved working in the industry. Those perks—event tickets, VIP access to parties, concerts, and shows—opened doors for me to meet a variety of actors, models, clothing designers, and athletes. So, it was a dream opportunity for a twenty-three-year-old, but I also needed money and I wanted my own space.

While I adored my aunt, it was difficult living with DeDe and the house rules prompted by her religion. She wrestled with transitioning to treating me like a young adult. Despite feeling like a visiting sixteen-year-old at times, we had a blast and enjoyed each other's company. She had always been a big supporter, and I think she liked having me around. We hung together, spending time getting our nails done and going to dinner or a movie. We became each other's companions in time.

When I wasn't hanging with my aunt or working, I spent time with Caty and reconnected with Darius. PJ had moved to another state with her boyfriend, and we hadn't talked in years. Darius and I reconnected through the website Myspace. (For my young readers, Myspace was the equivalent to Facebook back in 2006.) We had talked every now and then through graduation. Darius had blossomed quite nicely and said the same about me.

"You're far from that tomboy, black-lipstick-wearing hood chick. You grew up, Dee," he said with a laugh.

Chicago wasn't what I knew six years ago. Then again, I had changed so much. This time I was a grown woman with real responsibilities, a different mindset, and a better direction for my future. What used to be exciting to me was now terrifying. I hated public transit commutes, the wild activity, violence, and craziness of the city's Southside.

I moved there thinking I would easily gain work and take over the city. I had no concept of truly paying dues and that good things taking time. The transition from college to the real world blindsided me. In college, I'd studied, worked very hard, and seen instant results. That didn't happen in the real world; it was more difficult to see progress. In the real world, life happened. You could study hard, do everything right, be very talented, and still not see results. There was no report card or dean's list to aspire to.

Many of you may have experienced this transition or are currently going through it. I say, be kind to you. Give yourself some grace and time to learn, explore, fail (because it will happen), grow, and keep going. I wish I had known that at the time, but instead, I remained brutally hard on myself.

Kelly's words one visit to Houston changed my life. She held me as I panicked and listed my failures and shortcomings. "Dee, you're too hard on yourself. You are not perfect! Stop creating these self-imposed unrealistic expectations," she declared. She held me tighter as she introduced a concept I had hardly heard of, believed, or considered in my life.

It was her words that propelled my unofficial walk with Christ. Kelly told me that Jesus was forgiving, merciful, and faithful. I looked up at her with a confused look on my face. I had never thought of God or Jesus as any of that. As a matter of fact, I only viewed God as this powerful, mean person who judged and ruled. At least, that was what I'd been taught in the temple. My perception of God had been steadfast; however, Kelly's words really sunk in. I needed to know more about the forgiving God that Kelly had told me about. I had a lot of questions for Him.

I scored an interview with Harpo (Oprah Winfrey's) Studios and felt certain this was my big break. That interview happened to be my first industry professional interview. I figured I blew it when Oprah's team asked me to name my favorite show. It had been so long since I managed to catch daytime television. All my classes were during the day and I hadn't had time to watch TV since my relocation. My response simply wasn't satisfactory. The dead silence that followed was a dead giveaway, and there went my opportunity. On the bus ride home, I listened to all my family member's voicemails wishing me luck. I felt like I'd let them all down.

My commitment to succeed for them now felt so far away. And deep in my heart, I suspected that my motives weren't quite as pure as I liked to think. I can't tell you if I wanted to be a success for myself as bad as I wanted to do it for those watching me.

Aunt Bertha's message was the most heartfelt. She wished me luck and expressed her hopes that someday I would be able to ask Oprah to share my Cousin Lewis's story. Lewis was currently in the hospital, patiently waiting for a donor and transplant match. He had been there since my graduation. It was tough to process his rapidly progressing illness. He was the strongest, bravest, also one of the healthiest people I knew. He didn't drink or smoke, and his military background kept him physically fit. So, it was a mystery to us when he went to the emergency room with chest pains, only to learn he had a failing heart and needed a transplant.

Time spent at his bedside was usually filled with cracking jokes and laughter. According to him, he was one hundred percent well and would be out soon. His optimism and confidence made me a believer that he would push through and be back in no time. Lewis's health battle was another lingering question I had for God. I wanted to know why this happened to Lewis. I did enjoy the hospital visits with my cousin and telling him what I was up to. Aunt Bertha was truly a woman of faith, and her strength and that of Lewis in turn served to strengthen me.

Talking to God and asking for help became easier, and I started doing that more. It was waiting for responses that made each passing day so frustrating. I don't know that He really listened, and I didn't know Him well enough to trust Him. But just as I resolved that He didn't listen, Lewis was bumped to the top of the transplant list, followed by being matched with a donor and receiving a new heart. Miraculously, God had answered my repeated prayers, and my cousin would be heading home soon.

As expected, I didn't get the Oprah job, but I was hired part-time with the Chicago Bulls and found other gigs as well, including hosting an internet nightlife show. I had several balls rolling and juggled them quite well. Each of my gigs seemed to support the others. I was building transferable skills that would give me an advantage for my future endeavors. Slowly but surely, I started building a brand and a name for myself. My internet show allowed me access to people and places. Working in makeup provided exposure to different fashion brands and creative contacts. The makeup job stretched me the most and exposed me to a variety of different people, philosophies, and lifestyles. The cosmetic industry in downtown Chicago would be where I'd experience the most microaggression and racism in my working life. From older white women who bought a hundred-and-fifty-dollar eye cream to my idiot colleagues to offensive customers to flamboyant gay males prancing around like ballerinas, coming to work at times felt like a circus. The ignorant racial questions, touches of my hair, and hands were nonstop. I've never demonstrated so much restraint and grace while feeling violated. I was forced to respond differently in those uneasy situations, but each trying time provoked a little more growth.

There was this one colleague to whom I took a special liking. Everyone referred to her as "Church Girl." Church Girl wasn't invited when other coworkers went out for drinks after work. They made jokes and changed the subject when talking around her. Some were in good fun, I suppose. However, the more she was teased, the more fascinating I found her. Maybe because I was seeking answers, I wanted to know what Church Girl knew. So, I intentionally sparked a small conversation with her when we worked the same shift. I soon discovered I liked her. She was a sweetheart, funny with a sarcastic wit, just like me. Our birthdays were six days apart. We hit it off well, and she taught me a great deal about makeup.

Everything was on the up and up professionally. But personally, I found myself in an awfully traumatic situation with this one guy I met at work. He'd stop by my counter and ask me out. I turned him down — several times — but eventually, I agreed to meet up with him one night. He certainly wasn't anyone special — we'd just talked a few times and saw each other in passing, both working downtown. Although persistent, he seemed harmless.

I had adopted a more relaxed and open perspective my last few years in Houston. I wasn't the same street girl from the Westside of Chicago. Therefore, I had my guard down. When going out with new people, I had two rules: 1) Don't drink heavily with people I didn't know for safety measures, and 2) Text a friend the name and, if possible, license plate number of the person I was with.

While I had a system, it didn't include bringing my drink to the restroom with me. To my dismay, he slipped something in my drink and brought me back to his house and raped me.

Trigger Warning: This story may be startling and uncomfortable to some of you, but I believe it will be helpful and even freeing for others.

Shortly after returning from the ladies' room, I blacked out. Waking up in spurts, I have a vague memory of stumbling to his SUV, asking him to take me home. I woke up again to find myself riding in the passenger seat and recognizing from the expressway signage that we were heading north…and I lived on the far Southside. The next time I woke up, he was carrying me up a metal staircase while I demanded to be taken home. My next memory was of being unable to push him off of me and repeating "No!" before passing out again.

The final time I woke up, it was the next morning. I was fully awake but had the most massive headache ever. Looking around, I saw condom wrappers on the nightstand and my clothing strewn on the floor. I tiptoed out of bed, looking for my purse, which he'd refused to give me the night before. When I found it, I pulled out my phone, located a bathroom, got dressed, called Ophelia, and told her what had happened between sobs.

"He was supposed to take me home," I kept repeating. She told me to wash my face, get it together and calm down so I could get myself home. Tiptoeing down a flight of stairs, I sat on a gray couch in what I presumed was his living room. Rocking back and forth, I contemplated what to say. *Do I ask what happened? Do I ask why he didn't take me home and why was he on top of me?* I was terrified and didn't know what to say. I sat there in silence, trying to hold back tears as he came downstairs, sparking regular conversation as if nothing unusual had happened. The only words I managed to utter were, "Can you please take me home now?"

He grabbed his keys, and we left. I didn't say a word during the entire thirty-five-minute ride. The entire time, I looked out of the window, feeling humiliated, violated, and confused. I was afraid to tell DeDe and afraid to call the police. Truthfully, I didn't want to deal with the attention and drama that would have come with accusing him of raping me. *Maybe he'd lie and say it was consensual, and it'll just be a he-said/she-said.* I also told myself that because I was twenty-three, I shouldn't have put myself in that situation… in other words, I blamed myself. *I never should have met up with him in the first place.*

He never came back to my job, nor did I ever see him downtown after that. Mentally and emotionally, I was in shambles from carrying the guilt and shame associated with date rape. I simply couldn't undo what had happened. For months, I felt horribly dirty, robbed, and bitter. Wrestling old thoughts, I fought hard to dispel the belief of sex being the only thing I was good for. *God must be upset with me…how else could He allow this to happen?* I didn't want anyone else to know about it, so I tried my best to forget, to the point of pretending it never happened.

Now I know that nothing about that night was OK and that it wasn't my fault. That man was a predator and a monster. Had I known better and not been afraid, I would have called my aunt. I wouldn't have cared about being embarrassed or "bothering" her with my troubles. My aunt would have come in a heartbeat and would have called the police after whooping his a**. She would have contacted my uncles as well. If I had known better and not been intimidated, I would have called the police as well. Being raped, sexually harassed, or molested is *always* a big deal.

Ladies, it is never your fault that a man ignores your saying no, no matter how you got there. No always means no, and anyone who pushes beyond your no needs to be held accountable. Please do not suffer in silence, like I did. It's not healthy or fair to you or your emotions to harbor the guilt, shame, and embarrassment of someone else's behavior.

If you have had a similar experience, please understand that it was not your fault…and if you know someone with a similar situation, tell them it wasn't *their* fault. Hold the predator accountable; speak up, go to the police. By speaking up, you may likely be helping another young lady.

Working both late nights and early mornings, the days began to merge. As an outlet, I began hanging out in expensive, high-end stores. I tried on thousand-dollar furs from the shops on Michigan Avenue. Pretending I owned a black card, and I could afford anything I wanted: shoes, Tiffany jewelry sets, handbags, you name it. At my favorite fur shop, the staff was accustomed to me visiting. They knew I didn't have any money and that I was harmless, and they never followed me around or badgered me.

I think they were fascinated with me. "You are so beautiful," the manager of one store insisted every time I stopped in. He even kept my sizes handy. I stood in front of the mirrors near the dressing room, thinking, "Someday, I can buy a real one."

GOD, ARE YOU THERE?

One day, the owner slipped me his number. His name was Stefano, and he was an older, financially secure European, every bit of mid-fifties. He was charming but also very coy. Occasionally, he watched me try on furs, but only smiled and complimented me. He and a partner owned the shop and several buildings and nightclubs in the city. He lived next to the Trump International Hotel and Tower and drove the latest model Maserati. He certainly wasn't my type, but we chatted and ultimately went on a couple of dates. My mind was wired on him hiring or helping me land a real job. I worked tirelessly for pennies, my credit cards were maxed out, I was still living with my aunt and drowning in debt. My student loan lenders were hounding me as well. I wasn't in a good space emotionally. I felt like I needed cash and fast. And I knew he had connections and was capable of helping me secure a salaried job. But, of course, judging by his occasional comments, he had something else in mind.

I wasn't attracted to Stefano and wasn't the type to entertain men for money. I knew chicks who had sponsors and sugar daddies, but that wasn't me. I took pride in hard work and being independent, despite loathing where I was in life. Those high school days of getting free shoes were no more. I was grown, and I despised women who laid on their backs for material things and cash.

Admittedly, the city views from his forty-fourth-floor condo was stunning. With a glass of Merlot in hand, I stared out the window in admiration of how beautiful Lake Michigan looked. Tons of things went through my mind while standing there. I had a tendency to look up to the sky and ask God my purpose. He hadn't revealed it, and because I didn't know my purpose, I gathered life to be pointless. I wondered if I had done enough to make a real impact and if people would really miss my absence.

After the assault, I found myself thinking about death and purpose quite a bit. I became quite fixated on when I would die and what was my purpose in life. I wondered how it would feel to fly for several seconds if I were to jump out of a window.

My thoughts were interrupted by a kiss on my shoulder as Stefano stood very close behind me. "It's beautiful, isn't it?" he observed. "Just like you." I felt his words spoken in a deep, heavy accent vibrating against the back of my neck. His heavy accent made him difficult to understand at times. But I always understood his compliments. He had a way of making me feel special and was quite the gentleman on every date. I was exposed to things I'd never seen being around Stefano. I was impressed by the view from his condo, the cars he drove, and the one-hundred-thousand-dollar checks lying on the coffee table. For a moment, I thought, *This must be the life, and he could certainly put me a few steps closer to solving some of my money issues…*

He grabbed my waist and said, "Come, let's get in the Jacuzzi." I had brought a swimsuit with me that visit but wasn't comfortable getting in. I'd also known that sex would come up eventually, and it looked like this was it. I wondered how many other young girls like me had come to his place. I knew it wasn't any of my business, but still, I was curious. *Why me? What made me special from the other women?*

His cold hands touching my waist for some reason, reminded me of the date rape guy. My memories triggered, I started replaying portions of what I remembered from that awful night in my head, and I teared up. Then my help surfaced. "This is not you; there is better for you," it whispered softly, repeating it several more times before I told Stefano I was ready to go home.

He pouted in his accent. "Baby, you promised we'd get in the Jacuzzi this time." "Yes, I did, but I need to go. You don't have to take me. I can figure it out." I grabbed my bag, kissed him on the cheek, and left. That was the last time I saw him.

Making it back to the Southside, I avoided conversation with my aunt. I went straight to my room and retreated into deep thoughts. I was a wreck emotionally and felt homesick, missing my friends and life in Houston. Although that had been my most recent home, I didn't know where to call home. Nashville didn't feel like home, and neither did Chicago. I was in a weird space.

As a result of this weird emotional space, I gravitated more to Church Girl while at work. There was something inviting, trusting, and calm about her that I liked. She always seemed so positive and peaceful. So, I decided that I wanted to visit her church and kept promising that I would…but something always came up every time I tried to attend.

A friend suggested that I start manifesting into existence what I wanted in life. I had never heard of manifestation and wasn't sure I believed in it. He told me I had to think, speak, write it down and believe that I would obtain my desires. I took heed writing and searching for books on manifestation and stumbled across the book, *The Secret*. I must admit, I was desperate to find happiness and willing to try anything.

Moreover, I still had questions for God and curiosity about the Holy Spirit, who I had learned about months earlier. With all the emotional turmoil and temperamental feelings churning within me, I started reaching for God more. I figured He had to be why I was going through certain things or that He knew the answer. Still, I wasn't really sure if He heard me because He never spoke to me. I imagined all my prayers collecting like voicemails on an abandoned answering machine.

CHAPTER TWELVE

Who Said Experience Is the Best Teacher?

Shivering and sweating from flu symptoms, I had been sick since a few days after Christmas and spent New Year's in bed. I lay there having a recurring conversation with God. The ripping and running from hustling on the nightlife scene, multiple jobs, hardly sleeping, vodka cocktails, networking socials, and the city's cold weather shut my immune system completely down. I didn't even own a coat, and all my shoes were open-toed. My funds were low, and although I slaved, I barely made enough to keep skyrocketed interest paid on my maxed-out credit cards. I still had car insurance and my cellphone bill to pay.

My pride wouldn't let me ask my aunt for help. She had done enough just by allowing me to stay there rent- and grocery-free. So, Ophelia ended up sending money that I used to purchase a couple of sweaters, knee-length socks, and a coat. *God, what is my purpose? Will life get any better?* I lay there, thinking before dozing off and dreaming I was flying.

My vibrating cellphone alarm, nestled against my arm, woke me up from my dream, and I heard my help say, "Write it down." Crawling out of bed, I headed downstairs to the computer to find a pen and paper and look up the dream. Browsing through the web, searching "what flying dreams mean," I came across a book called *The Purpose Driven Life*, by Rick Warren (Zondervan, 2002). *Ah, I need this ASAP*, I thought. The next day, I purchased a copy.

It was still early in the New Year, and one of my resolutions was getting to know God, being celibate, and finding purpose. I also resolved to land a media job with a real salary.

A couple of days into reading my new book, I started action planning and gained momentum, but I encountered a very costly distraction just as I began to really take off.

His name was Duncan Pennihue, and he had a twin brother named Dorgan. I met them both while working for the Bulls. I remember the day very well; Brandon Roy led the Portland Trailblazers to a six-point victory over Chicago. The stadium was rocking, and it had been a great game despite the loss.

Occasionally, I pretended to be on the sidelines reporting in the United Center, doing postgame interviews with all the star players, as I had done back in college.

I spotted Dorgan in a different area than usual. I snatched a business card out of my pocket and applied a coat of lip gloss before approaching him. I walked up to him and with the warmest smile, said, "Hey." He looked at me. "Do I know you? Have we met?"

His reaction confused me. *OK, this dude is really trying to play me.* I didn't really know him, but we talked in passing every night during home games. "No, I guess we haven't," I said, and began to walk away.

"Wait. I'm Duncan," he informed me. "You must be looking for my brother, Dorgan."

"Your brother?"

"Yes, my twin. Identical."

I laughed. *He's got to be kidding me.* As if sensing my doubt, he quickly pulled out his phone and showed me a picture of the two of them.

I laughed even harder. "Oh wow, my bad. Yeah, I thought you were your brother. It was nice meeting you." "Wait," he persisted. "Can I call you sometime?"

I thought *He's thirsty, thirsty.* And before I knew it, I was engaged in a twenty-minute conversation about his week. He told me I looked gorgeous and that he wanted to link up and get to know me. I declined to go out with him and suggested I take his number instead. I smiled as I walked away. *What the heck was that?*

Duncan was a few years older than me, about six feet, brown-skinned, and wore a chin-strap goatee. He wasn't unattractive or bad-looking, just not my usual type. Physically, he lacked the athleticism I preferred. He also talked a lot, which made him less appealing as his brother. I sought out Dorgan, finding him talking with a girl. I joined them, complimented the girl's natural hair, and followed up by saying to Dorgan, "I didn't know you had a twin."

That was my first time seeing him with this young lady, who I later learned was his girlfriend. I turned to her and said, "Hi! I'm Dee, by the way." The three of us engaged in a good conversation and exchanged numbers. They suggested we meet up soon to talk business opportunities. Heading back to my post, I saw Duncan again and thought, *Well, they are twins...What the heck, his brother has my info now, anyway, so I'll give him a shout.*

We connected days later to chat. He was a character for sure, unlike anyone I've ever met. Duncan reminded me of Steve Urkel but a tiny bit cooler...not quite Stefan, but maybe a Carlton Banks. He came across as one of those kids who grew up really sheltered and pretentious. You know the type, so smart that they're stupid? He didn't have swag at all and lacked street smarts. He reminded me of the guys I had roasted in high school.

Duncan bragged about having a trust fund, being a devout conservative Republican, the property he owned in another country, and coming from an affluent family. He talked, talked, and talked. He left me both entertained and speechless. I didn't know what he'd say next; he appeared to be on Adderall or something. He was certainly different, and I wanted to be open to "different." I managed to ask him a few questions between his talking, like where he went to church and his goals and beliefs.

Ironically, he said he was a minister and had taken a semester off from seminary school. He held a degree in history and had no children. I found that rather appealing. *OK, cool, he has a pretty solid resume and is a minister. This must be a sign.* Given my spiritual quest, I loved that he was a minister, and his being in seminary school was a big plus. Duncan was charming, intelligent, and persistent, as well as a hopeless romantic. Those attributes gave him a foot in the door. He certainly seemed to be the type to spoil and cater to the women he courted.

Simply by listening, I learned so much about him. Then I noticed what appeared to be a woman's ring on the chain he wore around his neck…which should have been caution flag #1. I asked him about it, and a strange thing happened. After all that talking and energy, he shut down and became quiet. His nose flared, and he abruptly stood and said, "I think it's time for me to go."

I also stood, chuckling. "Um, no. Answer me. Are you engaged?"

He paused and finally answered, "I was," and promptly started to tear up. My smiled faded quickly once I saw the tears in his eyes. He brushed past me on his way to the door. I quickly followed, getting to the door before him and blocking it. "Are you OK? I'm sorry if I've offended you."

He looked me in the eye. "I didn't cheat Dee. I didn't cheat." I replied, "Um, OK," knowing the confusion I felt showed on my face. Even in his despair and sadness, the man still managed to be very animated. He started to explain what happened, and the tears that had pooled in his eyes now rolled down his cheek. I knew we needed to get his fiancée back ASAP.

Poor Duncan dressed like someone well over fifty and wore my favorite high school cologne. He had a gap between his front teeth, which my grandma called a liar's gap. She used to tell me to watch out for lying, gap-toothed men. I wish I had listened…

His tears not only shifted the energy but captivated my heart, and I hustled to the bathroom to grab a tissue. *Wow, this is heavy. I've never seen a man cry like this before.*

I handed him a tissue. "Hey, I'm here if you need someone to talk to. I'm also here if you just need a friend to hang with from time to time." My own breakup memories were still fresh, and I knew how hard that process was. Taking me up on my offer, Duncan asked me to lunch a few days later. It was low risk, and I was always hungry and down for free food, so I went.

Duncan was Mr. Chivalry and Mr. Confidence, thoughtful and charming. He showered me with compliments and roses, so much to where anyone would have thought we were an item. And I suspected he believed we were. "Hey, you know we're just hanging out, right?" I reminded him.

However, it was hard not to eat up the attention and romantic stuff. It had been forever since I had a man court me. I started bargaining with myself in an attempt to ward off my doubts…*He looks good on paper, has a degree, no kids, no felonies, is a minster, good family, and charming.* Certainly, he was different because a lot of the other guys I met in Chicago were hood dudes and polar opposites. Duncan checked off most of the boxes on my twenty-three-year-old list of my ideal man, including having a car and not living with his mom. Although he lived with a male cousin, he was still independent.

Duncan pulled out my chair, took my coat, walked closest to the curb, and told me I was beautiful every time we met. With each encounter, I learned something new, which made it hard on a sista.

Occasional texting turned into chatting regularly and him checking on and inserting himself in my whereabouts. Trampling my miserable attempts at setting boundaries with him, I was left scratching my own head. I started negotiating with myself harder for the buy-in. *He's a good guy, and his annoying personality quirks aren't too bad. Remember what auntie said: "A piece of man is better than no man"...* What I learned later in life, the hard way, was to never negotiate with yourself. Trust your instincts…if you have a bad feeling about something, don't do it!"

Furthermore, if you negotiate with yourself, you'll always come up short. That is a fact! I fully understood that dating him would make me his rebound girl. I was totally fine with that. I figured when his ex came back or he got back to being himself, that would be my way out. I had no intention of getting into a serious relationship with him. I mean, I wasn't seeing anyone and figured I would just enjoy being treated like a lady. Besides, I didn't have anything else going on, and all my friends lived in different states. I certainly wasn't trying to hang at the temple with my forty-one-year-old aunt. Besides, Duncan was very persistent; it was hard to evade him.

Unofficially, I joined his crew of friends, and Duncan's ex became a distant memory who we hardly talked about anymore. The longer I stayed connected to Duncan's world, the farther I drifted from shore. Our conflicts started as subtleties with innocent questions on my end. Still, I continued to bargain with myself. *I don't think he meant that. Nah, he ain't controlling. He just really cares about me. You need to be more open and go with the flow.* Slowly inhaling carbon monoxide and rationalizing the toxicity, I became entangled in a large web of lies and manipulation.

Sis, I had no clue of what I was really in for. The more time we spent together, the greater the soul tie, allowing him to set up shop in my head, emotions, and heart. The problem was that we both shared a commonality: to be loved and accepted, thus making it more difficult for me to leave.

Everything about him screamed, *Insecure!* Duncan was chauvinistic, egotistical, and controlling. I put in lots of time educating and creating teachable moments with him, unaware at the time, of course, that my brokenness was attracted to his brokenness. The fixer in me desired to resolve his issues while showing him that great women did exist, so I let my guard down. And although I questioned a couple of things, I didn't see the harm in spending so much time with him…at least not at first. I planned to avoid titles as long as possible, reasoning, *Technically, if I'm not his girlfriend, then I'm not tied to him.* Playing a set of my own game, I tried to have my cake and eat it, too…but in the end I played myself.

"I worship the ground you walk on. I love you and I need you," Duncan often tearfully said. While that, too, should have been a bright red flag to run, I ignored it. I had never met anyone who treated me like he did, but that was only a part of his manipulation strategy. Remember, I was the girl searching for love my entire life and yearning to hear words like that.

Furthermore, Duncan provided convenience and a false sense of fulfillment, a love that came with a price. When everything started unraveling and subsequently revealed his true character, I didn't run like I should have. Instead,

I questioned myself, fell for his tears, felt terrible about someone giving all that "love" and me not feeling the same. I didn't feel the same for a reason, but I coaxed myself into thinking that I should.

Duncan rolled out the red carpet for me the first couple of months. He brought me to and from work, helped me financially, funded outings, and assisted with anything I needed. Emotionally, he pretended to believe in and support me, as long as I stayed within his expectations, and that support kept me wrapped around his finger. He was strategic and masterful with the bait and switch...and after eight long months of celibacy, I gave in to intimacy with him. Aware of my desires to abstain, he vowed not to let it happen again, then in the next breath assured me it was OK because God had placed us in each other's paths for a reason. Yeah, I may have crossed paths with him for a reason, but God didn't send him. Duncan is the main reason that I'm convinced the Devil sends people, too, to distract us.

After being intimate, the tone of our relationship changed. He began showing up sporadically, unannounced. He became more aggressively controlling and emotionally manipulating. He started to feel entitled to my time and everything else about my life. His go-to move was to try and make me feel bad about not sharing the same feelings he had for me. Fights were rooted not only in character, personality, and value clashes but how much he cared for me and only wanted the same in return. He started accusing me of sleeping with other men because I wanted to continue abstaining. He was aware of my faith journey and intentionally fed me twisted truths. I regarded his words as a minister and seminary student, so he had me right where he wanted me, and the pressure was on.

Starting over, I began rereading *The Purpose Driven Life* while juggling Duncan's demands. I journaled specific habits that I wanted to work on. I believed that if I wanted to get right and be well internally, I first needed to be well spiritually. Trying to entertain Duncan while growing emotionally became a struggle.

I had successfully achieved a few things from my manifestation list, the first item being a car that Mel had gifted me with. Mel and I had always kept in touch. He knew I needed wheels, badly. *Surely, I can slow Duncan down now that I have wheels.*

The next piece of good news came the following month. I landed a job at one of the premier media companies after aggressively sending out resumes and practically stalking their employees. The new job was only part-time, but still exciting and in my chosen field. Part-time status allowed flexibility to keep my makeup and nightlife jobs. I didn't want to let either of them go.

Aside from my situation-ship with Duncan, life felt progressive until I got the call about Taylor. He had been arrested as a suspect in a deadly shooting! My chest and throat caved in and I felt suffocated after learning the news. Feverishly, I scoured the internet, looking for details of the shooting. "This can't be," I kept saying. I just knew they had to have the wrong person in custody. I flew to Tennessee immediately to be with Pee Wee and to find out what was going on.

I knew fighting for Taylor would be an uphill battle, especially in Tennessee. Not only did we not have anyone to truly advocate for Taylor, Tennessee has a history of modern-day lynchings of black men. Racial inequalities and systemic racism ran rampant there, especially for poor blacks. I also knew that Taylor's appearance and street associations wouldn't bode well for his character, despite him never being arrested or having a criminal history of any kind. There was nothing we could do until he received a court date.

The weeks were long and bleak, as court dates kept being postponed. I tried my best to compartmentalize and keep my mind clear. But the ongoing difficulties with Duncan and my lack of funds made it challenging. It created the perfect storm of vulnerability, hindrances, and wavering in my disciplines and values. Duncan gave me an ultimatum. He said he wanted titles and didn't want just to date anymore. He refused to continue seeing me without a commitment. I had already met his parents and started having feelings for him.

Figuring I couldn't straddle the fence forever, I agreed but cautioned it wouldn't happen until after my trip to Houston. I flew to Houston to celebrate my twenty-fourth birthday and Mother's Day with Tina that year. Taylor's situation had taken a massive toll on us all. Surprisingly, Tina was doing better than I could've hoped. She had her own place, had been sober a little over a year, had stopped smoking, had a job she loved, had lost over thirty pounds, and was planning to attend college that fall. She worked out consistently, was reading her Bible daily, and growing spiritually. I was so, so, so proud of her. She looked happy, healthy, and whole. I had a wonderful weekend planned and wanted to put a smile on her face… and I did.

Tina baked my birthday cake, just like old times. It was a perfect ending to that needed getaway. I couldn't have asked for a better birthday gift than her progress. Seriously, she managed to quit smoking after twenty-four years! That was big. Houston seemed to be shaping up to be her best move.

Duncan promised things between us would get better when I returned. He was so sure that having titles would fix everything…just like the people who think getting married can magically fix relationship drama, baggage, and broken people. Listen up, titles, marriage, waiting on the job, the bae, or moving to a new city will never fix character flaws, poor decisions, or broken people. And I was never convinced that having titles with him would do that; I simply went along. Not only did we regress, but all hell broke loose because of those titles. For him, they equated ownership.

Not only was Duncan a manipulator, but I learned he was also a masterful liar. He was financially incompetent, and those months of spending were courtesy of borrowed money, gambling wins, and maxed-out credit cards. He habitually over-drafted his checking account. I had no clue of any of this until the day he asked me to foot his phone bill. Paying that bill for him led to my discovery that he was unemployed and had been lying to me all along…and also explained why we abruptly stopped going out.

Nearly six months in, we had invested so much time in each other. I wouldn't have felt right ghosting him abruptly. Hence, I stepped in, supporting us, and Duncan became a project for which I'd sacrifice my development, growing faith, energy, and resources for several years. I wrestled, balancing my aspirations, plans, and personal goals with a competing Duncan. I ran out of gas being with him. That ambitious vibrant hustler who moved back to Chicago had disappeared. My identity had been shattered, and I no longer knew who I was.

Things finally crashed one day. After being intimate, I dozed off and woke up to Duncan touching my lower stomach. It looked as if he was praying over me. I grabbed his hand. "What are you doing?" He didn't answer right away. "I, um, have something to tell you." I sat up immediately, noticing tears in his eyes. He took another long pause, and I thought I saw his lower lip tremble.

"Come on, Duncan; you're scaring me. What do you need to tell me?" I was becoming more anxious by the second. "Dee, I'm sorry. I love you, and I know you love me, so we can work through this."

My breath caught in my throat. Oh my God, he has AIDS... "Spit it out," I demanded. He took a deep breath and announced, "Dee, I have herpes." I didn't hear anything after that, even though his mouth still moved.

My ears recovered in time to hear his repeated apologies. By then, he was crying harder, begging me not to leave him. I went through a myriad of emotions, primarily anger that he'd withheld that information for months despite my clean bill of health. I was angry at him for being such a cancer and angry at the amount of time I'd wasted with him. My mind racing, I grabbed my things and left.

It felt like I drove to Aunt DeDe's in slow motion. I entered my abandoned bedroom and dropped straight to my knees. I cried and pleaded with God to help me. "God, I want healthy children. Please don't let me have herpes. I promise I will leave that man alone! Please help me; I want to get back on track," I cried.

My knees were bruised from rocking and sobbing. I prayed for what felt like an eternity. The days that followed were brutal. I dodged my aunt as best I could; I didn't want her to sense something was wrong. Duncan called so often that I had to block him. I deleted his voicemails, unheard. I didn't want to hear his voice.

Overwhelmed by defeat, sadness, and depression, I had nothing left to give...until I heard a familiar voice. I hadn't heard from my help for so long...He whispered for me to grab my Bible. By this time, I had quite a few Bibles. Reaching for the larger one on my dresser, I missed, and it fell to the floor. I quickly snatched it up, and when I turned it over, the pages stabilized, and it fell open to Psalm 91. Immediately, my eyes locked in on the word "disease." *OK, that's weird. It must be a sign.* I read the scripture out loud. Psalm 91:3. "For He will rescue you from every trap and protect you from deadly disease." (New Living Translation). Tears flowed abundantly, and I felt as if God had heard my prayers.

The doctor's office called a week later with all the negative test results. The remaining months of that year were a conundrum of continuous stupidity on my part. Duncan lied, cheated, threw jealous fits, verbally abused me, put my health at risk, and continuously manipulated me into thinking I would never find anyone better. My relationship with him convinced me more than ever that specific people are assigned by the Devil himself to distract, derail, and disrupt us. Duncan had been assigned to me, and the hold was so strong that only my help could free me of it.

Duncan was a prime example of what dating a narcissistic man looks like. Some of those character traits include negative reactions to criticism, exaggerated achievements, expecting special treatment due to a belief of superiority, needing constant praise, entitlement, etc.

Ladies, hear me out; this is the thirty-seven-year-old me hindsight speaking now: Please pay attention and stop making excuses and giving passes. Your time is so valuable. These behaviors are not innocent or cute. Trying to control others is deliberate, selfish, and a major character flaw. Again, please don't make excuses for men and their behaviors! At twenty-three/twenty-four, I didn't recognize his deeds for what they were and felt horrible telling him no, trying to establish boundaries, and turning him away after he popped up without my consent. That's just crazy.

Setting and keeping boundaries and knowing your worth is so important. No man is ever worth choosing over your own wellbeing. I said it before in previous chapters, and I'll repeat it: You don't owe anyone anything! I don't care how bad they try to make you feel. If you've made them aware of how important something is to you and they don't respect it, that means they don't care about or respect you. Period.

Locking eyes with my brother for what felt like forever took me back to that kid I hooped with. Seeing Taylor behind bars was painful despite his positive attitude and optimistic smile. I told him I loved him, and I promised to return for his trial. After our visit, I went to see Taylor's son, my nephew. Handsome and growing, he looked more and more like Taylor. Holding and kissing my nephew's chubby cheeks helped to realign my ambitions a bit. It was a reminder of why I worked so hard in the first place—to break generational poverty.

I decided to apply to grad school after unsuccessful attempts to find salary employment. Figuring that another degree would open more doors, I went for it. I didn't know what else to do. Duncan had done a number on me emotionally, mentally, and physically. Student loan lenders stressed me out about repayment, and I was afraid of defaulting on my loans. I was tired and struggling to stay encouraged. While God protected my health, I was still upset with Him about Taylor's incarceration and the uncertainties of my purpose. I asked God almost daily for help, to no avail. Utilizing my last resort, I crawled out of bed one Sunday morning, hungover from a night out drinking with Lewis and Caty, and pressed my way to Church Girl's church.

I felt intimidated as I drove to church. It had been forever, and I know my pores reeked of Patrón. Despite my nervousness and uncertainty, I knew my current lifestyle wasn't working. I wanted help. I needed to find my purpose so life wouldn't feel so purposeless. I also wanted to find out about this Holy Spirit and to know God.

My coworker held a seat for me. The environment was warm and inviting; it was nothing like the temple. People were friendly, smiling and greeting each other. The choir was soulful with a Southern Baptist vibe, and it felt a bit like home. I left invigorated and picked up *The Purpose Driven Life* again and started reading.

Unfortunately, all those euphoric feelings from my renewed sense of possibilities came crashing down after Taylor's hearing. It was my tipping point. I took it personally and heavily blamed myself for leaving him in the first place. I blamed Tina for not being there. In that moment, I resented life. As a matter of fact, I was tired and wanted to end it all. Sitting in my lonely room, I decided it would be easier and best if I left the troubles of this world. Images of my smiling niece and nephews flashed before my eyes as I walked to the bathroom cabinet. The devil on the left was present and even more relentless. My help had appeared, too, and the two of them argued. I started writing:

December 2008

I'm grateful for living at this point, but I don't know the purpose. They say you are not to get attached to things of the earth, specifically people, but this becomes very hard when this world is all that you know. Yes, people say, "Get to know God," but how? When I try to, I still don't know Him; it's like I feel He doesn't hear me. I'm so tired of crying; my face hurts. I have a strong sense of loneliness and hurt that I carry with me daily. I wish I had one true friend who was here with me that could encourage and support and make me happy when I'm down. I just want to be happy in life while I'm stuck on this earth. If I can't be happy or enjoy it, it's like I'd rather not be here. I don't see purpose in living right now. Since I have to die anyway someday, why not now? I'm very sorry, and I know this is the easy way out. I don't know another way. I'm just overwhelmed with everything, physically and mentally beat.

After signing my letter, I thought more about my niece and nephews. I thought of how hurt they would be. But I was hurting as well. I lay there, taking the first dose of pills.

Honestly, I was afraid to take them all at once; I wasn't sure if I really wanted to kill myself. I spent too much time fighting with myself and trying to talk myself into it.

It broke my heart that I didn't want to live after making it to such an early point of my adulthood. I prayed one last time, asking God to help. I told Him I would never quit on anything but just couldn't fight anymore. "Where are you?" I asked angrily. Then my phone rang. It was an old friend from college who I hadn't spoken to in years. The first words out of his mouth were, "Whatever you're thinking, don't do it." I sat up and looked around, suddenly afraid. *How did he know?*

He told me that he felt something was wrong with me, and the Holy Spirit put it in his heart to call me. The irony in hearing that Holy Spirit name again got my attention. Perking up, I listened to him a bit before confessing what I was contemplating.

He shared a similar story, admitting he once ingested over twenty pills and drank a fifth of Hennessey but woke up the next morning like nothing happened. He said he believed that God didn't allow him to die because He still had a purpose for him. My friend's words calmed me to my core while providing a new perspective on purpose. He reminded me of how talented, beautiful, smart, and caring I was. He talked about all the wonderful accomplishments I'd made in college. He reminded me of all the people who looked up to me. He mentioned things I'd heard about myself but didn't quite believe or embrace. Finally, he assured me that it takes time to learn and discover purpose and urged me to be kind to myself until I discovered it.

The conversation went on for over an hour, and he prayed with me. The pills I'd ingested did put me to sleep. I rested without interruption that night. It was the first truly good rest I'd gotten all year. I woke up with an unexplainable joy in my heart. I couldn't put my finger on why I felt that way, but I did. I lay in bed, picturing my dreams and goals before hearing my help whisper, *"The Purpose Driven Life."* Jumping up, I rummaged through my things until I found the book and started rereading it. A week later, I wrote this in my journal:

Recently, I was so down. I felt purposeless, helpless, and ready to end my life. As I've been delivered and renewed, I reflect on the issues I am facing, and they don't seem as bad as they did a few days ago. Through prayer, encouraging words, and advice from friends, I've learned that without a purpose, I have nothing to look forward to in life. I've also learned that without God, life has no purpose, and without purpose, life has no meaning. Without meaning, life has no hope. You can pretty much guess what happens to a hopeless person. My 40-day journey to my new life began on December 8, 2008. I thought I was at my breaking point. I was dealing with a breakup, debt, no job, financial issues, family issues, and no plan. Since I've been reading The Purpose Driven Life, so far I've learned that: my life is not about me, I'm not an accident, living on purpose is the path to peace, and that life holds more than the here and now.

Invigorated, I was ready to move forward and excited to discover my purpose. I had convinced myself that reading *The Purpose Driven Life* would save my life...and it did. I started grad school the following month and planned to get myself together emotionally while picking up projects that I'd abandoned.

CHAPTER THIRTEEN

Purpose

It had been nearly ten years since I last set foot in a Chicago high school, and that would be the absolute last place I would've thought to look for purpose. I took a part-time tutoring job to supplement my income while in grad school. Duncan's mom worked for the school district and put a word in for me. Coincidentally, the job was within walking distance from home and freeway accessible to my night classes.

Tutoring at a high school, easy peasy, right? Seemingly, the job was perfect—convenient and low maintenance. But any new adventure brings its own set of challenges and opportunities to grow. As we all know, growth doesn't always feel good.

Let me tell you, working at that high school tested my character. I was bullied, harassed, disrespected, and forced to exercise discipline I didn't know I had. Therefore, I did a lot of growing. Luckily, God sent me a guardian angel (disguised as my boss) to assist me. Her name was Mrs. Hap, and she became my advocate, encourager, and supporter that year-and-a-half I worked at Harlan.

Harlan Community Academy, located in the Roseland neighborhood, had been in the news recently for shootings and gang fights. Harlan served some of the toughest communities on Chicago's South Side. I must admit, the thought of working there was intimidating, to say the least.

Despite having my own fair share of hood experiences, I was grown, college-educated and far removed from impoverished behaviors and "being on the block."

High school chaos didn't excite to me anymore. My concern was for my safety my ability to gain respect from teens not too far removed from me in age. I wasn't thrilled about tutoring in the first place, but I needed funds and the job came right on time. I just didn't want to fall into the teaching trap. A lot of people I knew ended up teaching when they couldn't find work in their chosen field.

Entering through metal detectors in my patent leather black stilettos, fitted pencil skirt, and matching blazer, I surveyed the lobby. My loosely curled hair fell to my shoulders, complementing my perfectly made-up face and accessories. Looking professional and well put together was very important to me, especially since I'd been a makeup artist and on-camera personality the last couple of years.

The school was reminiscent of my days at Farragut. I took note of the chipped wall paint, security cameras, and the loudly spoken profanity in the halls. *Wow, ain't nothing changed.* When it was my turn to be checked in, this brown-skinned lady rudely asked, "What you want?" Based on the glare I gave her, she followed up by asking if I was a student. Her demeanor was off-putting, causing a snarky response in my head: *Heffa, do I look like a student?* But instead, I merely smiled. "No ma'am, I'm here to meet Mrs. Hap."

"You know where you going?"

"This is my first time here, and it would be very kind of you to provide me with Mrs. Hap's room number. Thank you," I replied, forcing a smile.

This was one rude, unprofessional woman. I decided to kill her with kindness. Adapting to the environment was brutal. I had never experienced such inappropriate behaviors: staring, reluctance to speak, non-communication, and dirty looks from my female colleagues. Proactively, I created a strategy to disarm the women within the first five seconds of meeting them. I provided a warm smile, greeted them, and gave a compliment if I could find something worth complimenting.

Walking the halls to Mrs. Hap's office felt as if I was walking the green mile. Everyone just watched me: male staff, women teachers, boys catcalling, and girls openly admiring my attire. I overheard random chatter as people asked their companions if I was new and which class I was teaching. I proceeded to walk straight ahead my chest out and chin up, wearing my resting b*tch "try me" face.

I was stopped by another tutor, a man about 6-foot-1 with brown skin, a slim build, and pecan eyes. He had the most amazing smile and a head full of jet-black waves, the type of waves we called "360's" back in high school. Boys bragged that their 360 waves made the girls "seasick," and you had to wear a do-rag to achieve and preserve them.

He introduced himself. "Hi, I'm Trey. You look lost; are you looking for Mrs. Hap?" I laughed. "Yes, I am."

Nodding, he said, "Oh, you'll be working with me. You're here for the tutoring job, right?" "Yes, I'm Ms. Shelton."

Trey was a Harlan alumni. "There's Mrs. Hap now." Trey jutted his chin. I looked in the direction he pointed and saw an older lady with short gray hair and glasses, maybe in her late fifties. After thanking Trey, I approached the woman. "You must be Mrs. Hap."

She gave me a bright smile. "Yes. Ms. Shelton?" At my nod she said, "I was expecting you. When can you start?"

"As soon as possible. I'm in grad school but only have classes a couple of days a week," I replied. Mrs. Hap provided paperwork for me to complete, and I started immediately afterward.

The first few weeks were rough on me as I tried to get reacclimated to urban public school culture. The kids were loud, rambunctious, vulgar, violent, and disruptive. I could have sworn my generation was a lot better behaved growing up. We were more respectful and discreet around adults. These teens were like a new breed. They didn't give a flying poop. Guys rioted and fought in the halls; some were gang-affiliated, sagging their pants, smelling like weed, and violently quoting rap lyrics during instruction time.

Being so far removed from my rebel days, I couldn't imagine what we put our teachers through. Somehow, I didn't think it was as bad as what I encountered. Some of the girls looked me up and down before rolling their eyes, and some of the boys were disrespectful. Women teachers were the worst, behaving like jealous high school girls. They worked hard to bully and discredit me, usually in front of students. It took severe restraint to keep my cool, but I knew eyes were watching me, so I developed thick skin.

Sticking with my plan to kill people with kindness, I consistently greeted all staff with a cheery, "Good morning," even to those refusing to speak, who responded with reluctant waves. The male staff members—including both male principals—were fine; they greeted me warmly. I had no difficulties with any of them. Trey, the tutor I met on my first day, was especially helpful. We were the same age; our birthdays were just five days apart. He showed me the ropes, disclosing more about what I had gotten myself into.

What I learned over time was that my presence and appearance made many of the women uncomfortable, especially the insecure ones. There wasn't anything wrong with me per se. However, women who didn't know me but still gave me a hard time must have had an issue with themselves. Learning this the hard way, I wanted to prove that I was cool and likable, but the more flagrant their dislike of me, the more exhausting it became. It didn't matter what I did, and it won't matter what you do, either. Some people just won't like you, and that's fine!

What I do know about you, yes you (the one reading this), is that you're stronger than any scandalous behaviors or words spoken against you. I also know that you're courageous and mighty. How do I know? Easy. Because you're reading this book, learning from my mistakes, and choosing to empower yourself. Keep it up, sis. You've got this!

Now, I can't say it was the entire school staff, but about eight or ten teachers and other staff who were tightly knitted and seemed to have it in for me. They had an issue with how I spoke, dressed, looked, and how students gravitated to me.

My goal isn't to give the haters a lot of credit but rather to address the power and importance of being your authentic you even when you're hated.

I wholeheartedly believe that God placed me in that environment to develop my character. He wanted me to learn to navigate and overcome my issues with people-pleasing. As my uncle told me years earlier, "You can't please everyone, Dee," and his words were proven right time after time.

Ladies, there will come a time in your life where you're wrongfully targeted, even ostracized for absolutely nothing. The opportunity in that is to stand firm on who you know you are, what you have to offer, and to believe in yourself. Anyone who has a problem with you, especially if they don't know you, has a problem with themselves.

I continued to go to work dressed professionally and stylishly. Whether the height of my heels or my hair and makeup, the women remained rude, uninviting, or patronizing. The women in the office gave me a hard time every morning I checked in as if they hadn't seen me the previous day. Repeatedly, they asked if I was a student or ignored me when I asked for help in the office. Every day, I gave the same answer and politely stated my name. When I needed help, I would ask to speak to the assistant principal.

By the time my twenty-fifth birthday approached that spring, I had a more refined look. I had gained more weight, filling out my clothes far more than when I arrived from college. I kept my hair and makeup done, as my nonverbals (image) were important to me around the young girls. I realized there was an opportunity to demonstrate what an educated black professional woman looked like. Having that opportunity meant a lot to me because I didn't see many women like that growing up. I desired to set an example and provide young ladies with imagery they could aspire to, whether the staff liked me or not. And the more time I spent with the students, the more I reflected on where I had come from. Not only did I relate with many of the young girls, I knew where they were heading. I saw myself in them.

I changed for the better while working at Harlan. I had become even more compassionate and fulfilled while being there helping and encouraging youth. I felt most beautiful and most rewarded when serving the community. I developed a desire to reach each and every student with whom I came in contact. I hoped to encourage them much earlier in life than I had been inspired. My goals shifted to impacting the students, which helped me stay focused and ignore all the "extra-curricular drama." Some days this presented a real challenge, but I was on a mission, even though I didn't plan to stay at Harlan long.

I was carrying a heavy class load in order to complete my two-year program in one year. I shared my goals of maintaining a high GPA with my students. I understood that many of them barely knew anyone with a college education, let alone pursuing a master's degree. I realized it was my transparency and authenticity that garnered connectivity. I found my niche and gelled well with the teens. Although I was only their tutor, I had better control of the classes than some teachers. Not only did I demand respect and set clear boundaries between myself and the students, but in turn I respected them and their boundaries. I encouraged their thoughts, listened to them, and treated them like they were valuable. By my second month there, the young ladies gravitated to me heavily. My background bridged relatability and connectivity. I understood them, saw them how I wished someone had seen me at that age.

Having Trey as a colleague and sidekick made the year that much more enjoyable. We hit it off immediately, becoming super close. Trey was hilarious and very sweet. He was ambitious and cared passionately about the kids. His goal was to be a principal someday. I found his devotion admirable. We had lunch together and became great friends. I learned a lot about myself during our interactions. The lessons were never direct but gathered through reflection, which I believe are most powerful. Mrs. Hap and I also became awfully close. She was a mother bear, very helpful and honest.

Grad classes were going well, and my balancing act became much easier. I attended school near Darius and Lewis, and I often stopped by to see them before class. They became my primary sounding boards while working at Harlan. Nothing was off-limits; I could talk to them about anything, and I did. They were the two most influential men in my life at the time, always welcoming and supportive. Darius had been doing very well for himself and was attending barber college at the time. He aspired to open up his own shop. As for my cousin, Lewis had fully recovered but was still mindful of his health. He had aspirations to become a firefighter and in the meantime, worked odd jobs club bouncing and coaching youth. I loved them both dearly and enjoyed watching all three of us grow.

Taylor's trial was approaching soon, and Aunt Bertha and I traveled to Tennessee to attend. I took the stand as a character witness and taking the stand felt like a scene from *Law & Order*, but of course there was no one to yell, "Cut!" This was real life and a very sore spot for my growing faith. It was a heartbreaking time for me. Still, I struggled with compartmentalizing my emotions daily. I worked at it but struggled. I pretended to be stronger than what I was as that devastating verdict left the jury foreperson's lips. Taylor, my baby brother, had been convicted for a crime he hadn't committed. There was absolutely nothing I could do; I couldn't step in or fix this one. Holding his nearly four-year-old son, I felt hopeless and broken again. I became upset with God, bitter, and needed comforting, fast.

After the trial, I returned to Chicago more motivated to inspire the young men at my job. I was also preparing to move into my own place, so I hustled, working random promotional jobs on weekends. Darius helped me nestle into my new place. We shared a few laughs and stories while sipping Cabernet and listening to Duke Ellington.

Getting my own little palace just before my twenty-fifth birthday felt so rewarding. I had fought hard to make it happen. My new pad was within walking distance of the lake. Ironically, it was also down the street from the building I grew up in, making for the perfect nostalgia of life coming full circle. I felt blessed and grateful to be turning a new leaf again. My first grading period in my grad program ended with a 3.5 GPA and a little bottle of champagne solo. Sitting in my high-rise apartment that overlooked the city, I contemplated painting an accent wall. I'd missed my quiet time, and being by myself wasn't so bad after all. Considering my grief over Taylor's situation, I instead chose to relish the many things I had to be grateful for.

While the family took turns playing the blame game and being bitter, I learned a valuable lesson. I was able to see people differently, differentiating titles from the people to which they applied. This separation of titles from the person actually started with Tina when I graduated college.

Listen closely: It's so easy to get lost in someone's title, which in turn easily denotes a certain level of expectation. We forget that people are not their titles. People are flawed humans who carry titles. For example, the title of "Mother" denotes a certain expectation or assumption of specific behaviors, and when the one with that title falls short of those assumptions and expectations, our feelings are hurt. When you take that title away and aim to look at them in their true authenticity minus the title, it's easier to avoid being hurt. In other words, Tina is just Tina vs. looking at her by the title "Mother."

Viewing her as my mother (which, of course, she is) added the pressure of perfection to my view of her. Based on the mother definition and how we think of mothers, she possessed neither the skills nor the tools to provide that. I hope that makes sense.

Long story short, I learned that no one is superhuman, that I should extend grace, and that I should look at the person first and not their title. Now, I'm not saying that you can't still hold people accountable with this approach. You can, and please do. With the family feuding, I understood we were all just humans expressing our hurt over the severity of Taylor's sentence. Fighting my own hurt, I chose to focus on gratitude.

My students kept me positive and hopeful. I learned a different level of appreciation for family that my students benefited from. Each student became a younger sibling to me. I saw them as innocent younger beings full of hope, all of them with potential even if bruised. It was such a beautiful thing to see their curiosity. I took every opportunity to mold them, making every moment teachable. Subconsciously, I wanted to right some of my own childhood wrongs and give them the affirmations I never had. I wanted to protect them.

My following grew drastically. Students began stopping by my classroom. Some even skipped class to see me. Others asked permission to eat lunch with me or willingly stayed after school to speak with me. Even the students who initially gave me a hard time became fans. Privately, I was still so fixated on locating my purpose that I didn't realize it was right under my nose. Those children valued my every word. At times, it was a heavy responsibility because my advice was like a Bible for them. They told me everything, and I mean *everything*, challenging my mandated reporter status. Nothing was off-limits. I knew their secrets, fears, goals, their crushes, and their families' personal business.

I noticed the difference in their speech and in the way they carried themselves whenever I came around. Some actually told me they wanted to be like me. I felt burdened by what I considered both a gift and a curse of accountability through being a mentor. Deep down, I was still growing in many areas myself and still uncertain of many things. So, having those impressionable eyes on me was intimidating, but I was up for the challenge. They became my why, an additional reason for me to do better. They challenged me to grow, both professionally and personally. I knew I needed to practice what I preached to them, so I only engaged in progressive, encouraging, and substantial conversations with them. They inspired me, and touched my heart in ways I didn't know were possible. They made me a better person.

There were mornings when my personal life overwhelmed me and I didn't want to be at work. I still questioned my future career and purpose. *What am I doing?* I'd ask myself during the drive in. Before getting out of my car and entering the building, trying to overcome my personal frustration, I was approached by a student who'd been waiting to see me. The picture became clear: I didn't know what was next in my life, and I didn't like the work culture there. I didn't like the pay or having to hustle on the side to pay my bills. I didn't like not knowing if I would ever make it big in the television and film industry. But I also realized none of that mattered, that being at Harlan wasn't about me; it was about the teens and their future.

As I absorbed that knowledge, I began to see and feel my purpose every day! Each morning, someone waited for me to hang up my coat and tell them good morning. Each morning, someone needed a hug, an ear, or a positive affirmation. Each morning, at least one teen told me they wanted to quit, but wouldn't because they knew Ms. Shelton wouldn't quit. Some even confessed that I was the only one who believed in them. Such powerful words deeply affected me. There I was, so fixated on what was next in my own life when those kids desperately needed me in theirs. My issues frequently paled in comparison to the adult-sized issues some of my students faced. They had real-life happening and trusted me to be a part of it. They were fighting for their lives, working to avoid being a statistic.

Before the school year ended, I drafted a proposal to start a formal mentorship program for the girls. Mrs. Hap wholeheartedly supported me, and the principal signed off as well. Diva Talk was birthed out of my newfound love and passion for serving at Harlan. Diva was "AVID" (the name of the tutoring program) spelled backward. AVID stood for advancement, via, individual, determination. We met twice a week, covering life skills, financial literacy and self-esteem. We talked about demanding respect and honoring their bodies. The ladies were to compliment and encourage each other. I encouraged making better decisions than their parents. Nothing was off-limits. I taught respecting their elders as well. Whatever they needed, I provided. We discussed black history, politics, classism, finances, and college life. I brought my real bills to teach budgeting and my real self to teach humility.

I couldn't think of any other place to be in my spare time. Because of them, I found new joy and motivation. My program was self-funded, and I didn't have a lot of money. But it was important to me to feed them and oftentimes, I took them home, too. There were nights when a handful of us were talking well into the evening, until the janitors asked us to leave. The program was a success, and the times I'd drive home overwhelmed with gratitude and snot bubbles and tears were the best days. I went from driving in frustrated to driving home crying. As I turned on my block to park one day, my help whispered, *"This is your purpose."*

CHAPTER FOURTEEN

Believe 'Em the First Time

As incredible as my time at Harlan was, it revealed my empathetic nature, and my boundaries began to falter. I didn't properly balance my zealousness for serving my teens, and the fixer in me arose. Consequently, I carried the weight of their problems, taking home more than I should have each day. I found myself worrying and strategizing their lives on the regular. I shared my cell number with the students and received calls at night and on weekends ranging from suicidal thoughts, desires to run away, moms being gone for days, and other challenging matters.

My intentions were pure, and I wanted to be there for them as best I could, but I lacked professional training; I wasn't a therapist or even a social worker. I will say that some of my teens' issues actually fostered a stronger prayer life. I had this weird way of thinking in which I believed in God for others, but not as much for myself. I had no problem praying and believing for my teens or others. Prayer just seemed slower for me, although it was an essential part of my life at the time.

I was still seeking and looking for answers, hoping that I'd form a closer relationship with God along the way. Besides, finding my purpose still didn't help me to feel like I really knew Him. All the reading, searching and inching toward a closer relationship with my faith, and I still wasn't fully fulfilled. I didn't feel like I had arrived at a place of certainty with respect to God, but I was determined to keep trying. Furthermore, I needed His help to help my teens.

I spent my twenty-fifth birthday in Brooklyn, New York, dining with friends. The trip was brief but a much-needed getaway and reset to reflect, as well as ring in that milestone. I figured I would have gotten much further in my career by twenty-five. However, I was on track to graduate in a year as planned, and I began to give more thought to my next move. I can't say that I was really a strong visionary at that time. The last couple of years had me distracted and all over the place.

As difficult as it is to admit, I just didn't give much thought to the intricacies of obtaining future success. I thought about the future me, but I *didn't* think about the future me. I just knew I wanted to be successful, and I was relentless, talented, and very hardworking. But at the time, I lacked the strategic thinking, focus, and patience necessary to achieve success. Still, I wrestled occasionally with that thorn of hopelessness in my side. Sometimes it showed up as a fear of success; consequently, I played it safe when I shouldn't have. Other times, that thorn in my side materialized in the form of those devilish women at the job. I had finally reached my breaking point with them.

This particular day, I bought my makeup kit to work, as I had agreed to provide complimentary prom makeup services for the girls. The girls raved about it and couldn't wait to get to Diva Talk that evening. Their teachers were upset, not fans of either my connection with the girls or of Diva Talk. My boss, Mrs. Hap, was paged over the PA system to report to the main office. There, she was instructed to send me home for "inappropriate attire." One of the women accused me of parading throughout the school in a sheer top without undergarments.

She claimed that I was a distraction to the male staff and the student body. She went on to refer to me as tasteless and a few other names. Mrs. Hap pulled me aside to share what was going on. She didn't take well to the lie after seeing me fully and appropriately dressed. We both were furious at the blatancy, and I wanted to morph into the me of my fighting days on the Westside at Farragut. Unable to keep it together, I sat there in tears, no longer wanting to work in that hostile environment. After months on end of killing people with kindness, I was ready to quit. Only the words of Mrs. Hap and another guidance counselor convinced me to change my mind. They reminded me of the incredible work and impact I'd made in such a short time. The counselor looked at me in confusion, asking if I wasn't used to jealousy. "Look at you," she marveled. "You're beautiful and have so much going for yourself. Why wouldn't they be jealous of you?"

Her words realigned my spirit and affirmed the direction that I had already began walking in with purpose on my side.

I admitted, "No. I'm not used to jealousy, but I am used to being rejected, and that hurts." That moment revealed to me that I hadn't been created to fit in. As a matter of fact, my inability to fit in spoke to my intentional uniqueness. God purposely made me to stand out...and I'm more than convinced that He's done the same for you. So, if people are talking about you, let them. But if your environment is toxic to the point of it impacting your emotional health, it's OK to leave. Chosen, gifted, and beautiful souls will always stand out. Own your unique individuality, and don't apologize for it!

As the school year ended, I ran into a couple of familiar faces. A friend invited me to attend his play, and I accepted, not knowing my ex would be there. I could've run to the nearest exit when I saw him and his twin, but I played it cool, politely waving and mouthing a greeting from across the room. My ex's brother and his now-fiancée walked over and gave me warm hugs. Duncan stood in place across from us, looking. Managing a partial smile, I went ahead and acknowledged him. I didn't want to be rude or make things more awkward.

As if waiting for the perfect time, he made his way over to me while I was sitting solo. He casually started to chat, updating me on his life and telling me how much he missed me. I listened and discreetly told him, "I don't have anything to say." He asked if I would at least listen to him. So I sat there in silence, listening. He said he had cleaned up his credit, was handling his finances much better, and had a strong job lead. He told me he never stopped loving me and had never given up on us. He said he'd started going to church more and had a better prayer life. Most importantly, he said he'd consistently written to Taylor and placed money on his commissary.

The sound of my brother's name caught my attention. I looked into his eyes and asked, "How did you get my brother's address?" He said he looked it up, followed the case, and kept in touch ever since. He said he also kept in touch with Tina as well and that he'd asked them not to tell me; he wanted them to know he genuinely cared and wasn't out to make brownie points with me. He said he'd been praying for me and asking God to make him a better man for us.

While I didn't expect to hear any of that, the contact with Taylor did tug at my heartstrings. It had been over six months since I had seen or heard from Duncan. His words dug a hole under the wall I built specifically to keep him out of my life. But that wall still stood. "I'm praying for you," I responded, and I walked off.

I replayed everything he said over and over during the next couple of weeks. Seeing Duncan truly did a number on me, and I finally decided to deal with our breakup. I had successfully ignored him and stayed busy, blocking it out of my mind. Seeing him again opened a door I thought I had locked. That night, I went to all my blocked email folders and sure enough, he'd sent me hundreds of messages. He sent more emails after we saw each other at the show, creating several new email accounts because I'd blocked every other method of communication months ago. I talked to Taylor during those weeks as well. Both he and Tina verified Duncan's claims. So, I decided to go ahead and read one of Duncan's emails. *Big* mistake. I should have never read it, as it opened a door of destruction that I would need my help to close for me, for good.

Tears of confusion flowed all on my carpet that night. I didn't have my students' to distract me over the summer. I was left alone to address the thoughts and feelings I'd tried so hard to avoid. I wanted to believe every word he wrote. Most importantly, I was a firm believer of actions speaking louder than words, and his support of Taylor spoke volumes to me. I also believed in giving second chances. I missed the way he made me feel. I missed companionship. It was tiring, going on useless dates with different guys who didn't love me. Honestly, they only stagnated my growth. I understood that I was only hurting myself in that vicious roller coaster. I just didn't know how to stop it and get off.

Yes, I'd become far more polished and refined both socially and professionally. However, I still struggled privately with a couple of bad habits. I'd grown so much in the last couple of months but in my humanity, I occasionally medicated my hurts and emptiness with unhealthy vices. Yes, it felt rewarding to learn and walk in my purpose, but I was still lonely in my silence.

Hmm, what if Duncan is being honest? What if he was in church with me? Surely then things would change, and it could work. I mean, I really want to continue my spiritual growth.

My relationship with God had been one of curiosity, fear, and skepticism. I felt so conflicted. Although I professed to love God, I didn't really trust Him, and that kept me dancing on the fence. In my skepticism, I didn't expect Him to fill those holes, provide fulfillment, and comfort me in my silence. I am a woman who had never experienced a healthy father/daughter relationship. So to imagine God as a father, forget about it.

The moments I sought to comfort myself in male company only left me feeling ashamed, frustrated, and more skeptical. That shame and guilt kept me separated from God. Then the fear and belief of God being conditional, mad, and playing silly games kicked in. I was under a false notion that I needed to be perfect and have myself together before really trying to build a relationship with God. I had no clue that He loved me exactly how I was and that He wanted me to get to know Him exactly how I was so He could make me better. Instead, every time I thought I disappointed God, I stepped back, concluding that trying to have a relationship with God was too hard.

Maybe Duncan was right. Maybe he is who God has for me. That was part of the reason I agreed to see him. Another part of me wanted him to see how well I was doing without him, so I allowed him to come over. He concluded I had moved after riding by my aunt's so many times and not seeing me.

His career lead was with a police department. Ironically, he and Lewis happened to work out at the same gym during that time. Lewis, however, was training to take the firefighter exam. I knew they had crossed paths, as Lewis told me all the different ways Duncan tried to learn my whereabouts. Lewis attempted to put in a good word for Duncan every now and then, but it didn't work. I had done a good job moving on until that day I ran into him and heard him talk about Taylor. Duncan's writing my brother for months and sending money were serious actions to me. I couldn't get over it, and I wasn't one to go back and forth in relationships. I decided that this time, I would watch closely to see if he had truly changed. If he hadn't, I knew his actions would prove as much sooner rather than later.

After reconnecting with Duncan, he began showering me with expensive gifts, roses, and dinners. Just like Duncan himself, it was overwhelming. I hadn't received flowers in so long. They made me smile, but I remained on an even keel. Still very charming and poetic in his words, he talked his way back into my life. On the surface, he seemed changed and started off consistent. He had my undivided attention, and I gave two conditions: 1) I would remain abstinent, and 2) He needed to attend church with me. At the time, I attended church girl's church quite a bit—not consistently, but often. He agreed, and in his mind, we would marry, which he eventually suggested. Furthermore, he had no intentions of walking away this time, either.

Attending my family reunion that summer provided more time to reflect. It was held in my kindergarten hometown, so I traveled to Mississippi for the first time in over sixteen years. Being back in the city where new life started was eerily familiar. The area looked the same, painfully poverty-stricken and like something from a slavery movie. I thought about the little timid and uncertain kindergartener I'd once been. I had come such a long way since then. If I could've gone back to my past to talk to her, I would've told her that it gets better.

Visiting my old neighborhood warmed my heart. My favorite cousin from there brought me to Sandfield to see the projects where we had lived. Swinging by my elementary school reminded me of my teacher who taught me it was OK to smile and laugh in life. I thought of how far I had come and how my life story prepared me to be who I needed growing up. Mentorship came so easy for me. That moment was so powerful and encouraging. Going out at night with my cousin was reminiscent of us as children watching our mothers getting dressed. Now we were the adults, squeezing our frames into sexy mini dresses. That trip provided plenty of full-circle moments. I needed to be there. The end started to feel as if it was justifying the means. Mississippi provided a necessary closure for me; I was glad I went.

The following months were busy, to say the least. I took a heavier load in school, and both Duncan and Lewis were hired in their desired positions. They would be starting at the academy soon and were sworn in the day before Lewis's birthday. Words could not express my gratitude as I watched my cousin. His growth over the last couple of years helped increase my faith as well. It was such a proud moment and the best birthday gift ever. Attending his swearing-in ceremony a day before his twenty-eighth birthday brought tears to not only my eyes but Aunt Bertha's and everyone else who knew his journey. Just two years before, we didn't know if he would live. I found it pleasantly ironic that God blessed him with a new heart and a new life, putting him in a position to save the lives of others as a public servant. What an incredible moment!

The moment was impactful for Duncan as well. He had always struggled living in the shadow of a twin brother who was light years ahead of him. So it was essential for him to garner something of his own. Unfortunately, becoming a police officer inflated his already large ego. He started to change rapidly…maybe not so much change as returning to his old self.

Our relationship started to become overwhelming and stifling to my personal growth. I'd seen that show with him before and didn't want to see another episode. My confusion about why he reentered my life had me hold on longer than I should have. *God, why would You bring him back if he isn't the one?* Was God trying to see if I was still foolish? Was Duncan a test? Because I had been doing so well, maybe he was reassigned to try and derail me. I didn't get it and vowed to let time expose it.

I returned back to Harlan tutoring and mentoring that fall and spring while juggling another job, school, and supporting Duncan through the police academy. I helped him study, prepared his lunches, and was there emotionally. However, the more Duncan realized he couldn't control me, the more we feuded. Months before my graduation, he began petitioning for me to become a teacher and stop applying and pursuing my media aspirations. Our disagreements turned into heated arguments where he'd drink too much and become verbally abusive. The more time he spent at my place, the more I saw how slothful, controlling and poorly hygienic he was.

Duncan was all bad, an unnecessary stress, and became a larger problem. Realizing it had been a grave mistake to let him back into my space, I began plotting out my exit strategy. I had other things to focus on, like graduation and needing to identify my next career move. I refused to be in the same space as I was when exiting undergrad. I was open to relocating but also appreciative of the roots I planted at Harlan. Either way, I knew I needed to get focused; I used my next move and shedding my Duncan problem as motivation.

This is where I began tapping deeper into my faith. I needed God now more than ever. I needed His wisdom, guidance, and direction. I had nowhere else to turn. So I began journaling, reading, and praying over time. Converting to

Christianity, I officially joined Church Girl's church against Duncan's wishes. He was intimidated by my growth and every time I left that church, I felt empowered. For once in my life, my spiritual journey seemed interactive, better, and genuine. My feelings were more real than ever, and my fire burned brightly. The deeper I grew in my faith walk, the stronger I became. Not only was I able to see more clearly, but I overcame obstacles more confidently. My perspective started to shift rapidly.

I was determined to figure out how to merge my passion for media with my newfound purpose. I prayed, asking God to show me the way and to bless me to do both. Since God was my Creator, I rationalized who better to show and help me accomplish what I was created for. I made a final attempt to ensure I wasn't crazy, so I connected with Duncan's mom to garner clarity.

Astonishingly, Duncan's mom expressed admiration for the care and effort I put into taking care of her son. She was fully aware of all my concerns and told me straight up, "I know my son. Follow your dreams and move forward." She went further to validate my gripes, confiding that those were the same reasons she left his controlling father years ago. Her candor baffled me, but I appreciated her support and needed to hear it. She said she valued my work ethic and saw big things in my future. "Stay focused and take care of you," she said, ending the conversation. I had every intention to leave Duncan alone, but I just didn't know how to cut him off without him going crazy. He began acting erratically whenever I'd alluded to parting ways and focusing on our careers, and his drinking and verbal abuse worsened. I couldn't get him out of my place, either. Duncan had brought over so many of his things when we first resumed our relationship, and of course, he had a key. He used that as leverage over me. He'd stay away for a number of days and then would pop up at random times.

I realized I had to be direct and break it off completely and request my key. Having him there was the equivalent of a dark cloud hovering over my happy space. My spiritual journey was all I had. It was very much my safe haven during our spats. And fortunately, my faith helped me to worry less. I was thirsty for knowledge and growth in my relationship with God. The more I attended service, the safer, more comfortable, and more empowered I felt. God became my refuge and His peace was so fulfilling. I became engulfed with my desire to grow. Everything was new and intriguing. I learned so much about Jesus and what Christianity truly meant. I was able to study and cross-reference what I learned for my own understanding. My church was unlike the temple, where we weren't allowed to question anything.

My newfound enthusiasm and hope inspired a new hobby: reading the Bible. I wanted to know everything in it, and I challenged myself to read it from start to finish. Reading every chance I got, I carried one around with me to school, class, and work. My new desire to know God became all I thought about and wanted to talk about. My students, friends, and family noticed the shift, too. Duncan noticed it for sure became so threatened and insecure with his own faith that he taunted me, saying I thought I was better than him and closer to God. He went on these rants specifically after drinking. I found myself hiding when I wanted to read or pray when he was around. I didn't want to make him uncomfortable or be uncomfortable myself. I didn't want to fight about my growing faith, the one thing that made me happy.

CHAPTER FIFTEEN

Faith Is

A simple conversation I had with Church Girl shifted my entire way of thinking. She encouraged me to see my journey with God as a real relationship. The problem was that I hadn't truly been in any healthy relationships.

"Learning to walk with God is more about having a relationship than rules and going to church," she shared.

Hmm, I can dig it, I thought. More than digging it, those words changed my life and relationship. Previously, I focused on what I *couldn't* do in a relationship with God. I heard people talk about going to church as if it was court-ordered community service. I was used to hearing how hypocritical Christians were and even despised them at one point. It was the hypocrisy, rules, and my own church hurt that kept me on the outside looking in. I, too, shared in the misconception that church and Christianity were about rules and control.

Never before had I heard anyone highlight the fact that faith and Christianity are actually relationship-based. I learned that church was only the catalyst to help start, nurture, and encourage my relationship with God, and that "Church and hypocritical Christians" had nothing to do with my personal relationship with God. Besides, if that were the case, then I'd only see God once a week, and those hypocritical Christians would have a heaven or hell to put me in. Besides, I was a hypocritical Christian only because I wasn't perfect.

Viewing my faith as a relationship was game-changing. As we all know, relationships require time, communication, and trust. After gaining this new perspective, I knew I needed to communicate more, put in the time and work on trusting God.

Relinquishing my nearly twenty-six years of perspective wasn't going to be easy at all. I knew this new relationship required belief and this thing called faith that I had heard of so often. I also knew I couldn't be in a relationship with anyone who stifled my passion for pursuing God. I knew it would be different and challenging, but I was willing to try. I expressed these thoughts to Church Girl, and she totally understood my position. Actually, she was the most kind and non-hypocritical Christian I ever knew. She was patient, loving, gentle, and kind. She explained that my thoughts were normal and shared a few more simple words that made my new journey even easier.

"The key to having a relationship with God is understanding that it's not just one big decision, but a series of decisions," she said. "Building a relationship with Christ takes time, just like going to the gym to get in shape.

You can't give up when you don't see immediate results." She pointed out that because I am only human, I couldn't expect to do everything on my own. She concluded by saying that God loved me and desired to help me grow stronger.

Her gentleness kept me vulnerable and curious to learn so much more. I learned that God loved everyone so much that He gave His only son to die for me. I learned about grace, sin, salvation, and the importance of praying. While I attended church off and on for years, I don't recall learning any of that. The things I learned in Believer 101 blew my mind and were sometimes tough to digest, which is why I needed faith to believe. I learned that it was OK if I fell; I just needed to get up and continue striving. Learning that God loved me still, no matter how many times I fell, was incomprehensible.

"You've got to be kidding me," I often pondered. That was hard to accept, coming off my view of God as an angry judge who cuts people off. Church Girl really messed me up when she told me that was why Jesus died because He knew I would sin and mess up. It was too much to unpack and process all at once for me.

"Wait, you mean to tell me that grace is free, and I don't have to do anything to get it?" I asked her. "Yes, and God is consistent, always the same. He doesn't change His mind.

Once you accept Jesus Christ as your Lord and Savior, there is nothing that can separate you from His love," she replied. The more consistent I became in my journey, the more my help appeared and the less the spirit of hopelessness showed up. My help kept telling me to keep going, that every day brings new possibilities. My main problem at this point was my battle with perfection and being a high achiever. I took off as if my faith walk was a sprint. The more I learned, the more I wanted to implement and try to conquer. In time, I learned the impossibility of perfecting a growing relationship with God. I realized growth meant to change and understood that change was a constant. Therefore, I knew there was nothing I could do to perfect growth, since it meant change.

Classes and job hunting kept me occupied. The thrill and realities of graduating again dared me to stretch. That semester, I challenged myself more creatively and physically. Not only did I decide I would participate in my first twenty-one-day fast, but I also planned to produce my first full-length film for my thesis. I'd previously fasted every year for Yom Kippur, the Jewish holy day, when I belonged to the temple, but never for more than a day. Twenty-one days would be extreme, but I wanted to see what would happen.

I remembered reading somewhere that some things only come from prayer and fasting and thought, *Hmm, maybe a fast will get rid of Duncan.* He was certainly part of my motivation to fast. I also wanted answers to a couple of things I didn't understand. I remembered Angel's twenty-one- and forty-day fasts. She always talked about how great she felt afterward. I figured if it worked for her, it could work for me.

Midway through my fast, my computer crashed, deleting hours of footage of my film project. I lost the footage and had to start over from scratch...three days before it was due. Normally, I would've gone into a panicked frenzy, punching the air, but I remained calm. I believed it was the fasting and praying that kept me sane. Also, during the fast, I finally broke up with Duncan, but he refused to leave. He told me I couldn't afford to leave him and that I'd end up back at my aunt's again.

I got really good at blocking him out—my prayers had made me stronger. It was too exhausting, going back and forth with him. Part one of my plan was done. Now, I just needed to get my key back and toss his things. In the meantime, I was just trying to finish all my graduation requirements, and I figured I'd show him better than tell him.

I managed to reedit my whole film in days. I completed my other assignments as well. My professors were understanding and patient with me. I credit everything I went through at that time to my fast. Fasting had made me radiant, especially at Harlan. The hating coworkers were a nonfactor, and I murdered them with more kindness.

As my fast concluded, the pastor preached a powerful, game-changing sermon on faith. Let me tell you; it was eerie how the pastor seemed to have been in my business and prayers because every message seemed targeted at me, weekly! There wasn't a Sunday when he didn't seem to be talking specifically to me.

Every sermon felt like a game-changer, but that particular sermon changed my life. I had heard the word "faith" used so commonly in and out of church. The term had been thrown around casually all my life. I heard Tina, my aunts, uncles, and grandparents use it. Even before I knew the Bible, I knew how to quote those faith scriptures. However, I never knew the power of actually having and demonstrating faith. I didn't truly put it into action despite knowing the definition. Faith, in my opinion, is what we'd call manifestation today, the combination of action and belief.

One Sunday in particular, our guest pastor instructed us to turn our Bibles to Hebrews 11:1, which reads: "Now faith is confidence in what we hope for and assurance about what we do not see." (NIV). I had known that verse since I was a child. I read it again and again, reflecting on everything current in my life. You see, I hoped for so many things to happen or to change. The preacher went on to speak about these great biblical characters who demonstrated faith. All of the characters in the Bible shared the same common denominator: their belief in something they didn't see. They all had faith and believed God would work out their needs and the rest.

Because I've always considered myself a realist needing structure, organization, and a plan to function, their stories baffled me. *Wow, these people just kept doing things blindly, and it always worked out. Really?*

The more I thought about it, I realized I was uncomfortable winging even small details. I always had a plan for everything. I took pride in my ability to coordinate and plan well. I'd planned and worked hard to see results my entire life, so I wasn't sure about this "faith" thing. I needed to know for certain things would work.

Sitting in the church pew, I thought about what I was hearing. I wondered if the bible stories were realistic and practical, and then my help appeared and said, "Do you trust me?"

I considered the question. *Since I believe in God and He created me, I have to trust my Creator. Relationships need trust.* That sermon had a powerful enough effect on me where I reflected upon it that whole week.

The closer graduation got, the more nervous I became. I really needed stability and consistency in my career. I was approaching my third year in Chicago, and I wanted more to show for my time and effort. I needed a salary, full-time benefits, and a space to use my talents. I had so many prayers and requests for God at that time, I wasn't sure if His mailbox was full. I needed His help with finding my next steps because I didn't know what was next for me at all. My lease was ending soon, I'd broken off my relationship, I was graduating, and my job was ending as well. The parallels were startling, for that was exactly how things looked when I left Houston.

But this time, I had more expenses and little to no funds. I really needed to get Duncan out, too. Harlan had been an amazing ride, and I'd learned so much from the students. I learned a lot about myself and grew into a passionate youth advocate. I learned self-restraint, discipline, and how to practice what I preached. I laughed, cried, made lifelong friends, and created an amazing program that transformed lives. Harlan and all the youth there helped shape the person I am today. As incredible as it sounds, I chose not to return that fall. My work there was done. I wanted to have faith and to trust God for something greater. So, I started believing God for a career move.

What I prayed for specifically was a career that would allow me to work with teens, utilize my love for sports, and put my media background and communication degrees to use. Using my faith, I prayed for it daily and believed God would send exactly what I asked.

Ringing in my twenty-sixth birthday on my girlfriend's couch, I stuffed my face with candy. Duncan and I had gotten into a huge argument the night before, and I didn't want to go to my own home. I laid there, feeling frustrated and so alone.

I began to pray my same prayer, asking God to get me out of my mess. "God, where are you?" I cried. Continuing to talk to Him even though I didn't hear Him answer was the only hard part about our relationship. I wasn't even sure how or if God ever verbally responded to questions or prayers. I did know He listened, though.

In late spring, I got a timely and much-needed visit from Charles. He happened to be in Chicago for a potential job lead and hit me up. We connected, and it was great to see him. I needed to see a familiar face, and when I didn't feel anything upon seeing him, I knew things had changed. The usual effect Charles had on me was completely gone. We were just two old friends catching up. He promised we would connect the next time he came to town. We hugged, and he left.

Just as I suspected, Duncan refused to leave, although it had been months since our breakup. He threatened to take legal action if I didn't give him proper notice to vacate. He wasn't even on the lease, but that didn't stop him from insisting he wasn't leaving until my lease was up. My help interjected, "Step out on faith and trust me now." I didn't know exactly what that meant, but I had an idea deciding to move forward trusting God, which meant Duncan had to go ASAP.

Graduation was far more chill than undergrad. I finished with a 3.5 GPA from Governors State University. More than seventy guests packed into my apartment's clubhouse for the party. Tina decorated, and Aunt Bertha cooked. We had balloons, a program, poetry, interpretive dancing, music, and a special screening of my thesis film. My family and friends traveled from Mississippi, Michigan, Indiana, and Tennessee. Mrs. Hap and Trey came as well, as did some of the Diva Talk members. I felt so much love in that room. I couldn't believe I had reached another benchmark in life. I looked far more different than the girl I grew up as, and I felt purposeful and very grateful.

After everyone left, I took the money I received as graduation gifts and paid my rent and other bills. I didn't expect anything from Duncan and planned to refuse anything he offered. I said a quick prayer, and with the thirty-five dollars left in my account, I told Duncan he needed to leave and return my key. He did not take it well and put up a big fight. Our argument got so heated that I threatened to call the police if he didn't leave. I called Lewis to come over in case he hit me. I didn't want to draw more attention from the neighbors. I knew Duncan, as a police officer, didn't want any embarrassment, either. Calling me every obscene name in the book, he told me I would never make it or be anything in life without him. He stormed out with my key, refusing to return it. He picked the wrong time to try me. My first instinct was to throw his stuff outside, but I stayed mature. Instead, I contacted his mother, and she came over to bag up his items.

It took his mother less than twenty-five minutes to gather his things, and she returned my key as well. As soon as I had my place back to myself, I broke down crying on the floor. I told God, "This is my attempt at stepping out on faith and trusting you." I reminded God of my situation as if He didn't already know it. I sobbed, "OK, Lord, I have thirty-five dollars to my name, no job, tons of debt, and no idea what I'm supposed to do next. My rent is due again next month, and so are my bills. If you and this faith thing are real, please help me. I am afraid, and I don't know what to do next."

Tears fell from my eyes between slow blinks. I lay there, looking at the ceiling before hearing my help whisper, "God is with you." I needed to hear that and thought of the timeliness of my help's appearance. I pondered the idea that my help had something to do with God. And throughout the years, I still didn't know how to truly explain my help...I just knew when it arrived.

It felt different, readapting to life over the following weeks. I no longer had class to attend, a job to go to, or Duncan to fight about...or fight *with*. Although I felt lighter, I didn't know what to do with myself. Working out and job hunting became ritual. I bought a bike with one of my graduation gift cards and started riding over to the lake to begin my mornings. Lake Michigan was breathtaking in the early morning—refreshing and liberating. I ran into my neighbor on her way to work one morning. I noticed her dressed in promo attire, with a liquor bottle imprinted on her shirt, similar to what I used to do. I inquired about openings, and she gave me her boss's info. Her boss hired me on the spot because I had experience. That opened the door for another gig, which promised a ten-day stretch for none other than the Taste of Chicago (the world's largest food festival), and it paid well.

You may not believe this, but the total amount I earned between both opportunities was exactly what I needed to cover the following month's rent, bills, food, and gas. I landed both jobs in the same week, only days after my prayer! That was no coincidence; it was a blessing, and right on time. My expenses for the current and following months were covered, but I still needed something concrete. "So, is this what faith is, Lord?" I questioned. "Trusting you little by little when I don't see my way?"

Despite my need for answers, still, I felt lighter and at peace. I continued working out, job searching, and attending service, Bible studies, and my Bible readings. My life wasn't completely together but it was getting there, and I wasn't worried. I had the concept of faith down and was committed to exercising it. If I planned to be in a relationship with God, I knew I had to trust Him.

The following message I'd hear at church would not only radically redefine my perspective of God but drastically propel my understanding of Him and Christianity. The previous message on faith encouraged me to take action and step out on faith, and better understand the concept of faith. The following message completely blew me away.

As always, I arrived early to find parking. Eagerly setting foot in the building, I noticed my usual seat was taken, so I shifted to another side of the sanctuary. The choir sang, vibrant, roaring, and beautiful, as always.

As worship ended, the pastor finally took to the pulpit to begin delivering his message. "How God Speaks" was the title. Intrigued, that had been a looming question in my mind for years and something I remained curious about. As a newbie to Christianity, I didn't fully understand the Trinity. I mean, I'd heard of the Trinity, but I didn't truly know what it meant besides the Father, Son, and Holy Spirit. That was about it. Ever so graciously, the sermon focused not only on the roles of the Trinity but specifically the role of the Holy Spirit and how He lives inside of me. Ah, there went that "Holy Spirit" phrase, which reminded me of what Tina and DeDe said years earlier. The Holy Spirit's discovery was what started me on this entire quest to begin with.

I sat there, zoned out in my own world, trying to process what I was hearing and take the concept in. My mind flooded with scriptures I'd read regarding the Holy Spirit, and I began connecting the dots. Because I had practiced

FAITH IS

committing scripture to memory, there was one in particular that came to mind, 1 Corinthians 6:19, stating, "Do you not know that your bodies are temples of the Holy Spirit, who is in you, whom you have received from God? You are not your own." (NIV). *Oh, this makes sense and supports what the preacher is talking about.*

See, I'm a skeptic and logical by nature. I need proof and facts to understand and accept. However, I understood that faith also demonstrates blind belief and that it takes faith to be a true Christian. Heck, it takes faith to be an atheist, too, because it takes just as much faith to believe as not to believe.

That very moment changed my life. The biggest *a-ha* and epiphany was unveiled right before my eyes. Mentally, spiritually, physically, and emotionally I felt connected, locked in, as if something was downloaded into me. Think about a computer going through software updates before being rebooted. In that process, the installer program works hard in the background writing new files to the system, creating new registry entries, and in some cases, it will even download new files from the internet during that installation process. For me, God was the installer, and the scriptures, prayers, and the power of the Holy Spirit were equivalent to my updates, new files, and registry entries.

After my "restart," my thoughts were interrupted when the pastor said, "God speaks through thoughts, ideas, situations, dreams, and people, but primarily through His Word, the Bible."

It hit me like a ton of bricks, slapping me right in my face. *A-ha!* I felt emotional, vulnerable, and helpless at the same time. As I realized exactly who and what my Help (no longer my help with a lowercase "h") was all along, it made even more sense. I began to weep, sitting there frozen and statuesque in the sanctuary that suddenly stood still. Overflowing with images, scenes, and sounds, the highlight reel of my entire life played in my head, underscoring every time I heard my Help.

The scenes went as far back as my siblings and me as young children sleeping under carpets, the voice that spoke to Tina telling her to move, my time in elementary and middle school. I reflected back to being a child and hearing my Help for the first time. I thought of the times my Help warned me when I searched for love in the wrong places and felt depressed, scared, defeated, and uncertain. I remembered my friend who called out of the blue on the night I wanted to take my life. He'd said the Holy Spirit told him to call. I thought of scriptures my Help whispered to me and the Bible that appeared under my couch back in Houston. The countless times that I had been given instructions, the random people who encouraged me, the help from strangers, being favored in school, and all the countless other stories not listed in this book all flooded my memory. I knew my Help was responsible for it all. Realizing the identity of my Help rendered me speechless. My Help was the Holy Spirit—God all alone! Long before I even knew Him and pursued a relationship with Him, He was with me.

Continuing to weep, I remained seated in the pew while everyone else stood and sang. I felt overwhelmed with gratitude for finally putting it all together. Lil' ol' me, the master producer and planner who liked being in control and having everything figured out, was being helped by God even when I didn't know Him. How powerful it was to know the Holy Spirit had been the voice in my head and heart all along. Coming to that realization would only be a fraction of what God had up His sleeve. He performed another mindblower a few weeks later.

Not that He needed to do anything else for me or that waking up every day in good health wasn't enough. But He chose to bless me unexpectedly with my ultimate dream job.

That's right; He specifically created something for me. And it was everything I hoped, believed, asked, and prayed for. I couldn't have dreamed up anything better.

I received a call inviting me to apply for a teaching position at a nonprofit organization. While I wasn't thrilled about teaching, I was on the verge of desperation because I needed employment, so I scheduled an interview. In the interview, it soon became apparent that it wasn't a good fit, and I left feeling a little discouraged. A week later, that same interviewer called me back for a different position.

Not only did I nail the interview and accept an offer, but I negotiated a higher salary. My new role worked with inner-city teens and taught them about sports broadcasting and radio, television, and film production. I was to be executive producer and program coordinator of a high school sports show. My teens would utilize skills they'd learn under my instruction and package them into an hour-long television show that aired on public access television in Chicago.

This opportunity had been precisely what I prayed and believed God would deliver to me the year before. It represented the perfect culmination of my media passion, my sweet spot for sports, and my newfound purpose in mentoring teens. My dream job found me and fell in my lap, but once again, I knew it was not a coincidence but the work of God. It was too perfect. Before starting my new position, this verse came to mind: "Every good and perfect gift is from above, coming down from the Father of the heavenly lights, who does not change like shifting shadows." (James 1:17, NIV). Another scripture followed: "And we know that God causes everything to work together for the good of those who love God and are called according to His purpose for them." (Romans 8:28, NLT).

The dots connected as I reflected on how God made everything work together for my good. While Duncan was a terrible stain on my past, through him, I met his mom, who in turn introduced me to Harlan, where I found my purpose and passion for teens. Additionally, I was able to gain professional classroom experience and develop the necessary skills for working with young people. That was a prerequisite for the position. Also in my favor was my previous experience working on the sports broadcast at KTSU, which provided the necessary credentials to teach sports broadcasting.

My background and humble beginnings gave me a reliability factor with inner-city teens. I was able to reach them better than any of the other counselors and teachers. Therefore, teaching became easy, especially in a field I now had a master's in. My professional media work provided me with the experience needed to teach youth how to produce a weekly show. My Help had directed and sustained me until that opportunity came.

For example, getting a job in makeup introduced me to "church girl." Everything sprang from that encounter with her. I learned to appreciate all of my experiences. The dots continued to connect. Every experience, all I had been through, was preparation for the next chapter in my life. I learned my purpose existed long before I arrived. My Creator always knew what I was going to go through. He knew me long before I knew Him. He also knows what lies ahead of me.

I hope you can and will start to connect your own dots. Your Creator knows what's ahead for you, too. I have a long way to go and lots of growing to do still. I have more people to meet, to impact, to inspire, and to learn from. I understand that I'll continue making mistakes because I am human. You are, too. I know my faith will be challenged as well. I know I will hurt and have tough moments. I know the devil on my left will continue doing his job, too. However, I take comfort in knowing, "Greater is he that is in you, than he that is in the world" (1 John 4:4, NIV). The Holy Spirit that resides in me is greater than any evil. I am not alone, and neither are you.

Life isn't easy, but it can be beautifully enjoyable, even during the ugly times. I think it's more about how we view and respond to those ugly times. It's also about what we say to ourselves in those times. I encourage you to speak life and positive affirmations to yourself. I encourage you to find your place of peace.

Lastly, please understand that your past and current circumstances don't have to dictate your future. You have permission to rewrite your story. Find your reason to get up every day and fight to stick to it. Your purpose in life is bigger than where you currently are. And, you *do* have a purpose because you're here! You were created for a purpose. Nope, I'm not trying to convert you; I am simply sharing a portion of my life, my story, and my testimony. I hope it inspires you.

But...

If you are interested in developing a personal relationship and getting to know Jesus and the Holy Spirit, flip to the next page.

Congratulations for turning the page and deciding to take the next step.

Disclaimer: I am not a pastor or preacher, am not ordained, nor did I attend seminary school. I'm just an imperfect person delighted to share good news about one who *is* perfect. And contrary to popular belief, *all* Christians aren't as bad as those you may have encountered.

In the simplest definition, to be Christian means to be Christlike. That said, if you've encountered Christians who are not intentionally imitating Christ, that's a problem to be addressed between them and God. So, please don't let their personal problems impact your decision to have a relationship with Christ. Furthermore, God doesn't want you to keep score, be religious, or try to follow a lot of "rules." He simply wants a relationship with you and only you!

In other words, your personal relationship with Him is yours, not what the church or your family says. And He isn't mad at you or holding your past, bad decisions, or failures against you, either. He loves you more than you'll ever know and wants to help you find purpose and navigate your life easier. Say the prayer below, believe it in your heart, and you'll be saved! Lastly, be kind to yourself on this journey. It's a process but a rewarding one. Welcome to the family.

"Dear God, I want to be a part of your family and to start a relationship with You. The Bible says if I acknowledge that You raised Jesus from the dead, and if I accept Him as my Lord and Savior, I would be saved. So God, by faith, I believe You raised Jesus from the dead and that He died for my sins. I accept Jesus now as my personal Lord and Savior. God, help me to trust and to get to know you. I accept my salvation and believe I am now saved. Thank you, Father God, for forgiving me, saving me, loving and giving me eternal life with You. Amen!"

EPILOGUE

A Decade and a Year Later...

If you're anything like me, then you hate when a great movie, TV series, or story comes to an end, leaving you to wonder what happened to the characters we've fallen in love with. It happens to me every time, and I find myself thinking about those characters over and over, even if they are fictional. So, certainly, I couldn't leave you hanging like that. Let's just say the last decade and year have been nothing short of adventurous as the majority of life has been for me.

I'll start backward: I'm now married, still a newlywed, approaching my first anniversary in a few months. Finally, I got this love thing right. All along, I was my "love problem" and the missing link. I didn't know how to love and appreciate myself fully. I needed to learn to accept every inch, every curve, every flaw, and every part of my past. I needed to love me and all of me before I could invite external love in. Whew, honey, and coming to that conclusion is another book in itself. And as a married woman, I'm still learning to love myself more daily. My husband's love for me is overflowing and will never replace my love for myself. I'm learning that to love him, I have to be full of love before I can give some away. And guess what? God is love.

Speaking of God, I thank Him for sending my life partner and soulmate exactly when He did. Had I met my husband sooner, I wouldn't have been emotionally, mentally, or spiritually ready. We met at the height of the pandemic and of all places on Facebook. And guess what? We married eleven weeks after meeting. Did you hear that? We met in a pandemic and married in a little under four months. That was totally a God thing!

I'd actually been engaged to someone else seven months before meeting my husband. I know, I know, another story for another time. I recently blogged about this, and you can check it out on my website, www.rahkalroberson.com. It is sooo good! Anyway, my Help, the Holy Spirit, revealed to me that my husband was The One. My husband's Help revealed the same to him, thus creating magic for us. We have such a beautiful supernatural COVID-19 love story that we'll share publicly at some point, so stay tuned.

Atlanta is where I've called home for nearly eight years now. I resigned from my dream job (at the time) in Chicago back in May of 2013. My youth and I had an incredible three-year run exploring media and sports production together. I had grown tremendously as a professional, a woman, a creative mind, and a mentor. I quit with nothing lined up, only a nudging from my Help that it was time to leave. My Help and I had grown far more acquainted over those three years.

My dreams were more vivid, prayer more consistent since Church Girl's church became my home, and my knowledge, faith, and walk with God increased mightily. I got baptized there, joined a small prayer group, and attended worship conferences. I literally watched my life transform right before my eyes from the inside out. So when my Help said it was time to leave, I took another leap. Little did I know that God had something even greater in store for me and prepared me for my next dream job.

But before settling in Atlanta, I made a pitstop in DC. I was offered a position at a nonprofit just days after resigning. The job was at an organization I hadn't applied to or even heard of. Just as I prayed, asking God what was next, this popped up, and my help said, "Go." I figured, *What the heck.* I had wanted to live in DC since my undergrad years, and three days later, I was on a flight to Washington, with my apartment all packed. I had no clue that God was sending me on a particular assignment not only to save someone's life but to impact the lives of another set of youth.

Jumping right in, there I was, again teaching media production and scriptwriting to more inner-city teens. They were a creative, funny, and inspiring bunch. And as I suspected, I gelled with them quickly, and in no time, I became a big sister, mentor, confidant, and friend.

The teens were terrific, but the organization that employed me and its staff were horrendous. I am talking ridiculously unprofessional and disorganized. However, God was grooming me there, developing my faith and character for something else. After the first week, I was ready to quit but pushed for the kids. The youth alone kept me returning, in addition to my Help telling me to stay put. It was a good thing I had refined my relationship with God and was able to discern His voice.

The second week, the friend I stayed with had a gun pulled on her by her husband. I'd had no clue that she was in an abusive relationship. He towered over her as she sat on the couch nursing their baby. The sound of his fist colliding with her jaw sent shockwaves through my entire body. I was terrified when he ran after me, knowing he wanted to get my phone so I couldn't alert the police. I stood at the top of the stairs, calling the name of Jesus, and prayed loudly.

With every word I prayed, his anger subsided. My Help was present and covered us that night. The harder I prayed, the more he waved the gun at her, but eventually, he stormed out, taking the gun with him.

I know without a shadow of a doubt that my prayers and my Help's presence are what kept the three of us alive. I packed my bags and checked into a hotel in Baltimore, stranded with no place to go. For sure, I'm quitting and going back to Chicago. However, my Help advised me to stay, and God sent me an angel in the form of the receptionist in the building where I worked, who took me in after my Help instructed me to call her. Humbly, I asked that beautiful near-stranger if I could live with her for a few weeks. Not only did she happily oblige, but she was also a believer, and God used me to add value to her home as well. Nevertheless, I'm grateful that I finished the course. God was able to use me for His purpose, and DC forever changed my life in less than three months.

God sure has a funny way of allowing us to go through things for the benefit of others and when He's teaching lessons. This is the story of my life, being placed in spaces for the benefit of others, and, of course, for His glory. I'm constantly reminded that my life isn't about me. Months later, I accepted a job in Atlanta with Warner Media's (formerly Turner Broadcasting) NBA League Pass and eventually at Cable News Network, CNN. Talk about an absolute dream job (again, at that time).

Who would have known that little ol' me would one day be working for one of the largest media conglomerates in the country? God did, that's who. And I thought I'd found my dream job years prior. Reminded of Duncan's words, "You'll never make it without me or in media," I merely smiled.

Speaking of Duncan, after giving him the boot, I stayed single for several years, working on me, before meeting the next guy I dated. He had a great resume: no kids, educated, owned property, plus he was a gentleman who wore cufflinks. He was a believer, too, and we met at church. We had a lot in common but only dated a short while before I heard my Help say, "Not him; he's a mere preparation for your husband. Someone greater awaits."

I was, like, "Really?" *God, I've been trusting you for a minute. Why do you want me single again? It's hard out here.*

I consistently heard my Help nudge me "no" every time I prayed (as if He was going to change his mind), making it harder to leave the relationship. So I remained with him, praying, "God, please let him break up with me."

Ladies, please don't do this to yourselves! Whether you feel tension, are second-guessing, or have to keep praying about a man, he's likely not the one for you. If you heard or felt God saying no, but you continue the relationship regardless, that is called disobedience. Hear me out; you never have to talk yourself into a good or a God idea.

Pay attention to the tension, and don't settle! Maybe you love the man, have been with him a while, or even have kids with him; I get it. Starting over is terrifying, but you have to love yourself and know that you deserve more. Settling not only blocks God's will but causes resentment and more hurt in the long run.

I found myself bartering with God for my ex to be my husband, making things worse when the entire time God needed me single and in DC. If I didn't obey the Holy Spirit and break it off with my most recent ex, I would have never moved to DC or Atlanta. I wouldn't be married to the man God had chosen for me.

It's funny how life often repeats itself. Although it was difficult, I chose to listen to my Help, leaving my job and my man behind. Luckily, I've never been the type of woman who settled just to be able to say I had someone. My internal, ambitious wanderlust is usually hungry, anyway. I wanted what God had for me. Even though I didn't know exactly what that was, I knew it would be better than what I presently had. God's track record was just too excellent for me not to trust Him. As uncomfortable as things became at times, He had never let me down. So when He promised something greater lay ahead, I had to believe this.

Every so often, I'm urged to step out of my comfort zone to attempt to achieve something greater. Truthfully, I've always felt something significant waiting for me. I believe something powerful is out there for you, too. For me, it's like playing the hot-and-cold game. While walking through life, I constantly feel like I'm looking for something more significant, and when I think I'm getting hot or closer, I'm inspired and motivated…and when I'm cold, or going in the wrong direction, and feeling desolate, I know I need to move around. The writing is typically on the wall, but it isn't always easy to make out the words. Maybe this is the case for you, too?

Point blank, I needed to leave my location. In spite of this, I wasn't quite ready to move forward. I simply didn't foresee leaving Chicago, my friends, family, and church to move again. However, God did. It still amazes me that He had been guiding me all along, even before I knew Him.

Had I not made that move and been obedient, I wouldn't be where I am now. Just think: I had to leave where I was to get to where I am. So do you! The only guarantee in life is change. Change can be a good thing if we embrace it. It's often uncomfortable, even scary, but it's necessary. How do you grow if you're afraid to change or move forward? How can you get what you need and to where you need to be if you don't leave where you are?

Over the last eight years in Atlanta, my social circle has altered quite a bit. I don't have all the same friends, which

A DECADE AND A YEAR LATER...

is fine. Your social circle will shift as well, and that is often a healthy thing. We need people who mirror each level we advance to.

Speaking of social circles, I'm sure you're wondering what some of my family members and friends are up to. Angel and Kelly are happily married with beautiful children. Devita, Darius, and Ophelia are all mommies or daddies and successful business owners.

Pee Wee and her husband have been happily married for fifteen years now, living in Atlanta, not too far from me. My oldest nephew, Jamari, is leaving for college in a few weeks. Crazy, right, how time flies? The other kids are now teens and are doing very well academically as well as being fine young people. Daniel and his wife of seven years are also here in Atlanta with their lovely children. Daniel and I reconnected on my twenty-seventh birthday after nearly nine years of no contact with each other. We haven't lost touch since, and I don't expect we ever will.

Taylor was released from prison back in December of 2020 after serving thirteen years. He got out just in time to walk me down the aisle at my New Years' Eve wedding ceremony. God is so faithful for this. He and his son are also living here in Atlanta. As for Tina, she's growing and is still walking her unique path. She is here in Atlanta with us, too.

So, I suppose you can say I did an excellent job recruiting the family here to Atlanta. But the credit goes to God for answering my years of prayer to restore my family. He's still working on all of us. The first step was to get us all in the same city. We haven't been in such close proximity at the same time in over twenty years.

It's just the beginning, and we certainly have a ways to go in the areas of healing, growing, loving, and learning about each other as adults. Fortunately, Pee Wee's Sunday dinners are a great starting place.

My faith and new marital status have taught me the power and importance of healthy boundaries. Over the last few years, I've learned that I can't save or fix everyone. I've learned to back off, empathize as much as possible, and pray for people while no longer carrying the emotional loads of others. The fixer in me is dying. I mean, I didn't ask for super empath character traits, anyway.

I used to see being an empath as both a gift and a curse. Now I understand that I'm just gifted with the heart of God. However, He is the only and ultimate fixer; I'm not. I spent so much of my life trying to fix things. I agonized over what others thought and felt guilty when I couldn't fix their problems.

It took a series of events beginning in 2017 to teach me the value of surrendering and managing my inner fixer. The last four years since 2017 have also taught me so much about mental health and protecting my peace. Remember, being a fixer is intrusive to our peace.

After releasing the first edition of this book in 2016, I learned that Auntie Bertha was ill with stage IV lung cancer and had only weeks to live. She hid it from us because she didn't want Lewis to worry, which would be bad for his transplanted heart. Because I was already living in Atlanta by then, I didn't see her as often and was unaware she was sick.

Meanwhile, my little brother and sister were about to be taken away by the state. Years before in Chicago, Aunt Bertha introduced me to my father's youngest children, whom she helped care for (just like she did for us). Sadly, Carlos was—and still is—the same man he was when I was a child. Therefore, his younger children lived similarly to how we did: surrounded by drugs, violence, and filth.

From the moment I learned I had younger siblings, I became part of their lives, stopping by with food, helping with their school needs, and actively supporting and loving on them. They were roughly ages eight and five when I moved to Atlanta, and I vowed to keep in touch. Because of Aunt Bertha's illness, she couldn't bail out her brother again by taking them in. Someone called Child Protective Services on them.

Long story short, Aunt Bertha passed two months after I learned about her cancer. So, my fixer stepped up and moved the kids to Atlanta with me. Aunt Bertha had done so much for us, and it seemed fitting for me to carry on her legacy. Becoming an instant single mother marked the beginning of my breaking point.

Weeks after Bertha's passing, my grandpop died, and only four months later, my best friend, favorite cousin, life coach, and Bertha's youngest son, my cousin Lewis, passed away, too. He died of a heart attack while answering a call at work. Ironically, that year marked the tenth anniversary of his heart transplant and his eighth year as a firefighter. He died doing what he loved. I didn't have the opportunity to grieve or process either of those deaths, individually or collectively, because I had to keep going. The kids needed me.

Then, just three months after burying Lewis, I lost my grandmother. So, in under nine months, I lost four of the most influential people in my life and took in two children, consequently losing a fifth life…my own. Lewis dying so soon after his mom and the pain of losing him, period, caused me to lose my faith temporarily. I'm ashamed to say that I held a vendetta against God for nearly a year.

Angry, confused, bitter, and lost, I couldn't speak to God, but I had no place else to go and no one else to turn to. I still remember all the nights of laughter, celebrating, dancing, and even holding Lewis's baby girl during his funeral service. The year 2017 was a moment in my life that I'll never forget. I felt suffocated from battling grief, the stress and financial pressures of instant single motherhood, workplace pressures, and being in Atlanta solo. I was on my own; these events all took place years before my siblings and mother moved here.

The anxiety I felt daily nearly crushed me. My health declined rapidly; I was clinically depressed, chronically stressed, and fighting sleep deprivation. I had consistent heart palpitations, elevated blood pressure, stool bleeding, hair loss. I was on antidepressant medication while going about my activities of daily living: working, picking up the kids daily from school...all with a fake smile plastered on my face.

In one of my therapy sessions, a breakthrough exposed the bitterness I carried from caring for my father's children. The father who abandoned me lived his life, getting high and free of responsibility while I struggled to feed and clothe his children. All the stress and anguish terrified me; I was convinced I would die just like Lewis had from a sudden heart attack if I kept up my current stressful pace.

It was only the power of God and my Help who sustained me that entire time. Although I was upset with God, He wasn't upset with me, and He saw me through. There is no way I should be here today and still sane, after what I went through that year.

And, after nearly two years of caring for my young siblings, I had to wave the white flag to preserve my well-being and nurse myself back to health. They moved back to Chicago to live with another relative, and I started picking up the pieces of my life.

I've learned for sure that it's essential to be honest with yourself and pay attention to how you feel. Being honest about who you are, what you like, dislike, need, don't need, or can or cannot handle is crucial to your authentic health. And the more authentic you are, the more you can flow and experience peace. I've also learned that you can't be everything to everyone. I tried to fix my own childhood through the way I cared for my siblings, with a pure heart and great intentions. However, that was not my battle to fight, and it cost me a great deal. Nevertheless, I am reminded of Romans 8:28:

> "And we know that God causes everything to work together for the good of those who love God and are called according to his purpose for them." (Romans 8:28, NLT).

While having the kids took a toll on me physically, mentally, emotionally, and financially, my relatively short-term sacrifice forever changed their lives. They were exposed to a live example of what resilience looks like through someone who had walked in their shoes. They were exposed to the best Atlanta had to offer, academically and socially, while being affirmed, loved, and cared for. They learned firsthand that their past doesn't have to dictate their future. I also benefitted as well, for they helped prepare me for life, business, marriage, and helped me cope with my character flaws, dad issues and to see areas for growth.

They provided a reason for me to keep going while grieving and fighting depression. Honestly, losing Bertha was excruciating, and if I hadn't had them with me, I probably wouldn't have made it when Lewis died months later. The seeds planted in all three of us from our time together not only threatened to break me but broke off everything I needed to shed for my future while creating a more solid trust in God.

Today, I'm in excellent health. I'm still growing, embracing my uniqueness, and living my dream. I'm committed to turning all my pain into purpose and progress. And while I found my purpose in 2009, and my purpose exceeds far beyond my heart for youth. I know I was placed on earth to serve and inspire others. I do this through coaching, creative content, mentoring, and consulting. I've written other books since this one, and currently, I'm a full-time entrepreneur with a daily mission to be the inspired me. I believe in the power of sharing our stories with others. Sharing our personal story has a way of freeing someone else. It gives others the courage to embrace and share their own stories. It's a positive domino effect. Storytelling helps to connect, inspire, influence, and serve others. People need to know they are not alone. I pray my story has inspired you...

XO,
Rahk

About the Author

Rahkal Shelton Roberson is a certified professional life coach, speaker, author, and CEO of Be The Inspired You, a motivational personal and professional development lifestyle brand. She is passionate about helping girls and women gain confidence, self-esteem and break free of self-imposed restrictions to live a more fulfilling life. Rahkal is the author of *Woosah: A Survival Guide for Women of Color Working In Corporate*, *Dreams Bigger Than Texas: A Story of Faith, Purpose, Perseverance, and Growth Into Womanhood*, and *Blackbird: The Story of a SistaMom*. During her career as a project manager, professional coach, facilitator, and producer, she's found that success is achieved by intentionality, strategy, and a healthy mindset. Her coaching approach focuses on mindfulness, resilience, strategy, and identifying personal skills for professional success. She holds a Bachelor's degree in Radio, Television, and Film from Texas Southern University and a Master's degree in Media Communications and Training from Governors State University. With over a dozen years of corporate experience, Rahkal has worked for major companies, including CNN, Warner Media, iHeartMedia, and Fox Chicago News. Her expertise has been highlighted in *Forbes, HuffPost, WGN, VoyageATL, The Talk of*

Chicago, and *Radio One*. She and her husband, Dr. Joe L. Roberson, Jr., currently live in Atlanta, Georgia.

◎ Instagram: rcarladanielle

🐦 Twitter: rcarladanielle

f Facebook.com/rahkal.shelton

www.youtube.com/c/rahkalshelton

www.ingramcontent.com/pod-product-compliance
Lightning Source LLC
Chambersburg PA
CBHW071804080526
44589CB00012B/681